Early childhood and primary education

Readings and Reflections

Early childhood and primary education

Readings and reflections

Jane Johnston and John Halocha

Open University Press

Open University Press
McGraw-Hill Education
McGraw-Hill House
Shoppenhangers Road
Maidenhead
Berkshire
England
SL6 2QL

email: enquiries@openup.co.uk
world wide web: www.openup.co.uk

and Two Penn Plaza, New York, NY 10121-2289, USA

First published 2010

A catalogue record of this book is available from the British Library

ISBN-13: 978-0-33-523656-5 (pb) 978-0-33-523657-2 (hb)
ISBN-10: 0-33-523656-1 (pb) 0-33-523657-X (hb)

Library of Congress Cataloging-in-Publication Data
CIP data applied for

Typeset by RefineCatch Limited, Bungay, Suffolk
Printed in the UK by Bell and Bain Ltd, Glasgow.

Fictitious names of companies, products, people, characters and/or data that may
be used herein (in case studies or in examples) are not intended to represent any
real individual, company, product or event.

Mixed Sources
Product group from well-managed
forests and other controlled sources
www.fsc.org Cert no. TT-COC-002769
© 1996 Forest Stewardship Council

The **McGraw·Hill** *Companies*

Contents

Figures

Acknowledgements

The authors would like to thank: Emma Jordan for her persistent and efficient efforts in arranging the necessary permissions for the book; Fiona Richman for her patience and support in the writing process and for not badgering us; colleagues in school and the University College who have inspired us with their thoughtful discussions; Alan Stacey who helped us with IT solutions; and Vanessa Richards, the North East Representative for the National Association of Music Educators and Curriculum Support Teacher in Music in the Scottish Borders, who contributed to, and advised on aspects of the book.

Introduction

In this book the authors hope to support educational professionals in the early years and primary education to understand historical and current educational practice and their theoretical underpinnings and support them in developing their personal and professional practice. The rationale for this is that early years and primary are often seen as very separate stages of development, although children are expected to progress from one key stage to another in a seamless way and the historical and philosophical ideas underpinning practice at the different stages are often the same or similar. We believe that to be fully effective, professionals need to understand and reflect on children's experiences both before and after the stage they are currently working in and understand historical and current ideas and practice.

The theorists used in this book

The current drive is to equip professionals working with young children with higher-level understandings and skills and this involves consideration of the key historical and current theories and the development of the conceptual and philosophical frameworks that positively impact on current practice. In this book the main theorists we use are listed below in alphabetical order. We believe that it is important to read and understand their original work as often our understanding of the theories is based on knowledge passed down by word of mouth or read in more recent texts. Both these methods of dissemination of ideas is problematic, as the meaning of the theories become modified over time and are often assigned new meanings, which can distort the important ideas. It is also important for professionals to explore the origins of ideas currently used in practice so that the implications for current practice can be effectively critiqued and problems of application can be fully explored.

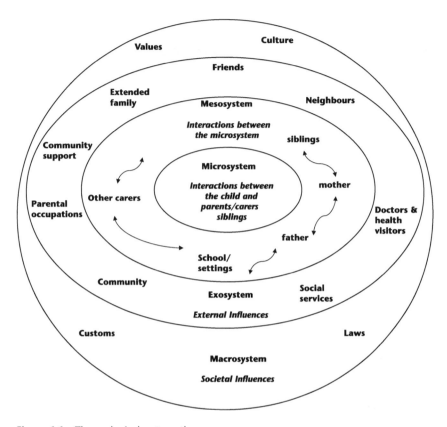

Figure 1.1   The ecological systems theory.

Source: reproduced with permission from Johnston and Nahmad-Williams (2008)

66   The Mesosystem and Human Development

In analyzing the forces that affect processes of socialization and development at the level of the mesosystem, we shall find ourselves using most of
the same concepts employed to delineate the structure and operation of
microsystems. Thus the basic building blocks will be the familiar elements
of the setting: molar activities, roles, and interpersonal structures in the
form of dyads and N + 2 systems varying in the degree of reciprocity,
balance of power, and affective relations. What is more, many of the
hypotheses derived will be analogous to prototypes previously formulated
for the microsystem. The difference lies in the nature of the interconnections involved. At the microsystem level, the dyads and N + 2 systems,
the role transactions, and the molar activities all occur within one setting,
whereas in the mesosystem these processes take place across setting
boundaries. As a result of this isomorphism, it is possible to formulate

most of our hypotheses in advance and then examine relevant research evidence.

I have defined the mesosystem as a set of interrelations between two or more settings in which the developing person becomes an active participant. What kinds of interconnections are possible, for example, between home and school? I propose four general types.

1. *Multisetting participation*. This is the most basic form of interconnection between two settings, since at least one manifestation of it is required for a mesosystem. It occurs when the same person engages in activities in more than one setting, for example, when a child spends time both at home and at the day care center. Since such participation necessarily occurs sequentially, multisetting participation can also be defined as the existence of a direct or *first-order* social network across settings in which the developing person is a participant. The existence of such a network, and therefore of a mesosystem, is established at the point when the developing person first enters a new setting. When this occurs, we also have an instance of what I have called an *ecological transition*, in this instance a transition from one setting to another.

When the developing person participates in more than one setting of a mesosystem, she is referred to as a *primary link*, as when Mary enters school. Other persons who participate in the same two settings are referred to as *supplementary links*; for instance, Mary's mother attends a PTA meeting, her teacher pays a visit to the home, or Mary brings home a classmate to play. As these examples indicate, direct links can operate in the direction of either setting.

A dyad in either setting that involves a linking person as a member is referred to as a *linking dyad*.

2. *Indirect linkage*. When the same person does not actively participate in both settings, a connection between the two may still be established through a third party who serves as an *intermediate link* between persons in the two settings. In this case, participants in the two settings are no longer meeting face-to-face so that we speak of them as members of a *second-order network* between settings. Such second-order connections can also be more remote, involving two or more intermediate links in the network chain.

3. *Intersetting communications*. These are messages transmitted from one setting to the other with the express intent of providing specific information to persons in the other setting. The communication can occur in a variety of ways: directly through face-to-face interaction, telephone conversations, correspondence and other written messages, notices or announcements, or indirectly via chains in the social network. The communication may be one-sided or may occur in both directions.

4. *Intersetting knowledge* refers to information or experience that

their own that persists when the participants are no longer together. When such activities occur in a variety of settings, this motivational momentum tends to generalize across situations. These effects are further enhanced if the participants are emotionally significant in each other's lives, that is, if they are members of primary dyads. The hypothesis has a corollary at the sociological level.

HYPOTHESIS 30
The positive developmental effects of participation in multiple settings are enhanced when the settings occur in cultural or subcultural contexts that are different from each other, in terms of ethnicity, social class, religion, age group, or other background factors. Underlying this hypothesis is the assumption that differences in activities, roles, and relations are maximized when settings occur in culturally diverse environments.

A critical case for the two foregoing hypotheses would be represented by a person who had grown up in two cultures, had participated actively and widely in each society, and had developed close friendships with people in both. If the two hypotheses are valid, such a person, when compared with someone of the same age and status who had grown up in only one country and subculture, should exhibit higher levels of cognitive function and social skill and be able to profit more from experience in an educational setting. I know of no research on this phenomenon, but it is certainly susceptible to empirical investigation by, for example, comparing the development of children with and without extensive experience of other cultures or ethnic groups, holding other aspects of family background constant. The hypotheses could also be tested by, for instance, assigning youngsters to work projects involving participation in subcultures within the community.

This line of reasoning is applicable not only at the level of the individual but also at that of the dyad. Just as it is possible for a person to engage in activity in more than one setting, so can the dyad do this. Such a migrating two-person system is referred to as a *transcontextual dyad*. From an ecological perspective, there is reason to expect this type of structure have special significance for development. It is probably even more conducive to the formation of primary dyads than a joint activity limited to a single setting. But more important, I suggest that the occurrence of transcontextual dyads in the life of the person may operate to enhance the person's capacity and motivation to learn. This possibility is based on the assumption that when a variety of joint activities are carried out in a range of situations but in the context of an enduring interpersonal relationship, the latter both encourages the development of higher levels of skill and tends to generate especially strong and persistent levels of motivation. This thinking leads to the following three hypotheses.

HYPOTHESIS 31
The capacity of the person to profit from a developmental experience will vary directly as a function of the number of transcontextual dyads, across a variety of settings, in which she has participated prior to that experience.

HYPOTHESIS 32
Children from cultural backgrounds that encourage the formation and maintenance of transcontextual dyads are more likely to profit from new developmental experiences.

HYPOTHESIS 33
Development is enhanced by providing experiences that allow for the formation and maintenance of transcontextual dyads across a variety of settings.
    Several hypotheses pertain to the optimal structure of additional links between settings beyond the primary connection established by the developing person. The first one is merely an extension of an earlier hypothesis (28) now expanded to encompass any additional persons who participate in the different settings under consideration.

HYPOTHESIS 34
The developmental potential of settings in a mesosystem is enhanced if the roles, activities, and dyads in which the linking person engages in the two settings encourage the growth of mutual trust, positive orientation, goal consensus between settings and an evolving balance of power responsive to action on behalf of the developing person. A supplementary link that meets these conditions is referred to as a *supportive link*.
    An example in which the conditions stipulated in this hypothesis were violated is found in the previously cited (chapter 8) account by Karnes of the unforeseen effects of combining home visits with a preschool program. The change in the staff's treatment of mothers as a result of the new arrangement decreased the mother's sense of her own importance and efficacy and her active involvement as a key figure in her child's development.

HYPOTHESIS 35
The developmental potential of a setting is increased as a function of the number of supportive links existing between that setting and other settings (such as home and family). Thus the least favorable condition for development is one in which supplementary links are either nonsupportive or completely absent – when the mesosystem is weakly linked.

or in studying the First World War, the focus can be on the altruistic behaviours of people during air raids. Discuss the behaviour of individuals within the example you have chosen and afterwards observe the behaviour of children over a period of time and identify any behaviours that they exhibit that could have been reinforced by the activity.

Reflection

- How successful was the activity in reinforcing, developing or supporting children's behaviours?
- Does the reinforcement of the activity have a greater effect on one type of function? If so why do you think this is?
- How could you use this type of activity to reinforce other behaviour or to provide resistance to behaviour?

Professional leader:

With your staff audit the behaviour that you want to reinforce and those that you wish to diminish. Prioritize the lists and choose the two positive behaviours that you consider the most important to reinforce and the two negative behaviours that you want to avoid. Identify the main factors that encourage and prevent the positive and negative behaviours. Develop an action plan for the medium (term) and long (year) term to reinforce and resist the behaviours that you have prioritized. This may include activities as part of the curriculum or modelling of behaviour, rewards and sanctions.

Try this out for one term and evaluate the success. You may then adjust the action plan and reassess after another term or at the end of the year.

Reflection

- How successful were the planned activities in reinforcing, developing or supporting children's behaviours over a short or long period?
- How do any changes in behaviour impact on the setting/school as a whole and the achievements of the children?
- How can you extend the use of this type of planned action to reinforce or resist other behaviours?

The social child today

The loss of opportunities for outdoor, loosely supervised play is also likely to have long term effects on children's social development.

Learning how to make friends, play as part of a group, and resolve minor conflicts used to take place out of adult view, meaning that children could take responsibility – and make mistakes – without incurring immediate adult judgement. Many of children's playmates now are screen-based virtual friends, from whom they don't learn social skills. And practically all real juvenile socialising goes on under the eagle eye of adults, who are naturally swift to intervene if things look dicey. Some children are thus being labelled 'naughty' very early in their social careers (and then going on to fulfil the prophecy), while others are learning to call for help at the first sign of danger.

(Palmer, 2006: 60–1)

Concerns about social problems in childhood have been expressed from a number of writers. Elkind (2001) is concerned that children today have less time to be children and play, with the obvious detrimental effects on their social development and in 2006, over a hundred child experts, academics, writers, and so on led by Baroness Susan Greenfield, Director of the Royal Institution, wrote a letter that was published in the *Daily Telegraph* (2006: 23) expressing concern at *'the escalating incidence of childhood depression and children's behavioural and developmental conditions'*, with little time to play *'in a fast-moving, hyper-competitive culture, today's children are expected to cope with an ever earlier start to formal schoolwork and an overly academic test-driven primary curriculum'* and calling for a long-overdue debate on childhood. *The Cambridge Review of Primary Education* (Alexander, 2009) provided a comprehensive review of the state of primary education, which included a clear endorsement for peer collaboration (Howe and Mercer, 2007) and play-based learning.

Children find that their relations with parents include elements of dependence, interdependence and independence. Over the primary school years, they become increasingly responsible – for self-care, organising their lives, jobs around the house and caring for family members. Parents (especially mothers) and siblings (also in some cases other relatives) provide children with confidants. Relations with siblings and friends vary widely, but help children understand their own identity. Siblings and friends are important for support, defence and fun, especially in public places and at school. Studies suggest that in times of hardship, including divorce and separation, children value being kept informed and participating in decision-making. Relational practices within the family are found to be crucial to children's well-being.

(Mayall, 2007: 3)

The United Nation's Children's Fund (Unicef, 2007) report on *The State of the* assessment of cognition, there are fewer opportunities than in previous generations. Interaction between home and setting (see Bronfenbrenner, 1979) also take time, if they are to be effective, and support children in their social development.

- Opportunities for children to be independent. Concerns about the physical safety of children have led to them having fewer opportunities to be independent (Palmer, 2006) and learn to be effective adults and citizens. Children can socialize with text messages and through social networking sites and when their parents arrange more formal play opportunities. However, there are fewer opportunities to socialize with peers in informal situations and to meet other peers.

- Encouragement and opportunities for children to take responsibility. The focus on positive behaviour strategies or positive reinforcement of behaviour (see Bandura, 1977) has created a situation where children find it less easy to take responsibility for anti-social behaviours and to blame others, events, or situations for things they do wrong; *'It is not my fault, I did not mean it'*, *'He made me'*, and so on etc.

Subject tasks

EYFS:
Puppets can be used in the EYFS to promote language, literacy and communication by encouraging children to speak and listen. Use a 'naughty' puppet to discuss a social issue. You may do this in conjunction with a children's book that focuses on a social issue, such as *It Wasn't Me: Learning About Honesty*, or *I'll Do It! Learning About Responsibility: Taking Responsibility* (Moses and Gordon, 1998a, b). The children can talk to the puppet and tell them why s/he should be honest, take responsibility, share with friends, and so on. The initial discussion could be part of a small group or larger group circle/carpet time and then the puppet could be left for the children to play with. Observe any subsequent interactions and note the children's dialogue with the puppet about social issues.

Reflection

- What do the children's interactions with the puppet tell you about their social development and development in language, literacy and communication?
- How could you use the puppet in the future to support social development?

KS1:
Role play can support development in a range of curriculum areas, as well as social development. For example, a post office can help children in English (writing, reading and speaking and listening) and mathematics (using and applying number, reasoning, and so on) as applied to money and also negotiating, manners, honesty, and so on in social development. Set up a role play area in your classroom that can support a number of aspects of the curriculum and social development. Observe the children as they play in the role play area and note the play for evidence of social development. You may wish to discuss some of your observations with the children to get them to consider the social interactions further.

Reflection

- What do the children's interactions with each other in the role play area tell you about their social development as well as development in curriculum areas?
- How could you use role play in the future to support social development?

KS2:
Hot-seating can provide children with opportunities to explore the reasons behind historical decisions. For example, a historical figure, such as Queen Victoria or Winston Churchill or King Henry VIII, can be asked by the children to explain why they chose to act in certain ways. The teacher may choose to be the historical figure and dress up appropriately, or a child may choose to be the historical figure and respond in a way they feel appropriate. Observation can tell you a lot about the children's social development and how the interactions and reflections develop them socially.

Reflection

- What do the children's questions, interactions and responses during the hot-seating activity tell you about their social development and understanding of history?
- How could you use hot-seating in the future to support social development?

References

Alexander, R. (ed.) (2009) *Children, their World, their Education: Final Report and Recommendations of the Cambridge Review*. London: Routledge.

Bandura, A. (1977) *Social Learning Theory*. Englewood Cliffs, NJ: Prentice Hall.

Barkow, H. (2001) *The Giant Turnip*. London: Mantra.

Bowlby, R. (2007) Babies and toddlers in non-parental daycare can avoid stress and anxiety if they develop a lasting secondary attachment bond with one carer who is consistently accessible to them, *Attachment & Human Development*, 9(4): 307–19.

Bronfenbrenner, U. (1979) *The Ecology of Human Development: Experiments by Nature and Design*. Cambridge, MA: Harvard University Press.

Bronfenbrenner, U. (1995) The bioecological model from a life course perspective: reflections of a participant observer, in P. Moen, G.H. Elder, Jr. and K. Lüscher (eds) *Examining Lives in Context*. Washington, DC: American Psychological Association, pp. 599–618.

Bronfenbrenner, U. and Evans, G.W. (2000) Developmental science in the 21st century: emerging theoretical models, research designs and empirical findings, *Social Development* 9: 115–25.

Daily Telegraph (2006) Letters to the editor – modern life leads to more depression among children, 12 September 2006, No. 47,049, p. 23.

Department for Children, Schools and Families (DCSF) (2007) *Extended Schools: Building on Experience – Every Child Matters, Change for Children*. Nottingham: DCFS.

Department for Education and Employment (DfEE) (1999) *The National Curriculum: Handbook for Teachers in England*. London:DfEE/QCA.

Department for Education and Skills (DfES) (2004) *Every Child Matters: Change For Children*. London: DfES.

Effective Provision of Pre-School Education (EPPE) (2003) Measuring the Impact of Pre-School on Children's Social/behavioural Development over the Pre-School Period: *The EPPE (Effective Provision of Pre-school Education) Project Technical Paper 8b*. London: Institute of Education.

Elkind, D. (2001) *The Hurried Child: Growing Up Too Fast Too Soon*, 3rd edn. Cambridge, MA: Da Capo Press.

Howe, C. and Mercer, N. (2007) *Children's Social Development, Peer Interaction and Classroom Learning: Primary Review Research Survey 2/1b*. Cambridge: University of Cambridge.

Johnston, J. and Nahmad-Williams, L. (2008) *Early Childhood Studies*. Harlow: Pearson.

Johnston, J., Halocha, J. and Chater, M. (2007) *Developing Teaching Skills in the Primary School*. Maidenhead: Open University Press.

Mayall, B. (2007) *Children's Lives Outside School and their Educational Impact: Primary Review Research Briefings 8/1*. Cambridge: University of Cambridge.

Moses, B. and Gordon, M. (1998a) *It Wasn't Me: Learning About Honesty.* London: Hodder Children's Books.

Moses, B. and Gordon, M. (1998b) *I'll Do It! Learning About Responsibility: Taking Responsibility.* London: Hodder Children's Books.

Palmer, S. (2006) *Toxic Childhood: How the Modern World is Damaging our Chldren and What we can do about it.* London: Orion.

Rose, J. (2009) *Independent Review of the Primary Curriculum: Final Report.* Nottingham: Department for Children, Schools and Families (DCSF).

Sammons, P., Sylva, K., Melhuish, E.C., Siraj-Blatchford, I., Taggart, B. and Elliot, K. (2002) The Effective Provision of Pre-School Education (EPPE) Project: *Technical Paper 8b – Measuring the Impact of Pre-School on Children's Social/behavioural Development over the Pre-School Period.* London: Department for Education and Skills (DfES)/Institute of Education, University of London.

Schwienhart, L.J., Weikart, D.P. and Toderan, R. (1993) *High Quality Preschool Programs Found to Improve Adult Status.* Ypsilanti, MI: High/Scope Foundation.

Sylva, K., Melhuish, E., Sammons, P., Siraj-Blatchford, I. and Taggart, B. (2004) *The Effective Provision Of Pre-School Education (Eppe) Project: Final Report. A Longitudinal Study Funded by the DfES.* Nottingham: Department for Education and Skills (DfES).

United Nation's Children's Fund (Unicef) (2007) *The State of the World's Children 2007.* Available online at www.unicef.org/sowc07/report/report.php.

2 Emotional development

This chapter discusses the attachment theories of John Bowlby and Mary Ainsworth and considers what the implications for emotional development are for children today as they develop in an increasingly complex world.

Emotional intelligence

Emotional development has a very important biological function in young children and problems with emotional development can seriously affect the development of older children and the function of adults in society. Our aim in early years and primary education is to support children to become emotionally intelligent adults. Emotional intelligence is the ability to be aware, judge and manage emotions in yourself and others. Salovey and Grewal (2005) identify five areas of emotional intelligence:

1   Perceiving emotions, the ability to tell emotions from facial expressions, voices, pictures and also to identify your own emotions.
2   Using emotions, the ability to use emotions in cognitive activities, such as thinking and problem-solving.
3   Understanding emotions, the ability to understand emotional language, relationships and the factors that affect emotions.
4   Managing emotions, the use of emotions to achieve goals.

Goleman (1998) identified four categories of emotional intelligence:

1   Self-awareness or the ability to understand your own emotions and the effect they will have on others and affect decision-making.
2   Self-management, or the ability to control emotions and impulses in changing contexts.

3   Social awareness, or the ability to perceive, understand, and react to emotions shown in other people.
4   Relationship management, or the ability to use emotions to lead, inspire, influence, and solve conflicts.

In this way the relationship between emotional and social development is strong and problems in one may create problems in the other. Emotional development begins in the womb and problems in early emotional development, especially in attachments are likely to be long lasting throughout childhood and into adulthood.

Attachment

The attachment that babies have with their mother is the primary attachment and has the function of providing support and care for the developing baby, who is born unable to care for itself. The reasons for human babies being born in this 'needy' state is thought to be because of the size of the head and brain, which would inhibit longer periods in the womb. If, when a baby is born, bonding does not occur for a variety and interrelationship of reasons, mother ill-health, including post-natal depression, the health of the baby, or social issues, such as single parent, or weak extended family support, then the effects can be quite severe for both mother and child. Babies can and do bond with others, such as fathers, grandparents and secondary carers and these bonds can be close and intense too and can overcome the problems of weak maternal attachment.

Bowlby (1958: 369) has been a major figure in the debate about young children's emotional development and in particular the debate about the importance of attachment as a biological response in the early years. He identifies '*instinctual responses*' in babies that help survival. These include, clinging, crying, smiling and following with eyes and once mobile following in actuality. Recent research (Mampe et al., 2009) has indicated that babies learn the intonation of their mother's voice in the womb and this is imitated in their crying, so national and regional accents are reflected in their crying. This crying response is shown in babies between 3–5 days old and is probably learned in the womb. It is likely to be a biological response supportive of attachment, making the baby and mother bond more secure at an early age.

> Although I have described these five responses as mother-orientated, it is evident that at first this is only potentially. From what we know of other species it seems probable that each one of them has the potential to become focused on some other object. The clearest examples of this in real life are where sucking becomes directed towards a bottle and not to the mother's breast, and clinging is directed to a rag and

not to the mother's body. In principle it seems likely that an infant could be so reared that each of his responses was directed towards a different object. In practice this is improbable, since all or most of the consummatory stimuli which terminate them habitually come from the mother figure. No matter for what reason he is crying – cold, hunger, fear, or plain loneliness – his crying is usually terminated through the agency of the mother. Again, when he wants to cling or follow or to find a haven of safety when he is frightened, she is the figure who commonly provides the needed object. It is for this reason that the mother becomes so central a figure in the infant's life. For in healthy development it is towards her that each of the several responses becomes directed . . . and it is in relation to the mother that the several responses become integrated into the complex behaviour which I have termed 'attachment behaviour'.

(Bowlby, 1958: 369–70)

Ten years after Bowlby (1958) wrote his thesis on 'The nature of the child's tie to his mother', he studied the effects of maternal deprivation on attachment and future emotional development and concluded that children have a bio-logical need for an attachment. Children are biologically adapted to form an attachment from seven months when a child begins to be able to crawl and move away from their carer and its importance continues until the child's third year. This attachment is normally with the mother, but can be with another significant adult and is primarily with one person (monotropic). Failure to form primary attachments has short- and long-term consequences to health and emotional development.

In the case of human personality the integrating function of the unique mother-figure is one of the importance of which I believe can hardly be exaggerated; in this I am at one with Winnicott who has constantly emphasized it. I also see the ill-effects stemming from maternal deprivation and separation as due in large part to an inter-ference with this function, either preventing its development or smashing it at a critical point . . .

In my experience a mother's acceptance of clinging and follow-ing is consistent with favourable development even in the absence of breast feeding, whilst rejection of clinging and following is apt to lead to emotional disturbance even in the presence of breast feeding. Furthermore, it is my impression that fully as many psychological disturbances, including the most severe, can date from the second year of life when clinging and following are at their peak as from the early months when they are rudimentary.

(Bowlby, 1958: 370)

Bowlby's research has been subject to criticism in that he did not consider the effects of privation (never having an attachment), problems in family relationships, attachments other than maternal attachments (paternal, peers, siblings, etc.) and multiple attachments on emotional development. Sir Richard Bowlby (2007) has continued his father's interest in attachment and has identified the problems that children face if they have insecure attachments and are cared for in their early years. These problems are likely to be greater in a society where children are 'cared for' in greater numbers and have a negative effect on the children's emotional development throughout their childhood and into adulthood, thus affecting development in other areas.

Reflective tasks

It seems important that children have initially good attachments with their own family and carers and later with peers and other adults such as the professionals who work with them. What appears to be important for professionals working with children in the early years and primary education are good secondary attachments that support not just emotional development, but also social and cognitive development. Field (1991) identified that key factors in emotional stability, contentment in early years and later achievements are stable childcare arrangements with a limited number of familiar carers or key workers, low staff turnover and low adult–child ratios.

EYFS:
We have known for some time about the importance of stable secondary attachments in the early years.

- What challenges do you face in your setting in maintaining stable key figures in young children's care?
- How could you improve secondary attachments in your setting?
- How do you think improving secondary attachments could support children's development, emotionally and in other key areas?

KS1:
Transition from the home/EYFS to KS1, from class to class in KS1 and from KS1 to KS2 can be critical times in children's emotional development, as secondary attachments with key workers are weakened or broken and children have to familiarize themselves with new class teachers.

- What are the major issues you face in supporting children through these transitions and in developing relationships with new teachers in KS1?

built up some kind of intraorganismic structure that we have hypoth-esized as attachment. Although such a structure can be conceived to be influenced also by the interactions that constitute the relationship, it is obviously different for each partner. On these grounds we hold that the attachment of child to mother is by no means identical to the attach-ment of mother to child, even though they both share an attachment relationship.

Attachment In Older Preschoolers

As we pointed out in Chapter 1, it is a misconception to believe that Bowlby was not concerned with the development of child–mother attachment beyond toddlerhood. To be sure, there had been very little research relevant to the later stages of development of child–mother attachment; thus, his formulations (1969, 1972) of such development were necessarily sketchy and programatic. He acknowledged that proximity-seeking behavior becomes less conspicuous in the child's inter-action with his mother as development proceeds. He did not equate this, however, with an attenuation of attachment itself. He emphasized the significance of the development of "working models" – inner represen-tations – that the child builds up both of himself and of his attachment figure, and the development of the capacity for making plans, both of which developments begin no later than the second year of life. In the final phase of development, in which a "goal-corrected partnership" is formed and sustained, the partners develop "a much more complex rela-tionship with each other" than is characteristic of a 1-year-old (Bowlby, 1969). In this phase the development of the capacity to take the perspec-tive of another is crucial. As this capacity develops, a child gains insight into his mother's plans, set-goals, and motivations, so that he can form increasingly complex plans that include influencing his mother to fit in with his plan. Indeed Bowlby's notion of "partnership" implies that both partners can negotiate mutual plans that comprehend the set-goals of each.

Obviously a child's cognitive development profoundly changes the specifics of the behaviors that mediate attachment in the older pre-schooler, as well as in still older children and in adults. Nevertheless, Bowlby (1973) conceived of the attachment of a child to his mother as enduring through a substantial part of life, even though it undoubtedly becomes attenuated, especially in adolescence, and supplemented with other relationships, including a number (a limited number) of other attachments. Furthermore, the fundamentally proximity-promoting nature of attachment behavior does not altogether disappear with increasing sophistication. Bowlby (1973) makes clear that even in infancy, proximity to the mother figure may come to be conceived in terms of her apparent availability – the degree to which she is believed by the child to be accessible to him and responsive to his signals and communications. Increasingly, therefore, proximity becomes less a matter of literal distance and more a matter of symbolic availability. Nevertheless, even in adult life, when the attachment system is activated at a high level of intensity – for example, by severe illness or disaster – the person seeks literal closeness to an attachment figure as an entirely appropriate reaction to severe stress.

To our knowledge, the only body of research that has picked up the threads of Bowlby's discussion of the development of attachment beyond the first year or two of life is that conducted by Marvin and his associates (Marvin, 1972, 1977; Marvin, Greenberg, & Mossier, 1976; Mossier, Marvin, & Greenberg, 1976), discussed in Chapter 10. They have shown that shifts in strange-situation behavior from one age level to another are associated with certain cognitive acquisitions. In particular, they have shown that the ability to take the perspective of another – at least in simple conceptual tasks – generally emerges between the third and fourth birthday. In recent, as-yet-unpublished research, Marvin (personal communication) has been investigating the way in which a child and his mother may negotiate a mutual plan – specifically, one in which the mother's plan (suggested by instructions) is to leave the child alone in a laboratory playroom for a few minutes. He demonstrated that when a mutual plan is negotiated, a 4-year-old shows no separation distress, although if (again according to instructions) the mother does not negotiate in response to the child's attempts to do so, the child is upset. The distress seems more likely to be angry distress, as a result of the mother's arbitrary unresponsiveness to his attempts to communicate his plan to her and to influence her plan, than attributable to mere separation. Furthermore, in the case of dyads who do successfully negotiate a mutual plan, a common compromise is the mother's acceding to the child's request to leave the door open, if only by "just a crack." The implication is that the child does not require his mother's actual presence as long as he feels that she would be accessible to him if he wanted to go to her. All of this is clearly in line with Bowlby's hypothesis about developments in the later preschool years.

As we have already pointed out, the strange situation does not activate attachment behavior at the same high level of intensity in 3- and 4-year-olds as in 1-year-olds. Consequently the patterning of behavior reflected in our classificatory system, dependent as it is on high-intensity activation of the attachment behavioral system (and also upon associated avoidant and resistant behavior), does not occur in older preschoolers in the same way that it does in 1-year-olds. In Chapter 10 we suggested several solutions to this problem. One solution is to use our categorical measures of interactive behavior, as Blehar (1974) did instead of employing our classificatory system – although this implies some loss of the patterning highlighted in classification. Another solution is to modify the classificatory system to make it more applicable to the behavior of the older preschoolers, as Marvin (1972) did. The other possible solutions considered in Chapter 10 involved devising new ways of assessing the attachment of older preschoolers to their attachment figure(s). Clues that might be useful might be found in the results of investigators such as Main, Bell, Connell, and Matas (reported in Chapter 9), who examined individual differences in later behavior of children who had been assessed in the strange situation at the end of the first year. Similarly, Lieberman's study (see Chapter 10) might give leads to variables relating to mother–child interaction at home that might substitute for strange-situation variables in the older preschooler. Marvin's current unpublished work seems likely to yield suggestions for ways in which laboratory assessments might be made more appropriate for the older child.

All of the foregoing implies that the situation-specific behaviors that reflect important qualitative differences in attachment in 1-year-olds may be replaced by a number of equally situation-specific behaviors in older preschoolers. Such a suggestion is akin to the concept of "transformation," proposed by both Maccoby and Feldman (1972) and Lewis and his associates (Lewis & Ban, 1971; Weinraub, Brooks, & Lewis, 1977); but it demands something less simplistic than their assumption that "proximal" behaviors become transformed into "distal" behaviors in the course of development. Both proximal and distal behaviors are involved in mother–infant interaction throughout the first year of life, and both may be viewed as contributing to the formation and later mediation of the attachment bond. Even though the relative balance between proximal and distal behaviors shifts with increasing age, the distal behaviors remain those that emerge only intermittently and for the most part under conditions of low-level activation of the attachment system, and hence less useful as indices of qualitative differences in attachment, even in the older preschool child. A more important consideration is that the most crucial differences in patterning, even in the 1-year-old child, pertain neither to proximal nor to distal attachment behaviors but to the way in which such behaviors are organized together with key nonattachment behaviors – specifically those that reflect avoidance of or resistance to the attachment figure. Our prediction is that those patterns of behavior in the older preschooler that will be found to link up with earlier strange-situation-based differences in attachment quality are patterns that include negative nonattachment behavior related to avoidance and resistance – and thus to anxiety and anger.

Attachments To Figures Other Than The Mother

One of the reasons that the concept of attachment has captured so much of the interest of developmental researchers and clinicians regardless of their initial theoretical starting-points is the implicit hypothesis that the nature of a child's attachment relationship to his mother figure has a profound effect on his subsequent development. (We, as well as Bowlby, emphasize the term "mother figure" to assert our belief that the child's principal caregiver in infancy and early childhood is most likely to become the principal attachment figure – and thus the most important initial influence on subsequent development – whether such a figure be his natural mother, a foster or adoptive mother, a grandmother, a "nanny," or father.) In the beginning stages of research into attachment, it made good sense to focus on attachment to the mother figure, without thereby implying that attachments to other figures were of no consequence, or that other later relationships, whether or not they could be classified as attachments, had little significance in influencing a child's development. It ought to be possible to assert the importance of research into other attachments and other relationships without thereby impugning the value or validity of the attachment theory. Thus it seems naive of Willemsen and associates (1974) to have concluded that their finding that the father serves as an attachment figure in the strange situation essentially as the mother does demonstrates the invalidity of attachment theory. It is undeniable that the young child, and indeed also the young infant, develops within the framework of a "social network," as Weinraub, Brooks, and Lewis (1977) have eloquently described. Undoubtedly it is important to trace through the characteristics and effects of relationships other than the child's attachment to his mother figure. It is clearly important to investigate children's relationships with siblings, playmates, teachers, and so on. But this does not mean that attachment theory is of no value.

It seems to us to be of more urgent importance, however, to investigate relationships an infant has with those figures who share the caregiving role with the principal caregiver (usually the mother) – whether these figures include the father, other adults resident in the household, or supplementary or substitute figures such as day-care personnel, long-term "baby sitters," and the like. We need to take advantage of cross-cultural studies and "experiments of opportunity" within our own culture in order to investigate how different patterns of infant care affect the attachments of the infant to those involved in a caregiving role, and how variations on the theme of principal caregiver with supplementary and secondary figures show support and reinforcement for each other, compensatory function, or conflict; and we need to show how at least the more common of the many possible variations affect the development of the child.

Let us pose a few of the questions that readily emerge when one contemplates investigating a child's social network, while still concerning oneself only with his major caregivers. Can a "good" relationship with the father compensate for a conflicted and anxiety-provoking relationship with the mother? Can a few hours of high-quality interaction with the mother compensate for the fact that she leaves the major responsibility for daily infant care to substitute or supplementary figures? If both parents share equally in the care of the infant or young child, does he become equally attached to both, and what influence does this pattern have on his subsequent social development? Does the nature of the attachment a child has to his principal caregiver (mother figure) affect his relationship with other attachment figures, and in what ways? Or is the nature of his relationship with different attachment figures affected only by the nature of his interaction with each figure in isolation from and unaffected by his relationship with other figures? Does a child form significant attachment relationships with day-care personnel, and how do such relationships affect his relationship with his principal attachment figure and indeed his subsequent development? Each of these questions would require very time-consuming and difficult research projects before we begin to know as much about them as we already know about infant-mother attachment, which indeed is all too little.

In short, the fact that ramifications of research into a wide variety of attachments and other relationships have been indeed sparse denies neither the importance of undertaking such research nor the commonsense of beginning with the infant's attachment to his principal caregiver, which, across many cultures and throughout history, implies attachment to his mother.   99

Source: Ainsworth, M., Blehar, M., Waters, E. and Wall, S. (1978) *Patterns of Attachment*. Hillsdale, NJ: Lawrence Erlbaum Associates, Inc., pp. 304–9

Reflection

In the early years and primary education, relationships are key to supporting emotional development. Through secure secondary attachments and positive relationships with adults and peers, children can develop emotionally and feel secure enough to develop cognitively. When children are put into social situations where they do not feel secure, they are more likely to experience emotional difficulties. In settings and schools, the times when children need emotional skills and understandings are playtimes, co-operative activities and movements between activities. We often expect children to have the emotional and social skills and understandings needed for the effective relationships in these situations but do not consider what those skills and understandings are.

Reflective tasks

Use Goleman's (1998) categories of emotional intelligence:

1 Self-awareness or the ability to understand your own emotions and the effect they will have on others and affect decision-making.
2 Self-management, or the ability to control emotions and impulses in changing contexts.
3 Social awareness, or the ability to perceive, understand and react to emotions shown in other people.
4 Relationship management, or the ability to use emotions to lead, inspire, influence, and solve conflicts.

- What emotional skills and understandings do you consider the children in the your setting/school need?
- What are the key emotional skills and understandings that you need to develop in the children in your setting/school?

Impact tasks

Relationships can be supported through co-operative and collaborative activities and through play.

Early career professional:
Use your reflections above to plan a play activity that will help the children to develop positive relationships with their peers. Observe the children as they play and make notes on their level of emotional development and abilities to gauge the emotions of others and manage their own emotions.

Reflection

- How successful is your activity in supporting peer relationships and emotional development?
- What other activities or interventions will support peer relationships and emotional development?
- How can you support the children as they develop their emotional skills and understandings and improve relationships with peers?

The development of self-identity

Erikson (1950) was concerned with self-identity and developed the psycho-social theory of development, which has eight stages of self-identity starting in infancy and developing throughout life:

1 trust vs. mistrust, which involves getting and giving in return
2 autonomy vs. shame and doubt, associated with determination and perseverance and involves holding on and letting go
3 initiative vs. guilt, associated with a sense of purpose and involvement
4 industry vs. inferiority, which involves making and completion and competence
5 ego identity vs. role confusion, associated with loyalty and involves 'being' yourself
6 intimacy vs. isolation, or to lose and find oneself in an emotional relationship
7 generativity vs. self-absorption, associated with caring and involving taking care of yourself and others
8 integrity vs. despair, or developing wisdom and understanding your-self through what you have and have not been.

Trust vs. mistrust

This stage begins in infancy and so much of the development of self-identity occurs at home or with primary carers in the EYFS.

> Mothers create a sense of trust in their children by that kind of administration which in its quality combines sensitive care of the baby's individual needs and a firm sense of personal trustworthiness within the trusted framework of their culture's life style. This forms the basis of the child's sense of identity which will later combine a sense of being 'all right', of being oneself, and of becoming what other people trust one will become. There are therefore (within certain limits previously defined as the 'musts' of child care), few frustrations in either this or the following stages which the growing child cannot endure if the frustration leads to the ever renewed experience of greater sameness and stronger continuity of development, towards a final integration of the individual life-cycle with some meaningful wider belongingness. Parents must not only have certain ways of guiding by prohibition and permission; they must also be able to represent to the child a deep, an almost somatic conviction that there is meaning to what they are doing. Ultimately, children become

neurotic not from frustrations, but from the lack or loss of societal meaning in frustrations.

(Erikson, 1950: 241)

Autonomy vs. shame and doubt

Children need to explore and manipulate their environment, with encouragement from adults so that they are developing a sense of autonomy or independence. The encouragement needs to be balanced so that children develop both self-control and self-esteem. However, if there is an imbalance the children may develop a sense of shame and doubt, resulting in poor independence. Children need encouragement and not ridicule, they need guidance and not unrestricted freedom, they need patience. However, Erikson (1950) says that some aspects of shame and doubt are beneficial and lead to impulsiveness, but too much can lead to compulsiveness. Balanced support can lead to independence and determination.

Initiative vs. guilt

Children need to be encouraged to take initiatives and try out ideas. Adults should accept and encourage curiosity and imagination in play. The ability to imagine can also lead to responsibility and guilt as children are able to imagine situations that they know are 'wrong'. It is important at this stage for children to learn that they are responsible for their actions, so encouragement to take initiative needs to be tempered by their understanding of responsibility. Too much initiative and too little guilt can lead to ruthlessness, while too much guilt can lead to inhibition, where the child will not venture for fear of the consequences. Where there is balance, the child has a sense of purpose and a clear understanding of limitations and past failings.

Industry vs. inferiority

This stage of Erikson's (1950) psychosocial theory of development occurs from about 6–12 years of age and here children need support and encouragement to develop a capacity for industry while avoiding feelings of inferiority. The industry Erikson refers to is that encouraged by education and learning and there is some thought that imagination needs to be curbed, although it can be argued that creativity and imagination can be supportive of learning. With encouragement children gain satisfaction and feelings of success from planning and carrying out their plans. Children at this stage will also strictly apply the rules of games and society. If there is an imbalance in this stage, maybe because adults or peers are too harsh, rejecting or discriminating, then the child will develop a sense of inferiority or lack of competence and they are unlikely to persevere with tasks if they think they will fail because of who they are rather than what they do or how well they do it. Children who are too industrious are those that grow up too quickly and are not allowed to be children; this termed *narrow virtuosity* by Erikson (1950). Too little industry results in inertia, so that children who feel inferior do not try again and persevere to succeed.

Growing up too fast

I recall seeing a group of boys racing along the street when one yelled 'Last one to the corner is a nerd'. One unfortunate youngster was tripping over his sneaker laces and had to stop to tie them. He shouted to the first boy 'Not included!' To which came the swift reply 'No say-backs'. Learning to create rules – even simple rules for otherwise uncomplicated street games – and to abide by those you have created is an important part of rule learning and of mature social behavior.

Children who have attained concrete operations are also able to enter the culture of childhood, which is in effect, a body of rules that has been handed down by oral tradition over hundreds of years . . . Hurried children are often deprived of this rich cultural heritage and the opportunity to interact with peers on a level that is unique to childhood and removed from adult concerns.

I am not advocating a romantic view of childhood that suggests that this period is free of conflict and anxiety. There are conflicts and anxieties that are appropriate to this age period – concerns about peer acceptance and about academic and athletic competence – that have to be faced and dealt with. What is crucial during this period is that young people learn to deal with peers on an equal footing as persons with reciprocal needs and interests. This is different from dealing with an adult where the relationship is unilateral – wherein adults have authority over children but not the reverse.

(Elkind, 2001: 127–8)

Subject tasks

There are a number of different ways to encourage and support emotional development in settings and schools through different key areas and subjects. Emotions are an important aspect of all learning as without the desire to learn, persevere and complete activities, children will not learn. Motivation is an important part of any learning experience and children need to be curious, questioning and have a desire to learn.

In these tasks, we focus on aspects of creative development to consider how emotional awareness and self-identity can be supported and encouraged.

EYFS:
Emotions are often triggered by the senses. Powerful emotions are evoked by smell, sound, colour and even taste. Playdough with the addition of lavender seeds can help calm and essence of cinnamon or frankincense can evoke memories of Christmas. Colour can be used in painting to indicate feelings with different colours and shades of colours used for different emotions. Music can also be used to evoke emotions and children can take a favourite book and produce a sound track to represent the different emotions in the story. For example, *The Snow Lambs* (Gliori, 1995) provides many opportunities to focus on different emotions (fear, sadness, relief, love).

Plan one activity that has both creative and emotional awareness learning outcomes. While children undertake the activity, collect evidence on the children's awareness of emotions in themselves and others.

Reflection

- How successful was the activity in developing emotional awareness in the children?
- What factors supported or inhibited the success of the activity?
- How else could you develop emotional awareness in the EYFS?

KS1:
Music and dance are good vehicles for expressing emotions. The starting point for dance can be the music or as Swindlehurst and Chapman (2008) have identified, action words. A combination of music and emotional words, such as 'happy', 'sad', 'frightened', 'angry', and so on can also be used as a starting point for dance.

Use music and/or dance to explore emotions with your children. Allow them to identify the way that music makes them feel or use emotions to help trigger their choice of dance. Observe their dance and question them about their feelings as they were dancing.

Reflection

- How successful was the activity in encouraging expression of emotions in the children?
- What factors supported or inhibited the success of the activity?
- How else could you encourage children to explore and express their emotions?

KS2:

Role play and drama can help children to explore self-identity and emotional problems in a non-threatening way. Children can explore difficult situations and encounters, including bullying or teasing and emotional and social experiences such as moving house, school or making or breaking up with friends. They can discuss the way they feel in these situations and explore their self-identity.

Children can start by brainstorming situations that make them feel good or bad about themselves. Allow children to work in a small group and choose one situation from the brainstorming list to enact. Through the drama the children can explore resolutions to help them create positive self-images in themselves and others.

Reflection

- How successful was the activity in the exploration of self-identity in the children?
- What factors supported or inhibited the success of the activity?
- How else could you encourage children to explore and support self-identity?

References

Ainsworth, M., Blehar, M., Waters, E. and Wall, S. (1978) *Patterns of Attachment.* Hillsdale, NJ: Lawrence Erlbaum Associates, Inc.

Alexander, R. (ed.) (2009) *Children, their World, their Education: Final Report and Recommendations of the Cambridge Review.* London: Routledge.

Bowlby, J. (1958) The nature of a child's tie to his mother, *International Journal of Psychoanalysis*, 39: 350–73.

Bowlby, J. (1969) *Attachment and Loss.* New York: Basic Books.

Bowlby, R. (2007) Babies and toddlers in non-parental daycare can avoid stress and anxiety if they develop a lasting secondary attachment bond with one carer who is consistently accessible to them, *Attachment & Human Development*, 9(4): 307–19.

Elkind, D. (2001) *The Hurried Child: Growing Up Too Fast Too Soon*, 3rd edn. Cambridge, MA: Da Capio Press.

Erikson, E.H. (1950) *Childhood and Society*. New York: Norton.

Field, T. (1991) Quality infant daycare and grade school behaviour and performance, *Child Development*, 62: 863–70.

Gliori, D. (1995) *The Snow Lambs*. London: Scholastic.

Goleman, D. (1998) *Working with Emotional Intelligence*. New York: Bantam Books.

Mampe, B., Friederici, A.D., Christophe, A. and Wermke, K. (2009) Newborns' cry melody is shaped by their native language, *Current Biology*. Available online at www.cell.com/current-biology/home (accessed 5 November 2009).

Maslow, A.H. (1968) *Towards a Psychology of Being*. New York: D. Van Nostrand Co.

Rose, J. (2009) *Independent Review of the Primary Curriculum: Final Report*. Nottingham: Department for Children, Schools and Families (DCFS).

Salovey, P. and Grewal, D. (2005) The science of emotional intelligence: Current directions in psychological science, 14(6): 281–5.

Swindlehurst, G. and Chapman, A. (2008) Teaching dance a framework for creativity, in J. Lavin (ed.) *Creative Approaches to Physical Education*. Abingdon: Routledge.

3 Physical and spatial development

This chapter considers children's physical and spatial development through the theories of the McMillan sisters (Rachel and Margaret) and Maslow's hierarchy of needs.

Children grow and develop physically from the moment of conception and although growth is rapid in the early stages of development (in the womb and in the early years) and slows down in later years, physical development can continue throughout childhood and into adulthood.

Physical development involves the control of the physical aspects of the body; gross motor skills such as crawling, walking, hopping, skipping and fine motor skills, such as holding, writing, painting, cutting, and so on. In this way physical development involves a link between the brain and the body and problems in the communication between the brain and muscles affecting physical development.

Brain development

Initial movements are not controlled by the brain, but are rather the result of reflexes and are designed with biological purposes to keep the baby safe and cared for. They include the grasp, suckle and startle reflexes. Some involuntary reflexes, such as blink, gag and startle continue into adulthood and again have a biological purpose.

There are two types of brain cell – neurons, or nerve cells – that send and receive information and glial cells that support and protect the neurons (Papalia et al., 2006). Neurons have two parts; the dendrite or receiver of signals and the axon or sender of information to other neurons, thus making a connection across the gap between neurons or synapse (Keenan, 2002: 79). The first year is crucial for the development of the brain and in the first two years of life, the pace of forming the connections between neurons is very rapid and occurs in bursts, followed by pruning of some connections. This is probably a result of experiences, but there may be some biological aspect to it. If, during the first year of life and important period of brain development, children are not stimulated, this can affect subsequent development of the brain (Nash, 1997). The developing brain is also capable of recovering from considerable trauma with neurons in other parts of the brain taking on new functions (Bukatko and Daehler, 2004).

The reflex movements seen in newborn babies are not really controlled by the brain but within one month the brain begins to control movements in response to sensory inputs; for example, the sight and sound of a parent elicits movements. By the time they are six months old the brain controls body movement and the instinctive reflexes seen in the newborn are replaced by increasingly controlled movements. The developing brain enables children to develop and use physical skills and has an impact on all areas of development. They can explore the world in which they live, make social contacts and fine-tune motor skills that lead to cognitive pursuits, such as reading, writing and measuring. In this way the physical child begins to be independent and social and supports a range of cognitive understandings and skills.

Reflection

There are a large number of disorders associated with physical and brain development and function. Consider the list below and identify conditions that you have encountered in your work with children and the effect on the children's development and your ability to support them:

- *Cerebral palsy*, where impairment in brain development affects movement.
- *Communication disorder*, which affects the ability to communicate due to problems in understanding, or producing verbal and non-verbal signals.
- *Down's syndrome*, where chromosome abnormalities affect both physical and cognitive development.
- *Dyslexia*, or problems in interpreting written language.
- *Fetal alcohol syndrome*, which causes a range of cognitive and physical problems.
- *Fragile X syndrome*, an inherited disorder that is associated with an abnormal X chromosome and causes moderate to severe cognitive problems and physical abnormalities such as large ears, chin and forehead.
- *Autistic disorder*, or impaired social development and communication and restricted physical activity and interests.

- *Rett's disorder*, or the development of multiple and specific problems that occur after a period of normal functioning after birth and characterized by a decrease in head growth and physical development.
- *Childhood disintegrative disorder*, which involves regression in a range of physical, social and cognitive functions after two years of normal development.

Reflective tasks

- How do the disorders you have experienced affect the child's social, cognitive and physical development?
- How can you support children with specific disorders to develop physically?

EYFS:
- Which disorders are more common or evident in the EYFS? Why might this be?
- How do the physical problems affect the children's emotional development?

KS1:
- How do the physical problems affect the children's ability to socialize?
- How can you support children with physical disabilities in the social interactions that occur at playtimes.

KS2:
- Are there some disorders that are more evident in later childhood? Why might this be?
- How do the physical problems affect the children in their cognitive development?

Spatial development

Spatial development, or the development of the ability to use space both physically and mentally, has strong links between the physical and cognitive. There are also thought to be differences in the male and female brain in spatial development, with these differences showing themselves by four years of age (Levine et al., 1999). Boys in middle childhood are more able than girls to mentally rotate three-dimensional figures and do considerably better than girls in spatial perception tasks and these differences continue to exist throughout childhood and into adulthood.

Spatial skills are thought to be a function of the right hemisphere of their brain and be the result of increased androgen hormones during brain development. Indeed, boys generally appear to be right brain dominant; that is, they use the right hemisphere of their brain more than the left. Children whose left hemisphere of the brain dominates tend to think more holistically, randomly, intuitively, concretely and non-verbally, as opposed to those whose right hemisphere dominates who tend to think in a linear, sequential, logical and verbal way.

The effects of brain on spatial and physical development

Cognition depends on language development, perceptual development and spatial development and children who enter school with poor spatial skills will have more difficulty in mathematical development.

> One critical factor for building a number system from these basic spatial and perceptual representations appears to be learning the count sequence. Counting appears to be learned first as a linguistic routine, like a nursery rhyme or the days of the week. The language of the count sequence captures number meaning in terms of both a distinctive individual quantity ('cardinality') and a quantity with a fixed place among other numerical quantities that is dependent on increasing magnitude ('ordinality'). A number label in the count sequence, such as 'four', represents the fact that 4 cats is the equivalent amount to 4 biscuits, and that 4 has a magnitude between 3 and 5. Learning to count enables children to organise their cognitive structures for number (subitizing and the analogue magnitude representation) into a coherent system. Accordingly, certain cross-cultural differences in the set of number names have some cognitive consequences, although these are brief and occur around age 2. . . . By around 3 years, children are developing the expectation that even unmapped number words refer to exact numerosities. Number knowledge such as the 'number facts' (for example the multiplication tables, 2 + 2 =4 et cetera) are stored in the language areas of the brain, and not in the spatial area where the analogue magnitude representation is found.
>
> (Goswami and Bryant, 2007: 17)

Subject tasks

EYFS:
Plan an activity that gives the children opportunities to explore conservation of number. This could be:

- counting and comparing five objects in a line, in a pile and in a plastic beaker
- making and comparing lines, towers and piles of five bricks
- making five fingerprints in a line, a circle, a random pattern and comparing.

Reflection

Observe the children as they undertake the task and encourage them to talk about their results.

- What does this activity tell you about the children's spatial development?
- How could you support them in their development?

KS1:
Plan an activity that gives the children the opportunity to explore the different ways to make 5 or 10 using small bricks, joined together. How many ways can they join the bricks together to make 5 or 10 (see Fig. 3.2).

Reflection

Talk with the children about what they have done.

- How did different children respond to the problem?
- How could support with their spatial development help children further in mathematics?

KS2:
Plan an activity that gives the children the opportunity to explore mental rotation. You could give them an object and ask them to draw what it would look like if it was rotated, or give them some odd one out visual spatial problems (see Fig. 3.1)

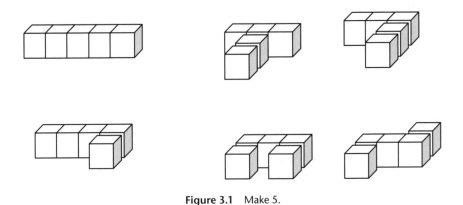

Figure 3.1   Make 5.

Motor skills

There are three types of motor skill: (1) gross motor skills; (2) locomotor skills; and (3) fine motor skills:

Gross motor skills

Gross motor skills are the large physical movements involving the whole body or limbs and include crawling, walking, running, skipping and hopping. Control of the head is the first gross motor skills that a baby develops and this is followed by control of other parts of the body.

Locomotor skills

Locomotor skills involve gross motor skills and movement from one place to another and start when children start to crawl and move around (Hughes, 2002). These gross and locomotor skills develop sequentially and are often

Find the one in each group that does not belong

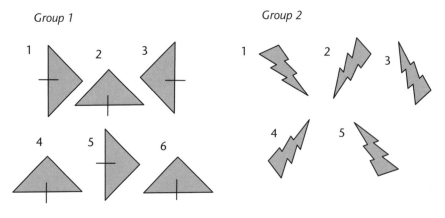

Group 1

Group 2

Answers

Group 1
4, each figure is turned 90 degrees counterclockwise to make the next figure

Group 2
3, each figure can be rotated so they coincide

Figure 3.2   Visual spatial problems.

identified as milestones in a child's life, which many child development books identify. Balance is important in physical development and crucial in the explosion of gross motor skills in childhood as children grow and become less top heavy. There are differences between boys' and girls' development of gross motor skills, with boys being more powerful and able to run faster, throw a ball further and girls being able to balance, hop and skip better.

Fine motor skills

Fine motor skills are those manipulative skills that involve small movements and small muscles in parts of the body, such as picking up, feeding themselves, threading, drawing, cutting and dressing. Fine motor skills develop slightly later than gross motor skills and need patience and practice to develop. As children grow and develop muscle and bone, they are able to use fine motor skills. The rate of development may also be different for boys and girls as the rate of growth of bones and muscles is different. For example, children have fewer bones in their wrist than adults and girls have developed a full complement by just over four years of age and boys by five and a half years of age (Bee and Boyd, 2007). This can mean that girls have developed the physical attributes for fine hand movements and may appear more advanced at writing and drawing at an earlier age.

The effect of physical development on the developing child

Maslow is a key figure known to all educational professionals. His hierarchy of needs has been used in many contexts and indicates the real problems that physical and emotional poverty and social conflict inflict on children's development. Maslow (1968) emphasized the importance of physical development by placing physiological needs as the foundation of his hierarchy of needs. Physical needs are the most important needs for the young child and if children do have the basic needs of sufficient food, sleep, warmth, and so on they are not able to develop physically nor move to develop emotionally, socially or realize their full potential in life. (See Chapter 2, Fig. 2.1, Maslow's (1968) theory of hierarchical needs.)

The following extract focuses on the basic needs that affect healthy physical development.

The concept "BASIC NEED" can be defined in terms of the questions which it answers and the operations which uncovered it. My original question is about psychopathogenesis. "What makes people neurotic?" My answer (a modification of and, I think, an improvement upon the analytic one) as, in brief, that neurosis seemed at its core, and its beginning, to be a deficiency disease; that it was born out of being deprived of certain satisfactions which I called needs in the same sense that water and amino acids and calcium are needs, namely that their absence produces illness. Most neuroses involve, along with other complex determinants, ungratified wishes for safety, for belongingness and prestige. My "data" were gathered through twelve years of psychotherapeutic work and research and twenty years of personality study. One obvious control research (done at the same time and in the same operation) was on the effect of replacement therapy which showed, with many complexities, that when these deficiencies ere eliminated, sickness tended to disappear.

These conclusions, which are not in effect shared by most clinicians, therapists, and child psychologists (many of them would not phrase it as I have) make it possible year by year to define need, in a natural, easy, spontaneous way, as a generalization of actual experiential data (rather than by fiat, arbitrarily and prematurely, prior to the accumulation of knowledge rather than subsequent to it simply for the sake of greater objectivity).

The long running deficiency characteristics are then the following. It is a basic or instinctoid need if

1. its absence breeds illness,
2. its presence prevents illness,
3. its restoration cures illness,
4. under certain (very complex) free choice situations, it is preferred by the deprived person over other satisfactions,
5. it is found to be inactive, at a low ebb, or intentionally absent in the healthy person.

It is these needs which are essentially deficits in the organism, empty holes, so to speak, which must be filled up for health's sake, and furthermore must be filled from without by human beings other than the subject, that I shall call deficits or deficiency needs for purposes of this exposition and to set them in contrast to another and very different kind of motivation.

(Maslow, 1968: 27–8)

Reflection

Is it the norm that children arrive in settings and school with their basic needs met and ready to learn?
Is the norm that family life is much more chaotic than we realize?

Reflective tasks

EYFS:
- Are there children entering the EYFS who have not had their basic needs met (Maslow, 1968)? Is there one basic need that is less well fulfilled?
- How do you think failure to meet basic needs impacts on other aspects of the children's development?
- How could you work with their family and other professionals to meet their basic needs?

KS1:
- What are the reasons why children start the school day not ready to learn?

- How do you think the problems that children encounter affect their readiness to learn?
- How could you ameliorate any problems that children have that affect their learning?

KS2:

- Are there children in your school who are failing because their basic needs are not met? What needs are most commonly not met?
- What are the short- and long-term effects of failure to meet basic needs?
- How can you support children and ameliorate the negative effects on learning?

Factors affecting physical development

Margaret McMillan, working with her sister Rachel, was the first professional theorist who recognized the importance of a healthy body for the development of a healthy mind and academic achievement. The following extract illustrates that as early as 1911, she was highlighting the importance of health for developing children.

> The facts that have met us in the first attempt at a survey have been overwhelming almost in their brutal nature. Who could have believed that weakness, defect, arrest, disease, deformity, semi-deafness and blindness were general in some places. Who could have guessed that these things are common even among the children of the well-to-do? Yet the first reports of the School Medical Officers do not leave us in any doubt on this point.
>
> In the last few years we have seen the "figure" so often. Can we not take them for granted now? Perhaps it may be well to give a few details here, if only to show how impossible it is to go on while pain and weakness and horrors unspeakable are right in front of us.
>
> Out of 372 scholars examined in the Boys' Department in a Deptford School, 168 are found to be in urgent need of Medical Treatment. In the Girls' Department, out of 412 examined 184 were declared to be cases for a doctor's immediate attention, and even in the Infants' Department 34 little children out of 105 are pronounced to be too ill to go on longer without treatment.
>
> These figures do not, however, reveal all the facts. They show, it is true, that out of nearly 900 children 400 stand in urgent need of

treatment. They do not show that the remaining 500 are in good health. Many of these are, as a matter of fact, on the way to becoming urgent cases, for the doctor turned again and again to mothers in order to warn them "not today, perhaps, but to-morrow your child will be in need of treatment".

(McMillan, 1911: 18–19)

Although McMillan is reporting on children a hundred years ago, there are some important lessons for us in today's society. First, the link between health and education was clearly shown by Macmillan's research and writing and needs to be remembered in today's society. Children are still malnourished, and sometimes this malnourishment is linked to obesity, as children's diet is not supportive of health and physical development. Illness of any kind has a negative effect on children's ability to learn and while medical advances mean that major illnesses of a hundred years ago can be treated, we have other challenges. These include life-style health problems, due to overeating and lack of exercise, resistance to drugs and children who have special needs that would not have been treatable in previous generations. MacMillan (1911) goes on to provide some mini case studies of children, whose physical problems do not appear to be so dissimilar to ones we can see today.

> Here is Marion, a small, but not ill-nourished child of ten. The teacher reports that she seems bright and intelligent, and unfit for the ordinary school only on account of eye-defect. The left eye is slightly inflamed. The child suffers also from nasal obstruction. The teeth are in a bad state.

(McMillan, 1911: 25)

The second important lesson concerns the way professionals work together to ensure that physical, social, emotional and educational needs are met and to enable all children to realize their full potential; self-actualization (Maslow, 1968). Extended and integrated services as identified in the *Every Child Matters* agenda (DfES, 2004) were introduced to provide opportunities for professionals to work together with families to support children (DCSF, 2009). This replaces the old system of school nurses, doctors and dentists and is not without its challenges, particularly to ensure that no child is 'forgotten' and every professional works effectively with others from different services. The children's centres and settings that provide integrated and extended services have a recognized place in the wider community, impacting on the physical, social, emotional, moral and educational development of children in the local community.

Many settings and schools provide extended services, such as breakfast clubs, after-school care, daily fruit and healthy school dinners. Some nurseries, in deprived areas, provide fresh fruit and drink 'on demand' so that children who may come to the nursery hungry may eat as and when they want. These children start by eating as much as they can as soon as they arrive in the nursery and after a while, when they realize that the food is always available, they eat when they need to rather than 'stocking up'. Other settings and schools provide clean, warm clothes and bathing facilities for children who do not get these basic needs met at home.

Impact tasks

Early career professional:
Consider how well your children are prepared for learning at the beginning of the day. Plan some changes to your day or practices to accommodate the children's needs. This may involve having a longer introduction to the day to allow children to settle into the day, or provide opportunities for children to talk about concerns that may affect their learning. Try out your idea and evaluate its effect on the children's readiness to learn.

Reflection

- What was the impact on the children's readiness to learn?
- What were the challenges you had to overcome to introduce the changes?
- How can you further support children to be prepared for learning?

Later years professional:
What are the reasons why children in your care are unprepared for learning? Plan some initiative to overcome the perceived problems. This may involve having a parents' session at the start of each day to allow the children to settle into the day, or introducing a class social breakfast at the start of the day. Try out your idea and evaluate its effect on the children's readiness to learn.

Reflection

- What was the impact of your initiative on the children's readiness to learn?
- What were the challenges you had to overcome to introduce the initiative and how did you overcome them?
- How can you extend the initiative to further support children to be prepared for learning?

Professional leader:
Introduce a new initiative to improve home-school liaison or extended services for children and families and which will improve children's readiness to learn. This may include a breakfast club, parents' club, or mother and toddler group. Evaluate the short- and longer-term impact of this initiative on the children in your setting/school.

Reflection

- How can you learn from reflection on the short-term impact of your initiative on the children's readiness to learn?
- How can you maximize the longer-term effects of your initiative on the children's readiness to learn?
- Are there any other initiatives that will support the children?

Modern challenges

In many ways the challenges for us in the twenty-first century are complex and numerous. These are illustrated by the United Nation's Children's Fund (Unicef) (2007) Report that looked at child well-being in 21 rich countries. Well-being was defined as being in six dimensions:

1 Material well-being. This is identified by three components: relative income poverty or the percentage of children living in homes with incomes below the national average; households without jobs; reported deprivation or children in families with few books and educational resources.
2 Health and safety, identified by health and mortality in the first year of life, low birth weight and age, health services available and deaths from accident or injury.
3 Educational well-being at school, indicated by achievement at age 15 in reading, mathematical and scientific literacy, the number of children who stay in education and the transition from education to employment (e.g. the percentage of young people in employment and skilled employment).
4 Family and peer relationships. This is identified by family structure (percentage of children living in single-parent families and the percentage of children living in stepfamilies), family relationships (percentage of children who report eating the main meal of the day with parents more than once a week and the percentage of children who

report that parents spend time talking to them) and peer relationships (finding peers 'kind and helpful').

5 Behaviours and risks. This is identified by three components: health behaviours (eating breakfast, eating daily fruit, being physically active, being overweight); risk behaviours (smoking, drinking, drugs, sex and teenage pregnancies); experience of violence (involvement in fighting, being bullied).

6 Subjective well-being, or perceived health, liking school life and personal well-being (feeling positive about their lives).

The results for the UK are frightening, as we came bottom overall with an average ranking of 18.2 and coming bottom (rank 21) for *family and peer relationships* and *behaviours and risks* and next to the bottom (rank 20) for *subjective well-being*. Indeed, *health and safety* is the only result where we do slightly better by being ranked 12, but we should not be pleased even with this result. The implications are equally frightening and pose big challenges for us as we try to support the physical, social, emotional and educational development of children (see Fig. 3.3).

Dimensions of child well-being	Average ranking position (for all 6 dimensions)	Material well-being	Health and safety	Educational well-being	Family and peer relationships	Behaviours and risks	Subjective well-being
UK	18.2	18	12	17	21	21	20

Figure 3.3 Results for the UK from the UNICEF report on child well-being.

Source: UNICEF (2007)

Reflection

Read the full UNICEF Report (2007) which can be found at www.unicef.org/sowc07/report/report.php

Reflective tasks

EYFS:
- What parts of the report specifically relate to issues that are part of the EYFS?
- How can you support children's physical and spatial development in

the EYFS by addressing some of the recommendations identified in the report?

KS1:

- What are the implications of the Report for your work with children at KS1?
- How can addressing some of the recommendations in the report positively affect children's physical and spatial development?

KS2:

- What aspects of the Report have implications for your work with children at KS2?
- How can you make changes in your provision for children to positively impact on children's physical and spatial development?

One of our biggest challenges is to move the current focus on narrow cognitive targets and create environments in which children can develop and learn in a holistic way and which recognizes the importance of all areas of development. This is recognized in initiatives that use the outdoor environment for holistic learning, such as improvements in the school grounds (WHO, 2003), outdoor education and Forest Schools (2009). The quality of the outdoor environment was recognized by McMillan (1930) when she identified the main features of the nursery garden to include:

- trees, for climbing and shelter
- other resources so children can use the garden as a gymnasium
- herbs and vegetables, which can be used to augment healthy eating.

Subject tasks

EYFS:
Grow some cress in pots on the windowsill and tomatoes in compost bags outside. Allow the children to care for the plants and pick when ripe. These can be used to make healthy food. Try making some bread rolls with the children and butter (by putting full fat cream in a jar and shaking vigorously until it separates and the whey can be drained away). Children can be involved in making the food, setting a table and then all the children can be involved in a social meal.

Reflection
- How does the activity support the children's development in the EYFS? In what key areas does it support development?
- How else could you support physical development in the EYFS?

KS1:
Introduce a new game for children, which involves them working together physically. This may be something like hopscotch, skipping games, or Twister (Hasbro Games). Allow the children to negotiate the rules between themselves.

Reflection

- How does the activity support the children's physical and social development in KS1?
- How else could you support physical and social development at KS1?

KS2:
This activity can start by a visit to the supermarket or greengrocer. As part of the visit, buy a collection of fruit and vegetables. Alternatively, children can dig, plant, care for and pick fruit and vegetables in a plot in the school grounds (you can use grow-bags and pots if you do not have a spare plot of garden). Sort the fruit and vegetables according to parts of the plant (Sc2 Life and Living Processes) and use to make a vegetable hotpot and fruit salad (D&T). Discuss healthy diets.

Reflection

- How does the activity support the children's understandings about healthy living?
- How else could you support science and physical development in a holistic way?

References

Bee, H. and Boyd, D. (2007) *The Developing Child*. New York: Pearson Education.

Bukatko, D. and Daehler, M. (2004) *Child Development: A Thematic Approach*. New York: Houghton Mifflin.

Department for Children, Schools and Families (DCSF) (2009) *About Integrated Services*. Available online at www.dcsf.gov.uk/everychildmatters/strategy/

deliveringservices1/multiagencyworking/integratedservices/integratedservices/ (accessed 18 November 2009).

Department for Education and Skills (DfES) (2004) *Every Child Matters: Change For Children*. London: DfES.

Forest Schools (2009) Available online at www.forestschools.com/ (accessed 18 November 2009).

Goswami, U. and Bryant, P. (2007) *Children's Cognitive Development and Learning: The Primary Review Research Survey 2/1a*. Cambridge: Cambridge University Press.

Hughes, L. (2002) *Paving Pathways. Child and Adolescent Development*. London: Wadsworth Thomson Learning.

Keenan, T. (2002) *An Introduction to Child Development*. London: Sage Publications.

Levine, S.C., Huttemlocher, J., Taylor, A. and Langrock, A. (1999) Early sex differences in spatial skill, *Developmental Psychology*, 35: 940–9.

Maslow, A.H. (1968) *Towards a Psychology of Being*. New York: D. Van Nostrand Co.

McMillan, M. (1911) *The Child and the State*. Manchester: National Labour Press.

McMillan, M. (1930) *The Nursery School*. London: Dent.

Nash, M. (1997) Fertile minds, *Child Growth and Development*, 1(2): 24–8.

Papalia, D., Olds, S. and Feldman, R. (2006) *A Child's World: Infancy Through to Adolescence*. New York: McGraw-Hill.

United Nation's Children's Fund (UNICEF) (2007) *The State of the World's Children 2007*. Available online at www.unicef.org/sowc07/report/report.php.

World Health Organization (WHO) (2003) *The Physical School Environment: An Essential Component of a Health-promoting School. Information Series on School Health Document 2*. Available online at www.who.int/school_youth_health/media/en/physical_sch_environment_v2.pdf (accessed 18 November 2009).

4   Cognitive development

This chapter looks at cognitive development today through an examination of Piaget's theory of cognitive development and a discussion of the work of Bruner and application of Howard Gardner's recent ideas on cognitive development.

What is cognitive development?

Cognitive development involves the development of conceptual knowledge and understanding; cognition. Cognition involves a number of skills and attributes, such as memory, the ability to abstract, solve a problem, think logically and reason. Much of our understanding about cognitive development in young children stems from Piaget's research that led to his seminal theory of cognitive development, part of which forms the following reading; chosen because of its relevance to children in the early and primary years.

> **66 Stages In The Construction Of Operations**
>
> In order to arrive at the mechanism of this development, which finds its final form of equilibrium in the operational grouping, we will distinguish (simplifying and schematizing the matter) four principal periods, following that characterized by the formation of sensori-motor intelligence.
>
> After the appearance of language or, more precisely, the symbolic function that makes its acquisition possible (1½ – 2 years), there begins a period which lasts until nearly 4 years and sees the development of symbolic and preconception thought.
>
> From 4 to about 7 or 8 years, there is developed, as a closely linked continuation of the previous stage, an intuitive thought whose progressive articulations lead to the threshold of the operation.
>
> From 7–8 to 11–12 years "concrete operations" are organized, i.e. operational groupings of thought concerning objects that can be manipulated or known through the senses.

Finally, from 11–12 years and during adolescence, formal thought is perfected and its groupings characterize the completion of reflective intelligence.

Symbolic And Preconceptual Thought

From the last stages of the sensori-motor period onwards, the child is capable of imitating certain words and attributing a vague meaning to them. But the systematic acquisition of language does not begin until about the end of the second year. Now, direct observation of the child, as well the analysis of certain speech disturbances, shows that the use of a system of verbal signs depends on the exercise of a more general "symbolic function", characterized by the representation of reality through the medium of "significants" which are distinct from "significates".

In fact, we should distinguish between symbols and signs on the one hand and indices or signals on the other. Not only all thought, but all cognitive and motor activity, from perception and habit to conceptual and reflective thought, consists in linking meanings, and all meaning implies a relation between a significant and a signified reality. But in the case of an index the significant constitutes a part or an objective aspect of the significate, or else it is linked to it by a causal relation; for the hunter tracks in the snow are an index of game, and for the infant the visible end of an almost completely hidden object is an index of its presence. Similarly, the signal, even when artificially produced by the experimenter, constitutes for the subject simply a partial aspect of the event that it heralds (in a conditioned response the signal is perceived as an objective antecedent). The symbol and the sign, on the other hand, imply a differentiation, from the point of view of the subject himself, between the significant and the significate; for a child playing at eating, a pebble representing a sweet is consciously recognized as that which symbolizes and the sweet as that which is symbolized; and when the same child, by "adherence to the sign", regards a name as inherent in the thing named, he nevertheless regards this name as a significant, as though he sees it as a label attached in substance to the designated object.

We may further specify that, according to a custom in linguistics which may usefully be employed in psychology, a symbol is defined as implying a bond of similarity between the significant and the significant, while the sign is "arbitrary" and of necessity based on convention. The sign thus cannot exist without social life, while the symbol may be formed by the individual in isolation (as in young children's play). Of course symbols also may be socialized, a collective symbol being generally half sign and half symbol; on the other hand, a pure sign is always collective.

In view of this, it should be noted that the acquisition of language, i.e. the system of collective signs, in the child coincides with the formation of the symbol, i.e. the system of individual significants. In fact, we cannot properly speak of symbolic play during the sensori-motor period, and K. Groos has gone rather too far in attributing an awareness of make-believe to animals. Primitive play is simply a form of exercise and the true symbol appears only when an object or a gesture represents to the subject, himself something other than perceptible data. Accordingly we note the appearance, at the sixth of the stages of sensori-motor intelligence, of "symbolic schemata," i.e. schemata of action removed from their context and evoking an absent situation (e.g. pretending to sleep). But the symbol itself appears only when we have representation dissociated from the subject's own action e.g. putting a doll or a teddy-bear to bed. Now precisely at the stage at which the symbol in the strict sense appears in play, speech brings about in addition the understanding of signs.

As for the formation of the individual symbol, this is elucidated by the development of imitation. During the serisori-motor period, imitation is only an extension of the accommodation characteristic of assimilatory schemata. When he can execute a movement, the subject, on perceiving an analogous movement (in other persons or in objects), assimilates it to his own, and this assimilation, being as much motor as perceptual, activates the appropriate schema. Subsequently, the new instance elicits an analogous assimilatory response, but the schema activated is then accommodated to new details; at the sixth stage, this imitative assimilation becomes possible even – with a delay, thus presaging representation. Truly representative imitation, on the other hand, only begins with symbolic play because, like the latter, it presupposes imagery. But is the image the cause or the effect of this internalization of the imitative mechanism? The mental image is not a primary fact, as associationism long believed; like imitation itself, it is an accommodation of sensori-motor schemata, i.e. an active copy and not a trace or a sensory residue of perceived objects. It is thus internal imitation and is an extension of the accommodatory function of the schemata characteristic of perceptual activity (as opposed to perception itself), just as the external imitation found at previous levels is an extension of the accommodatory function of sensori-motor schemata (which are closely bound up with perceptual activity).

From then on, the formation of the symbol may be explained as follows: deferred imitation, i.e. accommodation extended in the form of imitative sketches, provides significants, which play or intelligence applies to various significates in accordance with the free or adapted modes of assimilation that characterize these responses. Symbolic play thus always involves an element of imitation functioning as a significant, and early intelligence utilizes the image in like manner, as a symbol or significant.

We can understand now why speech (which is likewise learned by imitation, but by an imitation of ready-made signs, whereas imitation of shapes, etc., provides the significant material of private symbolism) is acquired at the same time as the symbol is established: it is because the use of signs, like that of symbols, involves an ability which is quite new with respect to sensori-motor behaviour and consists in representing one thing by another. We may thus apply to the infant this idea of a general "symbolic function", which has sometimes been used as a hypothesis in connection with aphasia, since the formation of such a mechanism is believed, in short, to characterize the simultaneous appearance of representative imitation, symbolic play, imaginal representation and verbal thought.

To sum up, the beginnings of thought, while carrying on the work of sensori-motor intelligence, spring from a capacity for distinguishing significants and significates, and consequently rely both on the invention of symbols and on the discovery of signs. But needless to say, for a young child who finds the system of ready-made collective signs inadequate, since they are partly inaccessible and are hard to master, these verbal signs will for a long time remain unsuitable for the expression of the particular entities on which the subject is still concentrated. This is why, as long as egocentric assimilation of reality to the subject's own action prevails, the child will require symbols; hence symbolic play or imaginative play, the purest form of egocentric and symbolic thought, the assimilation of reality to the subject's own interests and the expression of reality through the use of images fashioned by himself.

But even in the field of applied thought, i.e. the beginnings of representative intelligence, tied more or less closely to verbal signs, it is important to note the role of imaginal symbols and to realize how far the subject is, during his early childhood, from arriving at genuine concepts. We must, in fact, distinguish a first period in the development of thought, lasting from the appearance of language to the age of about 4 years, which may be called the period of pre-conceptual intelligence and which is characterized by pre-concepts or participations and, in the first forms of reasoning, by "transduction" or pre-conceptual reasoning.

Pre-concepts are the notions which the child attaches to the first verbal signs he learns to use. The distinguishing characteristic of these schemata is that they remain midway between the generality of the concept and the individuality of the elements composing it, without arriving either at the one or at the other. The child aged 2–3 years will be just as likely to say "slug" as "slugs" and "the moon" as "the moons", without deciding whether the slugs encountered in the course of a single walk or the discs seen at different times in the sky are one individual, a single slug or moon, or a class of distinct individuals. On the one hand, he cannot yet cope with general classes, being unable to distinguish between "all" and "some". On the other hand, although the idea of the permanent individual object has been formed in the field of immediate action, such is by no means the case where distant space and reappearances at intervals are concerned; a mountain is still deemed to change its shape in the course of a journey (just as in the earlier case of the rotated feeding-bottle) and "the slug" reappears in different places. Hence, sometimes we have true "participations" between objects which are distinct and distant from each other: even at the age of four years, a shadow, thrown on a table in a closed room by means of a screen, is explained in terms of those which are found "under the trees in the garden" or at night-time, etc., as though these intervened directly the moment the screen is placed on the table (and with the subject making no attempt to go into the "how" of the phenomenon).

It is clear that such a schema, remaining midway between the individual and the general, is not yet a logical concept and is still partly something of a pattern of action and of sensori-motor assimilation. But it is nevertheless a representative schema and one which, in particular, succeeds in evoking a large number of objects by means of privileged elements, regarded as samples of the pre-conceptual collection. On the other hand, since these type-individuals are themselves made concrete by images as much as, and more than, by words, the pre-concept improves on the symbol in so far as it appeals to generic samples of this kind. To sum up then, it is a schema placed midway between the sensori-motor schema and the concept with respect to its manner of assimilation, and partaking of the nature of the imaginal symbol as far as its representative structure is concerned.

Now the reasoning that consists in linking such pre-concepts shows precisely the same structures. Stern gave the name "transduction" to these primitive reasonings, which are effected not by deduction but by direct analogies. But that is not quite all: pre-conceptual reasoning or transduction is based only on incomplete dovetailings and is thus inadequate for any reversible operational structure. Moreover, if it succeeds in practice, it is because it merely consists of a sequence of actions symbolized in thought, a true "mental experiment", i.e. an internal imitation of actions and their results, with all the limitations that this kind of empiricism of the imagination involves. We thus see in transduction both the lack of generality that is inherent in the pre-concept and its symbolic or imaginal character which enables actions to be transposed into thought.

Intuitive Thought

The forms of thought we have been describing can be analysed only through observation, since young children's intelligence is still far too unstable for them to be interrogated profitably. After about 4 years, on the other hand, short experiments with the subject, in which he has to manipulate experimental objects, enable us to obtain regular answers and to converse with him. This fact alone indicates a new structuring.

In fact, from 4 to 7 years we see a gradual co-ordination of representative relations and thus a growing conceptualization, which leads the child from the symbolic or pre-conceptual phase to the beginnings of the operation. But the remarkable thing is that this intelligence, whose progress may be observed and is often rapid, still remains pre-logical even when it attains its maximum degree of adaptation; up to the time when this series of successive equilibrations culminates in the "grouping", it continues to supplement incomplete operations with a semi-symbolic form of thought, i.e. intuitive reasoning; and it controls judgements solely by means of intuitive "regulations", which are analogous on a representative level to perceptual adjustments on the sensori-motor plane.

As an example let us consider an experiment which we conducted some time ago with A. Szeminska. Two small glasses, A and A_2, of identical shape and size, are each filled with an equal number of beads, and this equality is acknowledged by the child, who has filled the glasses himself, e.g. by placing a bead in A with one hand every time he places a bead in A, with the other hand. Next, A, is emptied into a differently shaped glass B, while A is left as a standard. Children of 4–5 years then conclude that the quantity of beads has changed, even though they are sure none has been removed or added. If the glass B is tall and thin they will say that there are "more beads than before" because "it is higher", or that there are fewer because "it is thinner", but they agree on the non-conservation of the whole.

First, let us note the continuity of this reaction with those of earlier levels. The subject possesses the notion of an individual object's conservation but does not yet credit a collection of objects with permanence. Thus, the unified class has not been constructed, since it is not always constant, and this non-conservation is an extension both of the subject's initial reactions to the object (with a greater flexibility due to the fact that it is no longer a question of an isolated element but of a collection) and of the absence of an understanding of plurality which we mentioned in connection with the pre-concept. Moreover, it is clear that the reasons for the error are of a quasi-perceptual order; the rise in the level, or the thinness of the column, etc., deceives the child. However, it is not a question of perceptual illusions; perception of relations is on the whole correct, but it occasions an incomplete intellectual construction. It is this pre-logical schematization, which is still closely modelled on perceptual data though it recentres them in its own fashion, that may be called intuitive thought. We can see straight away how it is related to the imaginal character of the pre-concept and to the mental experiments that characterize transductive reasoning.

However, this intuitive thought is an advance on pre-conceptual or symbolic thought. Intuition, being concerned essentially with complex configurations and no longer with simple half-individual, half-generic figures, leads to a rudimentary logic, but in the form of representative regulations and not yet of operations. From this point of view, there exist intuitive "centralisations" and "decentralisations" which are analogous to the mechanisms we mentioned in connection with the sensori-motor schemata of perception (Chap. III). Suppose a child estimates that there are more beads in B than in A because the level has been raised. He thus "centres" his thought, or his attention; on the relation between the heights of B and A, and ignores the widths. But let us empty B into glasses C or D, etc., which are even thinner and taller; there must come a point at which the child will reply, "there are fewer, because it is too narrow". There will thus be a correction of centring on height by a decentring of attention on to width. On the other hand, in the case of the subject who estimates the quantity in B as less than that in A on account of thinness, the lengthening of the column in C, D, etc., will induce him to reverse his judgement in favour of height. Now this transition from a single centring to two successive centrings heralds the beginnings of the operation; once he reasons with respect to both relations at the same time, the child will, in fact, deduce conservation. However, in the case we are considering, there is neither deduction nor a true operation; an error is simply corrected, but it is corrected late and as a reaction to its very exaggeration (as in the field of perceptual illusions), and the two relations are seen alternately instead of being logically multiplied. So all that occurs is a kind of intuitive regulation and not a truly operational mechanism.

That is not all. In studying the differences between intuition and operation together with the transition from the one to the other, we may consider not merely the relating to each other of qualities forming two dimensions but their correspondences in either a logical (i.e. qualitative) or a mathematical form. The subject is first presented with glasses A and B of different shapes and he is asked to place a bead simultaneously in each glass, one with the left hand and one with the right. With small numbers (4 or 5), the child immediately believes in the equivalence of the two collections, which seems to presage the operation, but when the shapes change too much, even though the one-to-one correspondence is continued, he ceases to recognize equality. The latent operation is thus destroyed by the deceptive demands of intuition.

Let us line up six red counters on a table, supply the subject with a collection of blue counters and ask him to place on the table as many blue ones as there are red ones. From about 4 to 5 years, the child does not establish any correspondence and contents himself with a row of equal length (with its members closer together than those of the standard). At about 5 or 6 years, on the average, the subject lines up six counters opposite the blue. Has the operation now been acquired, as might appear? Not at all! It is only necessary to spread the elements in one of the series further apart, or to draw them close together, etc. for the subject to disbelieve in the equivalence. As long as the optical correspondence lasts, the equivalence is obvious; once the first is changed, the second disappears, which brings us back to the non-conservation of the whole.

Now this intermediate reaction is full of interest. The intuitive schema has become flexible enough to enable a correct system of correspondences to be anticipated and constructed, which to an uninformed observer presents all the appearances of an operation. And yet, once the intuitive schema is modified, the logical relation of equivalence, which would be the necessary product of an operation, is shown not to have existed. We are thus confronted with a form of intuition which is superior to that of the previous level and which may be called "articulated intuition" as opposed to simple intuition. But this articulated intuition, although it approaches the operation (and eventually joins up with it by stages which are often imperceptible), is still rigid and irreversible like all intuitive thought; it is thus only the product of successive regulations which have finally articulated the original global and unanalysable relations, and it is not yet a genuine "grouping".

This difference between the intuitive and the operational methods may be pinned down still further by directing the analysis towards the formation of classes and the seriation of asymmetrical relations, which constitute the most elementary groupings. But of course the problem must be presented on an intuitive plane, the only one accessible at this stage, as opposed to a formal plane indissociably tied to language. To study the formation of classes, we place about twenty beads in a box, the subject acknowledging that they are "all made of wood", so that they constitute a whole, B. Most of these beads are brown and constitute part A, and some are white, forming the complementary part A'. In order to determine whether the child is capable of understanding the operation A +A' i.e. the uniting of parts in a whole, we may put the following simple question: In this box (all the beads still being visible) which are there more of – wooden beads or brown beads, i.e. is A<B?

Now, up to about the age of 7 years, the child almost always replies that there are more brown beads "because there are only two or three white ones". We then question further: – Are all the brown ones made of wood?" – "Yes." – "If I take away all the wooden beads and put them here (a second box) will there be any beads left in the (first) box?" – "No, because they are all made of wood." – "If I take away the brown ones, will there be any beads left?" – "Yes, the white ones". Then the original question is repeated and the subject continues to state that there are more brown beads than wooden ones in the box because there are only two white ones, etc.

The mechanism of this type of reaction is easy to unravel: the subject finds no difficulty in concentrating his attention on the whole B, or on the parts A and A', if they have been isolated in thought, but the difficulty is that by centring on A he destroys the whole, B, so that the part A can no longer be compared with the other part A'. So there is again a non-conservation of the whole for lack of mobility in the successive centralizations of thought. But this is still not all. When the child is asked to imagine what would happen if we made a necklace either with the wooden beads or with the brown beads, A, we again meet the foregoing difficulties but with the following details: "If I make a necklace with the brown ones", a child will sometimes reply, "I could not make another necklace with the same beads, and the necklace made of wooden beads would have only white ones". This type of thinking, which is in no way irrational, nevertheless shows the difference still separating intuitive thought and operational thought. In so far as the first imitates true actions by imagined mental experiments, it meets with a particular obstacle, namely, that in practice one could not construct two necklaces at the same time from the same elements, whereas in so far as the second is carried out through internalized actions that have become completely reversible, there is nothing to prevent two hypotheses being made simultaneously and then being compared with each other.

The seriation of sticks A, B, C, etc. of different lengths, but placed side by side (to be compared in pairs), also yields an interesting lesson. Children of 4 to 5 years are able to construct only unco-ordinated pairs, BD, AC, EG, etc. Then the child constructs short series and achieves the seriation of ten elements only by groping his way from step to step. Furthermore, when he has finished a row he is incapable of interpolating new terms without undoing the whole. Not until the operational level is seriation achieved straight away, by such a method as, for example, finding the smallest of all the terms and then the next smallest, etc. It is at this level, similarly, that the inference $(A<B)+(B<C) = (A<C)$ becomes possible, whereas at intuitive levels the subject declines to derive from the two perceptually verified inequalities $A<B$ and $B<C$ the conclusion $A<C$.

The progressive articulations of intuition and the differences which still separate them from the operation are particularly clear where space and time are concerned, as well as being very instructive owing to the possibility of comparing intuitive and sensori-motor reactions. We are thus reminded of how the infant learns the action of turning a bottle round. To reverse an object by an intelligent action does not automatically lead to knowing how to reverse it in thought, and the stages of this intuition of rotation constitute largely a repetition of those of actual or sensori-motor rotation; in both cases we find a similar process of progressive decentralization from the egocentric point of view, this decentralization being simply perceptual and motor in the first case, and representative in the second.

Concrete Operations

The appearance of logico-arithmetical and spatio-temporal operations introduces a problem of considerable interest in connection with the mechanisms characterizing the development of thought. The point at which articulated intuitions turn into operational systems is not to be determined by mere convention, based on definitions decided on in advance. To divide developmental continuity into stages recognizable by some set of external criteria is not the most profitable of occupations; the crucial turning-point for the beginning of operations shows itself in a kind of equilibration, which is always rapid and sometimes sudden, which affects the complex of ideas forming a single system and which needs explaining on its own account. In this there is something comparable to the abrupt complex restructurings described in the Gestalt theory, except that, when it occurs, there arises the very opposite of a crystallization embracing all relations in a single static network; operations, on the contrary, are found formed by a kind of thawing out of intuitive structures, by the sudden mobility which animates and co-ordinates the configurations that were hitherto more or less rigid despite their progressive articulation. Thus, quite distinct stages in development are marked, for example, by the point at which temporal relations are merged in the notion of a single time, or the point at which the elements of a complex are conceived as constituting an unvarying whole or the inequalities characterizing a system of relations are serialized in a single scale, and so on; after trial-and-error imagination there follows, sometimes abruptly, a feeling of coherence and of necessity, the satisfaction of arriving at a system which is both complete in itself and indefinitely extensible.

Consequently, the problem is to understand what internal process effects this transition from a phase of progressive equilibration (intuitive thought) to a mobile equilibrium which is reached, as it were, at the limit of the former (operations). If the concept of "grouping" described in Chapter II has, in fact, a psychological meaning, this is precisely the point at which it should reveal it.

So, assuming that the intuitive relations of a given system are at a certain moment suddenly "grouped", the first question is to decide by what internal or mental criterion grouping is to be recognized. The answer is obvious: where there is "grouping" there will be the conservation of a whole, and this conservation itself will not merely be assumed

by the subject by virtue of a probable induction, but affirmed by him as a
certainty in his thought.   **99**

Source: Piaget, J. (1950) *The Psychology of Intelligence*. London:
Routledge & Kegan Paul, pp. 123–34 and 139–40

The relevance of Piaget's theories today

Piaget's theory of cognitive development (Piaget, 1950) has been influential in
education at all stages but is not without criticism. The first criticism is that the
theory used observations of his own children and so the sample was small and
his objectivity difficult to maintain. Other criticisms are concerned with the
assertive nature of Piaget's theories, the rigidity of the stages of development
in his theory and the ages assigned to the stages (Bruner et al., 1956). This is
because children's development appears to be more gradual and idiosyncratic
than Piaget's theory indicates.

Reflection

Piaget (1950) indicated that children could not abstract (solve mental problems)
until they were in the formal operations stage at about 11 years of age. As
children begin to abstract, they rely more on ideas than the need to manipulate
objects and are able to solve mental problems by building up mental models of
the world. However, children do seem to be able to think logically, make simple
hypotheses and to solve mental problems at a much earlier age, although
they will not be able to do it consistently or in every area at early ages.

Consider the children in your setting and make a note of all instances of
abstraction. This may involve them solving mental problems or hypothesizing.
You may wish to set up a problem-solving activity to see which children can
solve the problem.

Reflective tasks

EYFS:
- Are children able to solve mental problems in the EYFS? If so, when
  does this happen? If not why do you think this is?
- How do you think you can encourage the ability to solve mental
  problems and hypothesize in very young children?

KS1:
- What affects the children's ability to solve mental problems at KS1?

- How can you develop the ability to solve mental problems at KS1?

KS2:

- What opportunities do you provide to encourage children for mental modelling?
- How can you encourage abstraction and mental modelling in children at KS2?

Multiple intelligences

In *Frames of Mind: The Theory of Multiple Intelligence*, Gardner (1983) believes that there are a number of different intelligences:

- Bodily-kinaesthetic, where children use their body to solve problems and express ideas and feelings. Children who are physical and enjoy making things are likely to rate highly in this intelligence.
- Interpersonal, where children are able to gauge moods, feelings and needs of others and are good listeners and supportive friends.
- Intra-personal, where children have a well-developed knowledge about themselves and can use this knowledge to manage their own learning. They may be quite independent in the way they solve problems, doing it their way rather than copying others.
- Linguistic or the ability to use words, oral or written, where children are orally able; maybe telling stories, chatting away to others during activities.
- Logical-mathematical or the ability to understand and use numbers and reason well. Children will be good with numbers, think logically and solve problems.
- Musical, where children are likely to hum, tap their fingers and feet to imaginary beats even while they are working.
- Naturalist intelligence or the ability to organize and classify both the animal and plant kingdoms as well as showing understanding of natural phenomena. Children will enjoy outdoor education, animals, plants and environmental experiences.
- Spatial or the ability to perceive the visual-spatial world accurately, where children are able to orientate themselves and produce good painting, models and solve problems.

Many professionals have heard of Gardner's multiple intelligences, but fewer have actually read his work and so there has built up around this factor theory of intelligence a range of misunderstandings about what it means in practice. In *Multiple Intelligence: New Horizons in Theory and Practice*, Gardner (2006: 53–4) writes:

> Ever since I chose a career in scholarship, I have thought of myself primarily as a psychologist. My book Frames of Mind was written by a psychologist who thought he was addressing his fellow psychologists. In this book of some 400 pages, I included just a few paragraphs about the educational implications of the theory – and for the most part, these were ancillary thoughts.
>
> For reasons that I do not fully understand, the theory of multiple intelligences spoke immediately to educators – loudly and clearly. Many educators saw an evident relation between the theory, as they understood it, and educational practices that they embraced. In a sense, I had presented educators with a Rorschach inkblot, and they were trying to decipher it.
>
> I had read or heard about schools that had created seven or eight learning centers or even classrooms, one for each intelligence; schools that had decided to focus on one of the neglected intelligences; schools that taught subjects in seven or eight ways; schools that introduced new ways to assess intelligences; schools that put together all the students who were strong in one intelligence; schools that grouped students who were challenged in a particular intelligence; schools that believed the best education occurred when children representing different intellectual profiles were placed together in a classroom.
>
> None of these approaches was described or advocated in my book. I had not written as an educator: I did not know enough to be able to make cogent educational recommendations. Educators ere projecting their "projects" onto my uninterpreted inkblot tests; whatever they thought, they were not divining what I had *really* meant, nor what the theory had *really* meant.

Further reflection and interaction with education has led Gardner (2006) to identify three educational implications of the theory of multiple intelligences.

1   Individual centred education, which appears similar to personalized learning and 'takes the differences among individuals very seriously' (Gardner, 2006: 56) and had three roles, an assessment specialist collate individual formative assessments for parents, teachers and the child; a student-curriculum broker, who would facilitate differentiation to meet individual learning needs and the choice where options are available; a school community broker, who supports

children in vocational and non-vocational choices appropriate to their individual abilities.

2 The priority of educational goals, where schools prioritize their educational goals and have clear goals and success criteria. Trying to achieve everything is not a possibility, for 'if one seeks to be all things to all persons, the chances are high that one will not serve anyone well' (Gardner, 2006: 59).

3 Multiple representations of key concepts. Gardner identifies that the educational goals he most values is not literacy or numeracy, but skills of analysis and synthesis that can be applied to critique and understood in a few subject areas. His belief is that this is achievable if professionals focus on a few key concepts and explore them in some depth; that is, real understanding, rather than ephemeral and transitory knowledge needed to pass standard assessment tasks.

In a more recent publication, Gardner (2007) has identified five different ways of cognitive processing, which he calls 'minds' and which he considers will be important for individual cognition in the future. There is no hierarchy within these minds, but rather a rhythm, interrelationship and synergy between them. The first is the *disciplined mind*, that is developed through education and supports individuals in becoming 'expert' in one discipline. Being expert in one area/discipline was thought to be sufficient in the past, but the complexities of our current and future societies means that we need to become interdisciplinary or multidisciplinary, gain expertise in new disciplines and gain mastery over changing disciplines. This must not lead to a watering down of expertise, but rather the opposite.

The second 'mind' is the *synthesizing mind*. Synthesis involves the ability to survey a wide range of data or evidence, make decisions about the importance of that evidence, combine the data in a meaningful way and communicate the resulting synthesis in an understandable way. Synthesis is an intellectual skill of increasing importance in modern society and all professionals need to be able to synthesize huge amounts of information. A synthesizing mind will have an area of expertise (a discipline), know the trusted sources of information within the discipline, be able to keep an overview of the area being considered (the big picture) and consider the details. Gardner describes the synthesizing mind as being both a searchlight, having a broad overview, seeing and making use of the links between disciplines/areas, monitor changes in the area and also be a laser beam, having in-depth knowledge within the area. The *creating mind* is the third of Gardner's (2007) 'minds' and it involves the development of new ideas, practices and procedures, the solution to complex problems and innovation or engagement in creative pursuits such as problem-solving and risk-taking. It involves constant motivation to create and develop, even in the face of failure and involves aspects of both the disciplined and synthesizing minds in creation and innovative of new ideas in disciplines.

The fourth 'mind' is the *respectful mind*, which recognizes and embraces difference and inclusion and is important in a complex multicultural society, with the opening up of borders between countries and increasing pluralization. This mind encourages social contact, displays initial trust, gives individuals the benefit of the doubt, tries to form links, is tolerant and avoids making judgements. The final 'mind' is the *ethical mind*, which involves consideration of sophisticated moral issues in an abstract way. An ethical mind will not cut corners, will speak out if injustices are seen around them, at any expense and so there is a tension between the respectful and ethical minds.

Reflection

You may wish to read one or more of Gardner's books (1983, 2006, 2007) and consider your understanding of multiple intelligences, how you have used, or seen others use the theory.

- What are the implications of Gardner's (2006) educational implications for your future practice?
- How do the 'new look' multiple intelligences relate to the personalized learning agenda (DCSF, 2009).
- What do you consider are your educational goals? How do these fit in with Gardner's ideas?

Reflective tasks

EYFS:
- How are the educational goals for the EYFS different from other learning stages?
- How can you develop your practices in the EYFS to support individual learners?

KS1:
- How do your educational goals fit in with more personalized learning goals?
- What are the inhibiting factors that prevent you from developing a more personalized learning curriculum? How could you overcome these?

KS2:
  • How can you manage the tensions that exist between government agendas and more personalized learning goals?
  • How can you overcome the challenges and move towards more personalized learning and maintain standards?

Supporting children in cognitive development

Bruner (1966: 4–6) identified six features of cognitive 'growth':

1   Growth is characterized by increasing independence of response from the immediate nature of the stimulus, *or the ability to abstract.*
2   Growth depends upon internalizing events into a 'storage system' that corresponds to the environment; *memory.*
3   Intellectual growth involves an increasing capacity to say to oneself and others, by means of words or symbols, what one has done or what one will do; *metacognition.*
4   Intellectual development depends upon a systematic and contingent interaction between a tutor and a learner; *social interaction.*
5   Teaching is vastly facilitated by the medium of language, which ends by being not only the medium for exchange but the instrument that the learner can then use himself in bringing order into the environment.
6   Intellectual development is marked by increasing capacity to deal with several alternatives simultaneously, to tend to several sequences during the same period of time, and to allocate time and attention in a manner appropriate to these multiple demands; that is to solve complex problems.

Bruner has thus identified the important features that support cognitive development; metacognition, social interaction and language. Metacognition is the awareness and understanding of aspects of how you think. It is also one of the three pillars of cognitive acceleration, the process of supporting the construction of children's ideas (Shayer and Adey, 2002), based on Piaget's cognitive theories. Metacognition involves children in understanding their cognitive abilities and development and is greatly advanced by the second pillar of cognitive acceleration, social construction (see also Chapter 1). In social construction and through the medium of language (not writing), children share ideas, work through any muddled thinking, have greater metacognitive understanding and develop their ideas. It is important to note the distinction between children engaged in dialogic social constriction (Alexander, 2008) who develop understandings that can be applied in different contexts and children engaged in recording activities in written form so that they can be remembered to achieve the 'expected' standard in a test.

Another important feature of cognitive development is personalization, which again is a part of cognitive acceleration, so that children are treated as individuals, rather than as part of a group and activities are planned accordingly. This does not mean that teachers have to plan for each individual child, but rather that they differentiate appropriately for children who may need specific support or additional challenges.

Impact tasks

Early career professional:
Plan a cognitive learning activity with a small group of children and try and incorporate some peer and adult interaction. Carry out and evaluate the activity and identify how successful it was in developing the children's cognition.

- How important was the peer interaction in the success of the activity?
- How did your interaction support the children's learning?
- How could you improve your interaction to further develop the children's learning and your practice?

Later year professional:
Plan a cognitive learning activity for your class of children that incorporates both peer and adult interaction.

Carry out and evaluate the activity and identify how successful it was in developing the children's cognition.

- How important was the peer interaction in the success of the activity?
- How did your interaction support the children's learning?
- How could you improve your interaction to further develop the children's learning and your practice?
- How did the children feel about the activity? Did they learn best from the peer or adult interaction?

Professional leader:
Ask staff and children in your setting to identify what recent learning experiences they have liked/found most successful. Analyse their ideas and identify those that were individual activity, those that involved peer interaction and

those that involved more adult interaction. Try and identify what type of adult interaction was involved in the activities.

- Organizational; involved the adult in organizing the children;
- Motivational; involved the adult in motivating the children to learn for themselves;
- Instructional; involved the adult in didactic teaching of the children;
- Interactional; involved the adult in interacting with the children during the activity and learning with them;
- Other; not one of the above.

Identify what type of interaction you and your staff feel most comfortable with and why?

Subject tasks

EYFS:
Consider children in your setting with poor language development. Is there a link between their language and cognitive developments. How will development of one area support development in the other?

KS1:
Consider how language development is affecting the cognitive development of children in your setting. How could you develop their cognition through language?

KS2:
Analyse your current practice in your setting and consider how you develop cognition through and alongside other areas of development. What effect does poor language development have on the children's cognition and your ability to assess their cognition?

References

Alexander, R. (2008) *Towards Dialogic Teaching: Rethinking Classroom Talk*, 4th edn. York: Dialogos.

Bruner, J.S., Goodnow, J.J. and Austin, G.A. (1956) *A Study of Thinking*. New York: John Wiley & Sons, Inc.

Bruner, J.S. (1966) *Toward a Theory of Instruction*. Cambridge MA: Belknapp Press.

DCSF (2009) *Personalised Learning*. Available online at www.standards.dfes.gov.uk/ personalisedlearning/ (accessed 19 November 2009).

Gardner, H. (1983) *Frames of Mind: The Theory of Multiple Intelligence*, 2nd edn. London: Heinemann.

Gardner, H. (2006) *Multiple Intelligence: New Horizons*. New York: Basic Books.

Gardner, H. (2007) *Five Minds for the Future*. Boston, MA: Harvard Business School.

Piaget, J. (1950) *The Psychology of Intelligence*. London: Routledge & Kegan Paul.

Shayer, M. and Adey, P (eds) (2002) *Learning Intelligence: Cognitive Acceleration Across the Curriculum from 5 to 15 Years*. Buckingham: Open University Press.

5   Language development

This chapter focuses on the development of language in young children and the importance of early language acquisition on later development. It uses the theories of Chomsky (language acquisition) and Vygotsky (the link between social development, language development and cognitive development) and also links these to work by Bruner and Piaget.

Babies can communicate to their carers through crying and body language and animals can communicate with each other, but communication through language is unique to the developing human and sets us aside from all other animals. Language involves using a set of recognized symbols to communicate complex meanings and despite its complexity, it develops rapidly in the first few years of life, so that by the time a child is five years of age they can communicate complex emotional, social and cognitive meanings. Human language has three main features (Nahmad-Williams, 2007) being symbolic; grammatical; and having no single language system for different groups (Tomasello, 2003).

The development of language

In babies non-verbal communication, such as smiling, looking and touching, gives way to increasingly verbal communications by way of crying, gurgling and imitating sounds. In this way children are learning the complex rules associated with language and by the time they are a few years old they can not only recognize and use the symbolism and grammar associated with language, but they can also learn a number of different languages. We have seen three-year-old children who can speak fluently in three different languages, but we also know ourselves how difficult it is in older childhood or adulthood to learn a new language.

In our first extract, we consider Chomsky's (2006) ideas of language acquisition which have helped us understand how children develop language.

At the crudest level of description, we may say that a language associates sound and meaning in a particular way; to have command of a language is to be able, in principle, to understand what is said and to produce a signal with an intended semantic interpretation. But aside from much unclarity, there is also a serious ambiguity in this crude characterization of command of language. It is quite obvious that sentences have an intrinsic meaning determined by linguistic rule and that a person with command of a language has in some way internalised the system of rules that determine both the phonetic shape of the sentence and its intrinsic semantic content – that he has developed what we will refer to as a specific *linguistic competence*. However it is equally clear that the actual observed use of language – actual *performance* – does not simply reflect the intrinsic sound-meaning connections established by the system of linguistic rules. Performance involves many other factors as well. We do not interpret what is said in our presence simply by application of the *linguistic* principles that determine the phonetic and semantic properties of an utterance. Extralinguistic beliefs concerning the speaker and the situation play a fundamental role in determining how speech is produced, identified and understood. Linguistic performance is, furthermore, governed by principles of cognitive structures (for example, by memory restrictions) that are not, properly speaking, aspects of language.

To study a language, then, we must attempt to disassociate a variety of factors that interact with underlying competence to determine actual performance; the technical term 'competence' refers to the ability of the idealized speaker–hearer to associate sounds and meanings strictly in accordance with the rules of his language. The grammar of a language, as a model for idealized competence, establishes a certain relationship between sound and meaning – between phonetic and semantic representations.

(Chomsky, 2006: 115–16)

Reflection

Chomsky (2006) refuted the behaviourist view that language is learned by imitation and repetition and felt that children have an innate ability to learn the rules of language; the Language Acquisition Device (LAD). This occurs through application of the rules and after abstraction, indicating the part played by cognition in language development (see below).

We often underestimate what young children are capable of and yet knowledge about the way children develop language indicates just how capable they are. Consider the three characteristics of language: symbolism, grammar and the language system and how the children you care for are developing language. In the tasks below we have focused on one characteristic for each stage of learning, but this does not imply that each characteristic develops separately or that there is a hierarchy.

Reflective tasks

EYFS:
- How do you think children in the EYFS develop an understanding of the symbolism of language?
- How can you support the development of their understanding of symbolism in language?
- How does an understanding of language as symbolism affect other aspects of language; for example, grammar?

KS1:
- How do children in KS1 develop use of grammar in language?
- How can you support the development of grammar in speaking?
- How does an understanding of grammar affect other aspects of language; for example, symbolism or learning other languages?

KS2:
- Why might it be useful for children in KS2 to develop knowledge and understanding of different languages?
- How can you support children at KS2 to develop knowledge and skills of other languages?
- How might learning a second language help other aspects of language development; for example, an understanding of rules of grammar or roots of symbolism.

Language and thought

The second extract is from Vygotsky's important ideas about language and thought and which built on the work of Piaget (1929) which were discussed in the previous chapter.

    ❝ WE BEGAN our study with an attempt to discover the relation between thought and speech at the earliest stages of phylogenetic and ontogenetic development. We found no specific interdependence between the genetic roots of thought and of word. It became plain that the inner relationship we were looking for was not a prerequisite for, but rather a product of, the historical development of human consciousness.

In animals, even in anthropoids whose speech is phonetically like human speech and whose intellect is akin to man's, speech and thinking are not interrelated. A prelinguistic period in thought and a preintellectual period in speech undoubtedly exist also in the development of the child. Thought and word are not connected by a primary bond. A connection originates, changes, and grows in the course of the evolution of thinking and speech.

It would be wrong, however, to regard thought and speech as two unrelated processes, either parallel or crossing at certain points and mechanically influencing each other. The absence of a primary bond does not mean that a connection between them can be formed only in a mechanical way. The futility of most of the earlier investigations was largely due to the assumption that thought and word were isolated, independent elements, and verbal thought the fruit of their external union.

The method of analysis based on this conception was bound to fail. It sought to explain the properties of verbal thought by breaking it up into its component elements, thought and word, neither of which, taken separately, possesses the properties of the whole. This method is not true analysis helpful in solving concrete problems. It leads, rather, to generalization. We compared it to the analysis of water into hydrogen and oxygen – which can result only in findings applicable to all water existing in nature, from the Pacific Ocean to a raindrop. Similarly, the statement that verbal thought is composed of intellectual processes and speech functions proper applies to all verbal thought and all its manifestations and explains none of the specific problems facing the student of verbal thought.

We tried a new approach to the subject and replaced analysis into elements by analysis into *units*, each of which retains in simple form all the properties of the whole. We found this unit of verbal thought in *word meaning*.

The meaning of a word represents such a close amalgam of thought and language that it is hard to tell whether it is a phenomenon of speech or a phenomenon of thought. A word without meaning is an empty sound; meaning, therefore, is a criterion of "word," its indispensable component. It would seem, then, that it may be regarded as a phenomenon of speech. But from the point of view of psychology, the meaning of every word is a generalization or a concept. And since generalizations and concepts are undeniably acts of thought, we may regard meaning as a phenomenon of thinking. It does not follow, however, that meaning formally belongs in two different spheres of psychic life. Word meaning is a phenomenon of thought only in so far as thought is embodied in speech, and of speech only in so far as speech is connected with thought and illumined by it. It is a phenomenon of verbal thought, or meaningful speech – a union of word and thought.

Our experimental investigations fully confirm this basic thesis. They not only proved that concrete study of the development of verbal thought is made possible by the use of word meaning as the analytical unit but they also led to a further thesis, which we consider the major result of our study and which issues directly from the first: the thesis that word meanings develop. This insight must replace the postulate of the immutability of word meanings.

From the point of view of the old schools of psychology, the bond between word and meaning is an associative bond, established through the repeated simultaneous perception of a certain sound and a certain object. A word calls to mind its content as the overcoat of a friend reminds us of that friend, or a house of its inhabitants. The association between word and meaning may grow stronger or weaker, be enriched by linkage with other objects of a similar kind, spread over a wider field, or become more limited, i.e., it may undergo quantitative and external changes, but it cannot change its psychological nature. To do that, it would have to cease being an association. From that point of view, any development in word meanings is inexplicable and impossible – an implication which handicapped linguistics as well as psychology. Once having committed itself to the association theory, semantics persisted in treating word meaning as an association between a word's sound and its content. All words, from the most concrete to the most abstract, appeared to be formed in the same manner in regard to meaning, and to contain nothing peculiar to speech as such; a word made us think of its meaning just as any object might remind us of another. It is hardly surprising that semantics did not even pose the larger question of the development of word meanings. Development was reduced to changes in the associative connections between single words and single objects: A word might denote at first one object and then become associated with another, just as an overcoat, having changed owners, might remind us first of one person and later of another. Linguistics did not realize that in the historical evolution of language the very structure of meaning and its psychological nature also change. From primitive generalizations, verbal thought rises to the most abstract concepts. It is not merely the content of a word that changes, but the way in which reality is generalized and reflected in a word.

Equally inadequate is the association theory in explaining the development of word meanings in childhood. Here, too, it can account only for the purely external, quantitative changes in the bonds uniting word and meaning, for their enrichment and strengthening, but not for the fundamental structural and psychological changes that can and do occur in the development of language in children.

Oddly enough, the fact that associationism in general had been abandoned for some time did not seem to affect the interpretation of word and meaning. The Wuerzburg school, whose main object was to prove the impossibility of reducing thinking to a mere play of associations and to demonstrate the existence of specific laws governing the flow of thought, did not revise the association theory of word and meaning, or even recognize the need for such a revision. It freed thought from the fetters of sensation and imagery and from the laws of association: and turned it into a purely spiritual act. By so doing, it went back to the prescientific concepts of St. Augustine and Descartes and finally reached extreme subjective idealism. The psychology of thought was moving toward the ideas of Plato. Speech, at the same time, was left at the mercy of association. Even after the work of the Wuerzburg school, the connection between a word and its meaning was still considered a simple associative bond. The word was seen as the external concomitant of thought, its attire only, having no influence on its inner life. Thought and speech had never been as widely separated as during the Wuerzburg period. The overthrow of the association theory in the field of thought actually increased its sway in the field of speech.

The work of other psychologists further reinforced this trend. Selz continued to investigate thought without considering its relation to speech and came to the conclusion that man's productive thinking and the mental operations of chimpanzees were identical in nature – so completely did he ignore the influence of words on thought.

Even Ach, who made a special study of word meaning and who tried to overcome associationism in his theory of concepts, did not go beyond assuming the presence of "determining tendencies" operative, along with associations, in the process of concept formation. Hence, the conclusions he reached did not change the old understanding of word meaning. By identifying concept with meaning, he did not allow for development and changes in concepts. Once established, the meaning of a word was set forever; its development was completed. The same principles were taught by the very psychologists Ach attacked. To both sides, the starting point was also the end of the development of a concept; the disagreement concerned only the way in which the formation of word meanings began.

In Gestalt psychology, the situation was not very different. This school was more consistent than others in trying to surmount the general principle of associationism. Not satisfied with a partial solution of the problem, it tried to liberate thinking and speech from the rule of association and to put both under the laws of structure formation. Surprisingly, even this most progressive of modern psychological schools made no progress in the theory of thought and speech. For one thing, it retained the complete separation of these two functions. In the light of Gestalt psychology, the relationship between thought and word appears as a simple analogy, a reduction of both to a common structural denominator. The formation of the first meaningful words of a child is seen as similar to the intellectual operations of chimpanzees in Koehler's experiments – words enter into the structure of things and acquire a certain functional meaning, in much the same way as the stick, to the chimpanzee, becomes part of the structure of obtaining the fruit and acquires the functional meaning of tool. The connection between word and meaning is no longer regarded as a matter of simple association but as a matter of structure. That seems like a step forward. But if we look more closely at the new approach, it is easy to see that the step forward is an illusion and that we are still standing in the same place. The principle of structure is applied to all relations between things in the same sweeping, undifferentiated way as the principle of association was before it. It remains impossible to deal with the specific relations between word and meaning.

They are from the outset accepted as identical in principle with any and all other relations between things. All cats are as gray in the dusk of Gestalt psychology as in the earlier fogs of universal associationism.

While Ach sought to overcome associationism with the "determining tendency," Gestalt psychology combated it with the principle of structure – retaining, however, the two fundamental errors of the older theory: the assumption of the identical nature of all connections and the assumption that word meanings do not change. The old and the new psychology both assume that the development of a word's meaning is finished as soon as it emerges. The new trends in psychology brought progress in all branches except in the study of thought and speech. Here the new principles resemble the old ones like twins.

If Gestalt psychology is at a standstill in the field of speech, it has made a big step backward in the field of thought. The Wuerzburg school at least recognized that thought had laws of its own. Gestalt psychology denies their existence. By reducing to a common structural denominator the perceptions of domestic fowl, the mental operations of chimpanzees, the first meaningful words of the child, and the conceptual thinking of the adult, it obliterates every distinction between the most elementary perception and the highest forms of thought.

This critical survey may be summed up as follows: All the psychological schools and trends overlook the cardinal point that every thought is a generalization; and they all study word and meaning without any reference to development. As long as these two conditions persist in the successive trends, there cannot be much difference in the treatment of the problem.

The discovery that word meanings evolve leads the study of thought and speech out of a blind alley. Word meanings are dynamic rather than static formations. They change as the child develops; they change also with the various ways in which thought functions.

If word meanings change in their inner nature, then the relation of thought to word also changes. To understand the dynamics of that relationship, we must supplement the genetic approach of our main study by functional analysis and examine the role of word meaning in the process of thought.

Let us consider the process of verbal thinking from the first dim stirring of a thought to its formulation. What we want to show now is not how meanings develop over long periods of time but the way they function in the live process of verbal thought. On the basis of such a functional analysis, we shall be able to show also that each stage in the development of word meaning has its own particular relationship between thought and speech. Since functional problems are most readily solved by examining the highest form of a given activity, we shall, for a while, put aside the problem of development and consider the relations between thought and word in the mature mind.

The leading idea in the following discussion can be reduced to this formula: The relation of thought to word is not a thing but a process, a continual movement back and forth from thought to word and from word to thought. In that process the relation of thought to word undergoes changes which themselves may be regarded as development in the functional sense. Thought is not merely expressed in words; it comes into existence through them. Every thought tends to connect something with something else, to establish a relationship between things. Every thought moves, grows and develops, fulfills a function, solves a problem. This flow of thought occurs as an inner movement through a series of planes. An analysis of the interaction of thought and word must be in with an investigation of the different phases and planes a thought traverses before it is embodied in words.

The first thing such a study reveals is the need to distinguish between two planes of speech. Both the inner, meaningful, semantic aspect of speech and the external, phonetic aspect, though forming a true unity, have their own laws of movement. The unity of speech is a complex, not a homogeneous, unity. A number of facts in the linguistic development of the child indicate independent movement in the phonetic and the semantic spheres. We shall point out two of the most important of these facts.

In mastering external speech, the child starts from one word, then connects two or three words; a little later, he advances from simple sentences to more complicated ones, and finally to coherent speech made up of series of such sentences; in other words, he proceeds from a part to the whole. In regard to meaning, on the other hand, the first word of the child is a whole sentence. Semantically, the child starts from the whole, from a meaningful complex, and only later begins to master the separate semantic units, the meanings of words, and to divide his formerly undifferentiated thought into those units. The external and the semantic aspects of speech develop in opposite directions – one from the particular to the whole, from word to sentence, and the other from the whole to the particular, from sentence to word.

This in itself suffices to show how important it is to distinguish between the vocal and the semantic aspects of speech. Since they move in reverse directions, their development does not coincide, but that does not mean that they are independent of each other.

99

Source: Vygotsky, L. (1962) *Thought and Language*. Cambridge, MA: The MIT Press, pp. 119–26

Impact tasks

Vygotsky (1962) emphasizes the link between language development and cognition. These tasks will provide you with opportunities to reflect on these links.

EYFS:
Plan a problem-solving activity for the children and give them opportunities to talk to each other about what they are doing. You may use a problem-solving activity from Chapter 4, 'Cognitive development' or a shape puzzle, jigsaw or sequence activity. Ask the children to tell you about the problem and how they solved it.

Reflection

- What was the role of language in solving the problem?
- Why do you think language and cognitive development are mutually supportive?
- How can you use language to support cognitive development in the EYFS and vice versa?

KS1:
Plan to use speaking and listening to explore a story or historical character. This may involve hot-seating, where an adult or child can play the role of a character and be questioned by the children to help them understand the character and

the context, or use of a puppet for the child to speak to. We have used a 'Red Riding Hood' story doll to tell the story and for the children to quiz individual characters and Giant and Jack puppets to re-enact and question.

Reflection

- How did language enhance the activity for different learners?
- How did the activity develop an understanding of symbolism and grammar in language?
- Why do you think language and cognitive development are mutually supportive?

KS2:
Plan to use speaking and listening to communicate findings from another activity. This may be a science or geographical exploration or a mathematical investigation. After the activity, children should present the evidence they have and their interpretation as to what this evidence means. Other children should be encouraged to challenge the evidence and the interpretations of others. You may find this easier in the first instance to produce a set of statements about the results so the children can use the evidence to agree or refute the statements.

Reflection

- How does the development of argument support cognitive development?
- What does this activity tell you about the role of language in assessing cognition in all learners?
- How could you support language and cognitive development in other areas of learning?

Language and social development

Language is a complex interrelationship not only between cognitive development, but also between emotional and social development. The EYFS (DCSF, 2008: 41) identifies this interrelationship by identifying that:

> communicating and being with others helps children to build social relationships which provide opportunities for friendship, empathy and sharing emotions.

to become skilful communicators, babies and children need to be with people who have meaning for them and with whom they have warm and loving relationships, such as their family or carers and, in a group situation, a key person whom they know and trust.

Piaget (1959) was more concerned with cognition that language and the role that language plays in cognition was left to Vygotsky to uncover. Piaget believed that language supported cognition by linking symbols and thoughts, or labelling (Pinker, 1995). In this way language is used to describe and support schemas. This has been criticized by Pinker (1995) who feels, like Vygotsky (1962), that congnition is structured by the language. Piaget (1959) did, however, look at the role of social interaction and talk in cognitive development.

> In the preceding chapters we have tried to determine to what extent children speak to each other and think socially. An essential problem has been left on one side: when children talk together, do they understand one another?
>
> This question is not so easy to answer . . . and for a very simple reason. It is quite possible to determine immediately whether children are talking or even listening to one another, whereas it is impossible by direct observation to be sure whether they are understanding each other. The child has a hundred and one ways of pretending to understand, and often complicates things further by pretending not to understand, by inventing answers, for instance, to questions which he has understood perfectly.
>
> These conditions therefore oblige us to proceed with the utmost prudence; the different questions involved must be arranged in proper order, and only that one approached which concerns verbal understanding.
>
> (Piaget, 1959: 76)

Piaget goes on to describe case studies involving collaboration and argument both with and without reasoning; he calls these the acted and verbal cases.

> In the verbal case children collaborate or argue about a story to be reconstructed, a memory to be appreciated, or an explanation to be given (explanation of some phenomenon or other or of the words of an adult). Now discussions such as these take place on the verbal plane, without actions, without the aid of material object with which the speakers might have been playing or working, without even the present spectacle of the phenomena or of the events about which they are talking. In the acted case, on the other hand, the collaboration or argument is accompanied by gestures, by demonstrations

with the finger and not with words; it matters little therefore whether the talk is unintelligible or not, since the talkers have the object under their eyes. Hence the quaint character of much childish talk. ('That does that, and then it goes there, and it goes like that,' etc.) Were it not entirely outside the scope of this study, the connexion should also be established between these 'acted' conversations and the language by gesture and mime – language in movement, one might say – which is, after all, the real social language of the child.

Now in these two cases 'acted' conversation and 'merely spoken' conversation, children naturally understand each other in a very different manner. . . . In 'acted' conversation one gets the impression that the children understand each other well. Hence the success of the educational method (provided there is an adequate supply of educational games) which consists in letting one child explain to another, say, a certain way of doing sums, or a certain school regulation.

(Piaget, 1959: 77–8)

In this way Piaget advocated not only experiential experiences (Piaget, 1929) but dialogic learning and teaching (Alexander, 2008); a theme also developed by Bruner (1983: 39) when he identified that:

the development of language . . . involves to people negotiating. Language is not encountered dilly-nilly by the child; it is shaped to make communicative interaction effective – fine-tuned. If there is a Language Acquisition Device, the input to it is not a shower of spoken language but a highly interactive affair shaped, as we have already noted, by some sort of adult Language Acquisition Support System.

Such approaches indicate the importance of social interaction allowing young children to negotiate social boundaries (Broadhead, 2004) and develop conceptual understandings through cultural mediation (Bruner, 1991). This confirms Vygotsky's (1962) ideas concerning effective pedagogy for young children as including interaction between children, their environment and adults.

Bruner (1983: 39–42) goes on to look at the way children acquire language through social interaction.

There are at least four ways in which such a Language Acquisition Support System helps assure continuity from prelinguistic to linguistic communication. Because there is such concentration on familiar and routine transactional formats, it becomes feasible for the adult partner to highlight those features of the world that are already salient to the child and that have a basic or simple grammatical form . . . Events of this kind, we shall see, are a very frequent feature of mother-child formats . . .

And insofar as the 'fine tuning' of adult interaction with a child concentrates on these distinctions – both in reality and in speech – the child is aided in moving from their conceptual expression to an appreciation of their appropriate linguistic representation. Again they will be found to be frequent in the formats of the children we shall look at in detail.

A second way in which the adult helps the child through formatting is by encouraging and modeling lexical and phrasal substitutes for familiar gestural and vocal means for effecting various communicative functions . . .

What is striking is how early the child develops means to signal his focus of attention and his requests for assistance – to signal them by conventionalized means in the limited world of familiar formats. He has obviously picked up the gist of 'non-natural' or conventionalized signaling of his intentions before ever he has mastered the formal elements of lexicon-grammatical speech.

Thirdly, it is characteristic of play formats particularly that they are made of stipulative or constitutive 'events' that are created by language and then recreated on demand by language. Later these formats take on the character of 'pretend' situations. They are a rich source of opportunity for language learning and language use . . .

Finally, once the mother and child are launched into routinized formats, various psychological and linguistic processes are brought into play that generalize from one format to another. Naming, for example, appears first in indicating formats and then transfers to requesting formats. Indeed, the very notion of finding linguistic parallels for conceptual distinctions generalizes from one format to another. So too do such 'abstract' ideas as segmentation, interchangeable roles, substitutive means – both in action and in speech.

These are the mundane procedures and events that constitute a Language Acquisition Support System along with the elements of fine tuning that compromise 'baby talk' exchanges.

Impact tasks

Early career professional:
Tape yourself talking to a child or group of children. Listen carefully to the tape and analyse how you are supporting children in developing their language. Look also at the part played by peer dialogue in supporting language development.

Reflection

- How effective are the adult and peer interactions in supporting language development? Explain your reasoning for your answer.
- How can you improve the way you interact with children to improve language development?
- How can you incorporate dialogic teaching and learning into your planning to support future language development?

Later years professional:
Set up an activity that allows children to interact with each other and talk while they are working. This may involve some form of co-operation or collaboration. Observe the children closely (maybe using an observation schedule) or video the interactions during the activity. Use the evidence you collect to analyse the part played by peer dialogue in supporting language development.

Reflection

- How effective are the peer interactions and dialogue in supporting language development? Explain your reasoning for your answer.
- How do you use social interaction in your classroom to support language development?
- How can you incorporate social interaction and dialogic teaching and learning into your planning to support future language development?

Professional leader:
Audit the planning in your setting/school to analyse the current use of social interaction and dialogic teaching. Plan some activities that support language development through adult and peer social interaction and discussion and argumentation. Analyse the effect of the changes on language development at different ages.

Reflection

- How effective were the activities in supporting language development? Explain your reasoning for your answer.
- What was the effect on other areas of development/subject areas?
- How can you incorporate social interaction and dialogic teaching and learning into future planning for different age groups?

Subject tasks

EYFS:
Set up a shop as a role play area. This can be a post office, garden centre or optician and have learning outcomes in the following key areas:

- language, literacy and communication
- problem-solving, reasoning and numeracy
- knowledge and understanding of the world
- personal, social and emotional development.

Observe the children as they play and analyse the way they communicate with each other. You may wish to tape or video the interaction so you can watch it at your leisure.

Reflection

- How did the opportunity to talk support the more cognitive learning outcomes?
- How did the social interaction support language development?
- How could you use play opportunities and talk to support language development in the future?

KS1:
Plan some literacy or mathematical games as part of your literacy or numeracy session. These could be word or number lotto, fish for word/number, rhyming word or shape snap. Observe the children as they interact and analyse the way they communicate with each other.

Reflection

- How did the opportunity to talk support the more cognitive learning outcomes of the games?
- How did the social interaction support language development?
- How could you use games to support language development in the future?

KS2:
Ask the children to work in groups and plan a small drama based on a moral or social issue. This may be something based on the children's real life experiences, such as bullying, getting into trouble, jealousy, anger or joining a gang. After

the performance, allow other children to question the group. Observe the way the children interact through the planning, performance and questioning/discussion.

Reflection

- How did the interaction at different stages of the activity (planning performance and questioning) support language developments?
- How did the talk support social development and other areas of development?
- How could you develop this type of experience to support language and social development in the future?

References

Alexander, R. (2008) *Towards Dialogic Teaching: Rethinking Classroom Talk*, 4th edn. York: Dialogos.

Broadhead, P. (2004) *Early Years Play and Learning: Developing Social Skills and Cooperation*. London: RoutledgeFalmer.

Bruner, J. (1983) *Child's Talk: Learning to Use Language*. New York: Norton.

Bruner, J.S. (1991) The narrative construction of reality, *Critical Inquiry*, 18(1): 1–21.

Chomsky, N. (2006) *Language and Mind*, 3rd edn. Cambridge: Cambridge University.

Department for Children, Schools and Families (DCSF) (2008) *The Early Years Foundation Stage: Setting the Standard for Learning, Development and Care for Children from Birth to Five; Practice Guidance*. London: DCSF.

Nahmad-Williams, L. (2007) Language development, in J. Johnston and L. Nahmad-Williams (eds) *Early Childhood Studies*. Harlow: Pearson Education Limited.

Piaget, J. (1929) *The Child's Conception of the World*. New York: Harcourt.

Piaget, J. (1959) *The Language and Thought of the Child*. London: Routledge & Kegan Paul.

Pinker, S. (1995) Language acquisition, in L.R. Gleitman and M. Liberman (eds) *An Invitation to Cognitive Science*, 2nd edn (vol. 1). Cambridge, MA: The MIT Press.

Tomasello, M. (2003) *Constructing a Language: A Usage-based Theory of Language Acquisition*. Cambridge, MA: Harvard University Press.

Vygotsky, L. (1962) *Thought and Language*. Cambridge, MA: The MIT Press.

PART 2
The changing world of childhood

6   The family

This chapter looks at the changing world of childhood and attempts to make sense of the importance of childhood on child development.

The family serves a biological function to help support the developing child until they are able to fend for themselves. Childhood, the time when families care for children, is a long period; until 19 years of age according to the *Every Child Matters* initiative (DfES, 2003a). During this time children develop emotionally, socially, physically, cognitively and linguistically supported by their family. The length of childhood appears to be in direct proportion to the complexity of society and so children may be physically capable of caring for themselves, but socially need a great deal more support from adult family members. The structure of the family has also changed over time, again reflecting changes in society.

Another changing feature of families has been changing opinion and legislation concerning children's rights. Legislation has protected the child from exploitation by families and other adults (e.g. the Factories Act of 1833), identified rights for all regardless of age (the United Nations Declaration of Human Rights of 1948) and identified specific rights of the child (the Children Act of 1989). Burr and Montgomery (2003) identify children's rights to be provision, prevention, protection and participation. Provision rights entitle all children to have their physiological needs met and provide the right to education. Prevention rights are concerned with the systems in society to ensure children are safe. Protection rights protect children from any exploitation by adults, society and cultures. Participation rights allow children to be involved in decision-making and be full participants in society.

The history of the family

Our first extract from Aries (1972) illustrates the changes in childhood and helps us make sense of childhood today through consideration of the differences between childhood historically and childhood today.

> In the Middle Ages, at the beginning of modern times, and for a long time after that in the lower classes, children were mixed with adults as soon as they were considered capable of doing without their mothers or nannies, not long after a tardy weaning (in other words, at about the age of seven). They immediately went straight into the great community of men, sharing in the work and play of their companions, old and young alike. The movement of collective life carried along in a single torrent all ages and classes, leaving nobody any time for solitude and privacy. In these crowded, collective existences there was no room for a private sector. The family fulfilled a function; it ensured the transmission of life, property and names; but it did not penetrate very far into human sensibility. Myths such as courtly and precious love denigrated marriage, while realities such as the apprenticeship of children loosened the emotional bond between parents and children. Medieval civilization had forgotten the *paideia* of the ancients and knew nothing as yet of modern education. That is the main point: it had no idea of education. Nowadays our society depends, and knows that it depends, on the success of its educational system. It has a system of education, a concept of education, an awareness of its importance. New sciences such as psycho-analysis, pediatrics and psychology devote themselves to the problems of childhood, and their findings are transmitted to parents by way of a mass of popular literature. Our world is obsessed by the physical, moral and sexual problems of childhood.
>
> This preoccupation is unknown to medieval civilization, because there was no problem for the Middle Ages: as soon as he had been weaned or soon after, the child became the natural companion of the adult. The age groups of Neolithic times, the Hellenistic *paideia*, presupposed a difference and a transition between the world of children and that of adults, a transition made by means of an initiation or an education. Medieval civilization failed to perceive this difference and therefore lacked this concept of transition.
>
> (Aries, 1972: 395–6)

Reflection

Consider the functions of the family and the changes in these over the last century and your lifetime. Some of the functions appear to have been taken over by the state and settings/school and it does seem that each week, the media, politicians and the general public expect more from professionals working with children.

Reflective tasks

EYFS:
- Are there any functions of the family that the EYFS is expected to deliver? Why might this be appropriate or inappropriate?
- How is the EYFS expected to support families to fulfil their functions?

KS1:
- What are the challenges in KS1 for professionals and schools who have to fulfil some functions previously undertaken by the family?
- How can you overcome these challenges?

KS2:
- Are there any functions of the family that you feel are appropriate or inappropriate for professionals and schools at KS2? Explain your reasoning.
- How can you overcome the challenges of fulfilling these functions and your educational remit?

Modern families

There are many different types of families. They can be:

- nuclear, consisting of parents and siblings
- extended, consisting of parents, siblings, grandparents, aunts and uncles, living under one roof or in close proximity
- blended or reconstituted, where adults and children from different family groups combine to make a new family (or stepfamily)
- multi-families, where more than one family share a household
- single parent, consisting of one parent and children (maybe because of separation, divorce or bereavement).

Montgomery (2003) identifies four views of childhood within the family structure.

1   The Puritan considers children as evil and wild and needing to be disciplined and punished.
2   The Tabula Rasa, the blank slate as described by Locke (1632–1704), which considers children as developing with the support of the family.
3   The Romantic view (Rousseau, 1911) considers children as innocent.
4   The final view of Globalisation (see Giddens, 1997) considers that children are increasingly dependent on the world society and need support from their family in this respect.

The UK scored the lowest in the Organization for Economic Co-operation and Development (OECD) countries for relationships in the United Nation's (International) Children's Fund (Unicef, 2007) report on *The State of the World's Children 2007*. Relationships were difficult to measure but their importance was too great to allow this to influence the decision to attempt to measure them. Quality of family relationships was measured using evidence on family structures, plus children's (aged 15 years) own answers. Evidence on family structure considered the percentage of children living in single-parent families and stepfamilies. This is not a fully helpful indicator, as it does not take into account that relationships in single-parent families are not the only ones that can have problems and that many single-parent families provide secure bases for developing children. However, the statistics do indicate that there is a greater risk to well-being 'including a greater risk of dropping out of school, leaving home early, poorer health, low skills and low pay) for children growing up in one-parent families' (Unicef, 2007: 23).

Evidence on family relationships considered the percentage of children who identified that they ate the main meal of the day with their parents more than once a week and the percentage of children who identified that parents talk to them. This evidence was taken from the *Programme of International Student Assessment (PISA)* (see Currie et al., 2004). Here the UK did not fare so badly being in the top half of the countries studied for having parents who talk to them regularly. The results indicate that 'girls, find it easier to talk to their mothers than to their fathers and that difficulty in communicating with parents rises significantly between the ages of 11 and 15' (Unicef, 2007: 24). However, the UK was fourth from the bottom for eating their main meal of the day with their parents, although this actually meant that more than two-thirds of their main meals were eaten with their families. There is likely to be a cultural dimension to this evidence as family, but concerns about diminishing childhoods (Elkind, 2001; Palmer, 2006) still exist.

Reflection

If settings and schools are fulfilling more of the functions of the family and supporting wider developing relationships, should they also support families in the relationships they have with their children?

Consider the different family structures of children in your setting/care.

- How do the different structures affect the children's holistic development?
- Do you find it easier to understand and accommodate some types of family structures? Why might this be?
- Does your setting accommodate one type of family structure over others? Why might this be?
- What factors affect your ability to accommodate different family structures and support children and families?

Reflective tasks

EYFS:
- How should settings in the EYFS work with families to support relationships?
- What is the biggest challenge you face in supporting family relationships?
- How can you overcome this challenge?

KS1:
- What are the family relationship issues that affect children at KS1?
- What are the advantages for the children, you and the school of positive family relationships?
- How can you work with families to support relationships?

KS2:
- How do family relationship problems affect children educationally at KS2?
- How can you support families and children at KS2?
- What additional resources (time, expertise, etc.) do teachers need to support family relationships? Explain your reasoning.

Parenting

Diana Baumrind's (1971) work has helped us to understand the effect of different parenting styles on childhood. Her research looked at over 130 pre-school children and parenting styles and identified four areas of parental behaviour: control, nurturance, clarity of communication and maturity demands, and she found that parenting could be best described as a combination of these and this resulted in a taxonomy of parenting styles.

66 Pattern Definitions

Subjects were assigned to groups on the basis of their patterns of scores on the PBR clusters. The bases for assignment are given below. Out of a possible 73 families of white boys, 54 were assigned to patterns. Out of a possible 60 families of white girls, 48 were assigned to patterns.

Patterns were defined so that they would fit the following definitions. These definitions differed from each other as did the Authoritarian, Authoritative, and Permissive patterns described in the report of the previous study using the group-comparison method (Baumrind, 1967), and conceptualized in two previous papers (Baumrind, 1966, 1968a).

Authoritarian

The *authoritarian* parent attempts:

> to shape, control, and evaluate the behavior and attitudes of the child in accordance with a set standard of conduct, usually an absolute standard, theologically motivated and formulated by a higher authority. She values obedience as a virtue and favors punitive, forceful measures to curb self-will at points where the child's actions or beliefs conflict with what she thinks is right conduct. She believes in inculcating such instrumental values as respect for authority, respect for work and respect for the preservation of order and traditional structure. She does not encourage verbal give and take, believing that the child should accept her word for what is right.
>
> (Baumrind, 1968a, p. 2611)

Two subpatterns corresponded to this description and differed only in the degree of acceptance shown to the child.

Authoritarian (Not Rejecting) – Pattern I. Pattern I contained families who were authoritarian but not rejecting. In defining this pattern operationally, it was required that (a) both parents have scores above the median in Firm Enforcement or one parent score in the top third of the distribution, (b) both parents have scores below the median in Encourages Independence and Individuality, or one parent score in the bottom third of the distribution, or the father score in the bottom third on Promotes Nonconformity and In the top third on Authoritarianism, (c) both parents score below the median in Passive-Acceptant or one parent score in the bottom third, and (d) the father score in the bottom third on Promotes Nonconformity or the top third on Authoritarianism. Conceptually, one would have preferred that parents in the Authoritarian group not differ from parents in the Authoritative group on rejection scores. However, only two families of girls otherwise Authoritarian were not Rejecting. Eight families of boys were Authoritarian but not Rejecting.

Authoritarian-Rejecting Pattern VIII. Pattern VIII, with eight boys and eight girls, contained families that were authoritarian and also rejecting (i.e., parents met the criteria for inclusion in Pattern VII, Rejecting-Neglecting, as well as Pattern I, Authoritarian). It should be understood that the term "rejecting" is used relatively, since the sample was drawn from normal (concerned and caring) parents. With eight boys each in Groups I and VIII, differences in boys' behavior, where Authoritarian parents were relatively Rejecting and where they were not Rejecting, can be evaluated. Because of the small N for girls in Pattern I, such pattern comparison would be meaningless.

Authoritative

The Authoritative parent, by contrast with the Authoritarian parent, attempts to direct the child's activities but in a rational, issue-oriented manner. She encourages verbal give and take and shares with the child the reasoning behind her policy. She values both expressive and instrumental attributes, both autonomous self-will and disciplined conformity. Therefore, she exerts firm control at points of parent-child divergence, but does not hem the child in with restrictions. She recognizes her own special rights as an adult, but also the child's individual interests and special ways. The authoritative parent affirms the child's present qualities, but also sets standards for future conduct. She uses reason as well as power to achieve her objectives. She does not base her decisions on group consensus or the individual child's desires; but also, does not regard herself as infallible or divinely inspired [Baumrind, 1968a, p. 261].

Two subpatterns correspond to this description and differ only in degree of nonconformity.

Authoritative (Not Nonconforming) – Pattern II. In defining Pattern II operationally, it was required that (a) like the Authoritarian Patterns I and VIII, both parents have scores above the median in Firm Enforcement, or one parent score in the top third of the distribution (as in the previous study, the scores on Firm Enforcement of Authoritative parents were actually higher, although not significantly so, than those of Authoritarian parents), (b) both parents score above the median in Encourages Independence and Individuality or one parent score in the top third of the distribution, (c) like the Authoritarian parents, both parents score below the median in Passive-Acceptant or one parent score in the bottom third. (Pattern II fathers, in fact, scored very high on Firm Enforcement but not on Authoritarianism. They were also not Nonconforming.) The pattern membership consisted of 12 families of boys and 7 families of girls.

Authoritative-Nonconforming – Pattern III. A small group of Authoritative families whose parents just barely met the criterion of above the median scores on Firm Enforcement, required for Pattern II, also met the criteria for Pattern IV, Nonconforming (Not Permissive and Not Authoritative). Pattern III, then, contained the four families of girls and two families of boys who were Authoritative-Nonconforming. Because of the small N, tests of significance using this group are not very meaningful except when Pattern III subjects are combined with other subjects.

Permissive

The Permissive parent attempts:

> to behave in a nonpunitive, acceptant, and affirmative manner toward the child's impulses, desires, and actions. She consults with him about policy decisions and gives explanations for family rules. She makes few demands for household responsibility and orderly behavior. She presents herself to the child as a resource for him to use as he wishes, not as an active agent responsible for shaping or altering his ongoing or future behavior. She allows the child to regulate his own activities as much as possible, avoids the exercise of control, and does not encourage him to obey externally-defined standards. She attempts to use reason but not overt power to accomplish her ends.
>
> (Baumrind, 1968a, p. 256)

The next three patterns discussed reflect different facets, and correspond to different degrees with the prototypic permissive parent described above. As in the previous study, the author had difficulty finding a group of parents who corresponded to the ideal permissive parent. The author sought but did not find a group of parents who would score low on Firm Enforcement, high on Encourages Independence and Individuality, high on Passive-Acceptant, and high on Promotes Nonconformity. Instead, the data required that we define three patterns corresponding to different facets of this definition. Consider Pattern IV, Nonconforming (Not Permissive and Not Authoritative). Five of the seven Pattern IV fathers of girls did not have standard scores below the mean in Passive-Acceptant, and more than half of the mothers of both boys and girls scored rather high in Firm Enforcement and/or Expect Participation in Household Chores. Pattern IV parents then were democratic, but were not totally acceptant or nondemanding.

The parents in Pattern VI, labeled Permissive (Not Nonconforming), did indeed score very low on Firm Enforcement, high on Passive-Acceptant and low on Expect Participation in Household Chores, and on Directive, but they did not score high on Encourages Independence and Individuality, and the fathers were generally Rejecting, often even when they were also Passive-Acceptant.

The scores of individual parents as well as the mean standard scores of parents of girls in Pattern V, Nonconforming-Permissive, best met the definition for girls. However, there were only four families of boys who fit this pattern and, surprisingly enough, although all fathers scored high on Promotes Nonconformity, three of the four fathers of boys did not score above the median on Encourages Independence and Individuality.

The empirical realities then required modifications in the operational definitions of patterns corresponding most closely to the prototypic definition of the Permissive parents. For boys, Pattern IV, and for girls, Pattern V, parents came closest to meeting the prototype of the Permissive parent. For both boys and girls, Pattern VI parents came closest to duplicating the behavior of parents designated as Permissive in the last study (Baumrind, 1967).

Nonconforming (Not Permissive and Not Authoritative) – Pattern IV. In defining Pattern IV, it was required that (a) at least one parent have scores in the bottom half of the distribution for Firm Enforcement, (b) at least one parent have scores above the median for Encourages Independence and Individuality, (c) the father score below the median on Rejecting, (d) both parents score in the top third on Encourages Independence and Individuality or the father score in the top third of the distribution on Promotes Nonconformity, and (e) the father score below the median on Authoritarianism. Pattern membership consisted of eight families of boys and seven families of girls.

Permissive (Not Nonconforming) – Pattern VI. In defining Pattern VI, Permissive, it was required that (a) both parents have scores below the median on Firm Enforcement, (b) at least one parent score in the top third of the distribution on Passive-Acceptant, (c) at least one parent have scores below the median on Rejecting (in order to define permissiveness so that it was not synonymous with neglect), and (d) two out of three of the following criteria be met – Expect Participation in Household Chores, below median score; Directive, below median score; Discourage Infantile Behavior, low third. Seven boys and seven girls and their families composed this pattern.

Nonconforming-Permissive – Pattern V. Families in Pattern V, Nonconforming-Permissive, met the criteria for both Patterns IV and VI. Four families of boys and seven families of girls made up the pattern membership.

Rejecting-Neglecting

Rejecting-Neglecting (Not Authoritarian) – Pattern VII. There were six families of girls and five families of boys in this pattern. These parents were Rejecting, relative to other parents sampled, but they did not meet the criteria set for Pattern I, Authoritarian. There were families in Pattern VII who were noncontrolling and in that sense "permissive," but no family in the Permissive group (by definition) met the criteria described below for Pattern VII. The requirements for membership in Pattern VII were that (a) both parents have scores below the median for Encourages Independence and Individuality, (b) both parents have scores above the mean in Rejecting, and that (c) one parent score in the top third of the distribution on Rejecting, or that the family on the Joint clusters score in the bottom third on Enrichment of Child's Environment, and the top third on Discourage Emotional Dependency. Parents who were also highly controlling and authoritarian were placed in Pattern VIII, Rejecting-Neglecting-Authoritarian.

More than three-fourths of the 133 white families could be assigned to one of the eight patterns of parental authority on the basis of the criteria just described. Most of the families not assigned had cluster scores which resembled one or another pattern in shape, but failed to meet the criteria set with regard to magnitude of score. A few families had unique configurations of scores which deserve special study; for example, in one family the father had an extremely high score on Encourages Independence and Individuality, but also had high scores on Rejecting and Authoritarianism, while the mother met the criteria for inclusion in Pattern VI, Permissive (Not Nonconforming).

In summary, patterns of parental authority were defined to produce contrast groups of families whose configuration and magnitude of scores on the Parent Behavior Clusters were of interest because they corresponded to more refined definitions of three prototypes described in a previous study. The operational definitions of patterns included Mother, Father, and Joint cluster scores. The Mother and Father cluster scores were used interchangeably since the author lacked a sufficiently large pool of subjects to take into account the interaction of sex of parent and child. 〝

> *Source*: Baumrind, D. (1971) Current patterns of parental authority, *Developmental Psychology*, Monograph 4.1, Part 2, pp. 22–4

Impact tasks

Early career professional:
Consider the following behaviours that you may see in your setting/class:

- a child who has little self-control and wants and expects and demands
- a child who when reprimanded cowers
- a child who willingly accepts guidance and co-operates in class
- a child who shows independence and will find something to do if the professional/teacher is busy
- a child who when reprimanded listens and discusses why their behaviour is unacceptable.

Reflection

- Can you assign a style of parenting to each behaviour?
- Is there a style of parenting that is more supportive to the professional work that you are engaged in (more supportive of care and education)? Explain your reasoning.
- How can you adopt aspects of this style of parenting as a professional?

Later year professional:
Look at the children in your care and try and find examples of children who are the recipients of the different parenting styles identified by Baumrind's (1971) taxonomy. Provide an example of behaviour to justify each decision.

Reflection

- How does the style of parenting affect the children's ability to develop in your setting/class?
- How can you modify/change your style of teaching to accommodate the positive parenting styles and support children's development?

Professional leader:
Consider the style of parenting exhibited by the families of children in your setting.

Reflection

- Which style of parenting is more like the style of behaviour management in your setting? Explain your reasoning.
- How can you support the development of children who have experienced different styles and who may be alienated by the styles used in your setting?

Education and care

Jean-Jacques Rousseau (1712–1778) was a French philosopher who is considered to be the 'Father of Education'. Rousseau believed that humans are born free and good, but influenced by society, its conventions and through the process of socialization so that children are constrained by the rules of society and develop inhibitions, vices and ideas during childhood.

> ❝ In the natural order men are all equal and their common calling is that of manhood, so that a well-educated man cannot fail to do well in that calling and those related to it. It matters little to me whether my pupil is intended for the army, the church, or the law. Before his parents chose a calling for him nature called him to be a man. Life is the trade I would teach him. When he leaves me, I grant you, he will be neither a magistrate, a soldier, nor a priest; he will be a man. . . . The object of our study is man and his environment. To my mind those of us who can best endure the good and evil of life are the best educated; hence it follows that true education consists less in precept than in practice. We begin to learn when we begin to live; the ancients used the word "Education:" in a different sense, it meant "Nurture." "Educit obstetrix," says Varro. "Edueat nutrix, instituit pedagogus, docet magister." Thus, education, discipline, and instruction are three things as different in their purpose as the dame, the usher, and the teacher. But these distinctions are undesirable and the child should only follow one guide.
>
> We might therefore look at the general rather than the particular, and consider our scholar as man in the abstract, man exposed to all the changes and chances of mortal life. If men were born attached to the soil of our country, if one season lasted all the year round, if every man's fortune were so firmly grasped that he could never lose it, then the established method of education would have certain advantages; the child brought up to his own calling would never leave it, he could never have to face the difficulties of any other condition. But when we consider the

fleeting nature of human affairs, the restless and uneasy spirit of our times, when every generation overturns the work of its predecessor, can we conceive a more senseless plan than to educate a child as if he would never leave his room, as if he would always have his servants about him? If the wretched creature takes a single step up or down he is lost. This is not teaching him to bear pain; it is training him to feel it.

People think only of preserving their child's life; this is not enough, he must be taught to preserve his own life when he is a man, to hear the bullets of fortune, to brave wealth and poverty, to live at need among the snows of Iceland or on the scorching rocks of Malta. In vain you guard against death; he must needs die; and even if you do not kill him with your precautions, they are mistaken. Teach him to live – rather than to avoid death: life is not breath, but action, the use of our senses, our mind, our faculties, every part of ourselves which makes us conscious of our being. Life consists less in days than in the keen sense of living. A man may be buried at a hundred and may never have lived at all. He would have fared better had he died young.

99

Source: Rousseau, J.-J. (1911) *Emile*. London: J. M. Dent & Sons, pp. 9–10

Reflection

Rousseau believed that children should be accommodated educationally and that the setting (in Rousseau's day this would have been the family) should employ the principles of child-centred, differentiated, experiential learning.

In considering these principles of care and education for children and how appropriate they are today, we need to consider the wealth of evidence from theorists (e.g. Froebel, 1826), policy (e.g. DES, 1967; DfES, 2003b) and research (e.g. Alexander, 2009).

Reflective tasks

Early career professional:
What do you consider experiential learning to be? Identify which of the following would be part of experiential learning.

- finding out for yourself
- being taught something
- learning through your own experience
- thinking through a problem
- being supported by another person (adult or peer)

- learning through practical activities
- discussing with others
- learning from a book or the media.

Think about a positive learning experience you have had. What made it so positive? Was it experiential?

How do you incorporate Rousseau's principles into your own practice?

Later years professional:
Think of a successful learning experience you have provided for children. What were the features that made it successful? How could you have made the experience more experiential? Would this have made it even more successful? Why?

Professional leader:
Consider the future planning of your setting/school. Does it contain aspects of experiential learning? How can you work with your staff to develop the planning further to enhance children's experiential learning? Why might this be beneficial to the children?

Clearly, the context now is very different from Rousseau's over two hundred years ago. However research into early years care by the Families, Children and Child Care Study (FCCC, 2005) and evidence from the Cambridge Review of Primary Education (Alexander, 2009) indicates that the principles are still very valid today.

Whatever aspect of quality is considered, it is clear that more information is needed concerning the relationships between different types of child care, including maternal, parental or familial care, and their quality, and a range of outcomes for different children. Without more information, and information relevant to the present-day UK, overall assessments of the relative merits of different forms of child care, or of particular practises within them, cannot be relied upon. Research on the quality and outcomes of child care has advanced our knowledge, usually demonstrating better child outcomes in paid care of higher quality compared to paid care of lower quality (NICHD, 1998). However a growing body of results from the USA have shown that it is not solely the form of care, or even its form and quality together, which determine the outcome for a child. Whatever the nature of the care provided, it is the quality of parent–child relationships which shape developmental outcomes. When the NICHD Early Child

Care Research Network team (1997d) set out to unravel the effects of different forms of child care, including home care, on toddlers' attachment to their mothers, they found that the attachment outcomes could only be understood in the context of child care if the security of each child's relationship with the mother, and the sensitivity of her parenting, were also understood. In statistical terms, the "interaction effects" in that American study are as powerful as the "main" ones.

(FCCC, 2005: 9–10)

Subject tasks

These family learning activities can help families to understand how children develop and learn, the types of experiences that are conducive to learning and development and support settings in achieving educational and developmental goals for children. They can be on any subject of the curriculum or be cross-curricular.

EYFS:
Plan a parent's play session when parents, carers, siblings and the wider family can come and play with the children. This may be a special day or a regular slot each week to accommodate the family and children. For example, you may set up some water play, baking activity or physical play activity that will give parents and carers ideas that they can use in the home.

Reflection

- How successful was the session in helping families in understanding learning and development in the EYFS?
- How can you build on the successes and ameliorate the challenges of such a session?
- How else can you support families to support the education and development of their children?

KS1:
Plan a family learning activity. This may be on a theme and involve problem-solving activities that the whole family can join in with. For example, a theme of shopping could involve making a box, producing an advert and jingle for a product.

Reflection

- How successful was the session in helping families in understanding learning and development at KS1?
- What are the issues/challenges that you face in setting up such a session? How could you overcome these?
- How else can you support families to support the education and development of their children?

KS2:
Plan some problem-solving activities that children can take home for the family to undertake. This may be making a bridge out of A4 paper, making a plasticine boat or writing an article for a newspaper.

Reflection

- How can you evaluate the success of the activity in helping families to understanding learning and development at KS2?
- What are the implications for both families and schools of improved liaison at KS2?
- How else can you include children and their families more successfully in learning?

References

Alexander, R. (ed.) (2009) *Children, their World, their Education: Final Report and Recommendations of the Cambridge Review.* London: Routledge.

Aries, P. (1972) *Centuries of Childhood.* Harmondsworth: Penguin.

Baumrind, D. (1971) Current patterns of parental authority, *Developmental Psychology,* Monograph 4.1, Part 2, pp. 22–4.

Burr, R. and Montgomery, H. (2003) Children's rights, in M. Woodhead and H. Montgomery (2003) *Understanding Childhood: An Interdisciplinary Approach.* Chichester: John Wiley & Sons/Open University.

Currie, C. et al. (eds) (2004) *Young People's Health in Context: Health Behaviour in Schoolage Children Study* (HBSC). International Report from the 2001/2002 Study. Copenhagen: World Health Organization (WHO) Regional Office for Europe.

Department of Education and Science (DES) (1967) *Children and their Primary school: A Report of the Central Advisory Council for Education (England)* (vol. 1). London: Her Majesty's Stationery Office (HMSO).

Department for Education and Stills (DfES) (2003a) *Every Child Matters*. London: DfES.

—— (2003b) *Excellence and Enjoyment: A Strategy for Primary Schools*. London: DfES.

Elkind, D. (2001) *The Hurried Child: Growing Up Too Fast Too Soon*, 3rd edn. Cambridge, MA: Da Capio Press.

Families, Children and Child Care Study (FCCC) (2005) *A Prospective Study of the Effects of Different Kinds of Care on Children's Development in the First Five Years*. Available online at www.familieschildrenchildcare.org/fccc_static_PDFs/fccc_protocol.pdf (accessed 27 November 2009).

Froebel, F. (1826) *On the Education of Man*. Keilhau, Leipzig: Wienbrach.

Giddens, A. (1997) *Sociology*. Cambridge: Polity Press.

Montgomery, H. (2003) Childhood in time and place, in M. Woodhead and H. Montgomery (2003) *Understanding Childhood: An Interdisciplinary Approach*. Chichester: John Wiley & Sons/Open University.

Palmer, S. (2006) *Toxic Childhood: How the Modern World is Damaging our Children and What We Can Do About it*. London: Orion.

Rousseau, J.-J. (1911) *Emile*. London: J.M. Dent & Sons.

United Nations (International) Children's Emergency Fund (Unicef) 2007) *The State of the World's Children: An Overview of Child Well-being in Rich Countries. A Comprehensive Assessment of the Lives and Well-being of Children and Adolescents in the Economically Advanced Nations*. Florence: UNICEF.

7 Play

This chapter considers play through the theories of major theorists, such as Rousseau, Paiget and Froebel. Play is a term that is equally misunderstood, underused and undervalued. It is often considered to be an informal aspect of childhood, rather than an important developmental tool. It can be considered to be messing about with no purpose, rather than the purposeful activities that we engage in throughout life. Play is often thought to be of some use in early childhood, but less in later life and to be of value by professionals, but not so much by policy-makers and the general public.

The importance of play

The importance of play in all areas of child development is well recognized by professionals. Advocates of play include Rousseau (1911), Froebel (1826), Steiner (1996), Piaget (1976) and Vygotsky (1962) all of whom recognized play as a supporting emotional, social and cognitive development.

> ❝ As Froebel (1826) says play is the highest phase of child development – of human development at this period; for it is self-active representation of the inner-representation of the inner front inner necessity and impulse.
>
> Play is the purest, most spiritual activity of man at this stage, and, at the same time, typical of human life as a whole – of the inner hidden natural life in man and all things. It gives, therefore, joy, freedom, contentment, inner and outer rest, peace with the world. It holds the sources of all that is good. A child that plays thoroughly, with self-active determination, perseveringly until physical fatigue forbids, will surely be a thorough, determined man, capable of self-sacrifice for the promotion of the welfare of himself and others. Is not the most beautiful expression of child-life at this time a playing child? – a child wholly absorbed in his play? – a child that has fallen asleep while so absorbed?

As already indicated, play at this time is not trivial, it is highly serious and of deep significance. Cultivate and foster it, O mother; protect and guard it, O father! To the calm, keen vision of one who truly knows human nature, the spontaneous play of the child discloses the future inner life of the man.

The plays of childhood are the germinal leaves of all later life; for the whole man is developed and shown in these, in his tenderest dispositions, in his innermost tendencies. The whole later life of man, even to the moment when he shall leave it again, has its source in the period of childhood – be this later life pure or impure, gentle or violent, quiet or impulsive, industrious or indolent, rich or poor in deeds, passed in dull stupor or in keen creativeness, in stupid wonder or intelligent insight, producing or destroying, the bringer of harmony or discord, of war or peace. His future relations to father and mother, to the members of the family, to society and mankind, to nature and God – in accordance with the natural and individual disposition and tendencies of the child – depend chiefly upon his mode of life at this period; for the child's life in and with himself, his family, nature, and God, is as yet a unit. Thus, at this age, the child can scarcely tell which is to him dearer – the flowers, or his joy about them, or the joy he gives to the mother when he brings or shows them to her, or the vague presentiment of the dear Giver of them.

Who can analyze these joys in which this period is so rich?

If the child is injured at this period, if the germinal leaves of the future tree of his life are marred at this time, he will only with the greatest difficulty and the utmost effort grow into strong manhood; he will only with the greatest difficulty escape in his further development the stunting effects of the injury or the one-sidedness it entails.

99

Source: Froebel, F. (1826) *On the Education of Man.*
Keilhau, Leipzig: Wienbrach, pp. 53–6

Reflection

Research on play (e.g. BERA, 2003: 13) identifies that:

play is an almost hallowed concept for teachers of young children. It is richly cloaked in idealogy which emphasizes its fundamental role in early learning and development. Among the tenets of this ideology is the idea that children need to play, and in doing so, reveal their on-going needs which, ideally, should inform the curriculum offered.

However, they go on to say that in practice, the use of play in pedagogical approaches is 'problematic' (BERA, 2003: 13) because many teachers feel pressurized by the curriculum, play is often unsupported by adults and so of less value and that 'parents' expectations are that children will "work" when they come to school and not "play" ' (BERA, 2003: 14).

In 2004, Johnston (2004) argued that play and discovery learning, both of which had been subject to misunderstanding and devaluing, were redefined and used more effectively to support children's development. This article is reproduced in the EYFS (DCSF, 2008) CD-ROM, together with research articles on play, which provide a very useful resources for professionals wishing to develop play in their settings/schools.

Reflective tasks

EYFS:
- How do you use play to support different key areas of the EYFS (DCSF, 2008)?
- How do you think your use of play indicates the value you place on it? Explain your reasoning.
- What aspects of play do you think need developing/strengthening/introducing in your setting? Why?

KS1:
- How is play used in your school/class? Is play fully incorporated into all aspects of learning and teaching, an extra or incidental part of learning, or not used at all outside playtime?
- Why do you think you should use play more effectively in learning and teaching?
- How can you fully incorporate play into one aspect of learning and teaching?

KS2:
- How is play relevant for learning and teaching at KS2?
- How can you use play more in learning and teaching at KS2?
- What are the challenges for using play in learning and teaching at KS2 and how can you overcome them?

Impact tasks

Try these tasks to implement and reflect on play in your context.

Early career professional:
Plan a play activity to support the achievement of specific learning outcomes. This may be a role-play area to develop writing skills (Post Office, Book Shop) or understanding of shapes (architects office, builder's yard). It can be small world play to support scientific understanding (minibeast environment box, with plastic minibeasts, a collection of materials and stones to create an environment) or historical understanding (Roman figures and fort). The play can be augmented by factual or fictional books on the subject to help focus the play.

Observe the children while they play and collect evidence to assess them against the learning outcomes.

Reflection

- How did the play support the achievement of the learning outcomes for different learners?
- How could you vary the play to support the less able and extend the more able?
- How could you use play in other learning activities?

Later years professional:
Look at your planning for the next half-term and consider how you can include a variety of different play activities to support achievement of the planned learning outcomes. This may be a role-play area as above or to support history (an air raid shelter), or small world geography play (a farm or seaside toys). It could be water play to support capacity in mathematics or changing materials and prediction in science. It could be drama to support aspects of personal, social, health and economic (PSHE) education or citizenship.

Over the course of the half-term, collect evidence to assess the children against the learning outcomes. Ask the children to identify what they have learned and how the play has supported learning. Combine your own and the children's evaluation to ascertain how play supports learning.

Reflection

- How did the different types of play support the achievement of the learning outcomes for different learners?
- How did the children feel that the play had supported their learning?

- How did the evidence indicate the value of play in supporting different learners?

Professional leader:

With your staff, audit the play activities used to support learning in different learners and at different stages of learning.

Plan some different play activities in all classes. Try and include some play activities that you would not usually consider using with this age group. This may be sand or water play with KS2 children, self-initiated play with early years children and supported exploration with KS1 children.

Evaluate the impact of the play on children's learning, social development, behaviour and motivation. Use the children to help you with the evaluation.

Reflection

- How did the different types of play affect children's learning, social development, behaviour and motivation?
- What have you and the children learned about play?
- How can you develop play in your setting/school in the future?

The development of play

Piaget's work on play is less well known than his theories on cognition, but is of equal importance and helps us develop our practice with children, not just in the early years but in later primary stages as well.

❝ The beginnings of play

When does play begin? The question arises at the *first stage*, that of purely reflex adaptations. For an interpretation of play like that of K Groos, for whom play is pre-exercise of essential instincts, the origin of play must be found in this initial stage since sucking gives rise to exercises in the void, apart from meals. But it seems very difficult to consider reflex exercises as real games when they merely continue the pleasure of feeding-time and consolidate the functioning of the hereditary set-up, thus being evidence of real adaptation.

During the *second stage*, on the other hand, play already seems to assume part of the adaptive behaviours, but the continuity between it and them is such that it would be difficult to say where it begins, and this question of boundary raises a problem which concerns the whole interpretation of later play. 'Games' with the voice at the time of the first lallations, movements of the head and hands accompanied by smiles and pleasure, are these already part of play, or do they belong to a different order? Are 'primary circular reactions' generally speaking ludic, adaptive, or both? If we merely apply the classical criteria, from the 'pre-exercise' of Groos to the 'disinterested' or the 'autotelic' character of play, we should have to say that everything during the first months of life, except feeding and emotions like fear and anger, is play. Indeed, when the child looks for the sake of looking, handles for the sake of handling, moves his arms and hands (and in the next stage shakes hanging objects and his toys) he is doing actions which are an end in themselves, as are all practice games and which do not form part of any series or actions imposed by someone else or from outside. They no more have an external aim than the later motor exercises such as throwing stones into a pond, making water spurt from a tap, jumping, and so on, which are always considered to be games: But all autotelic activities are certainly not games. Science has this characteristic, and particularly pure mathematics, whose object is immanent in thought itself, but if it is compared to a 'superior' game, it is clear that it differs from a mere game by its forced adaptation to an internal or external reality. In a general way, all adaptation is autotelic, but a distinction must be made between assimilation with actual accommodation and pure assimilation or assimilation which subordinates to itself earlier accommodations and assimilates the real to the activity itself without effort or limitations. Only the latter seems to be characteristic of play; otherwise the attempt to identify play with 'pre exercise' in general would involve the inclusion in it of practically all the child's activity.

But although the circular reactions have not in themselves this lucid character, it can be said that most of them are continued as games. We find, indeed, though naturally without being able to trace any definite boundary, that the child, after showing by his seriousness that he is making a real effort at accommodation, later reproduces these behaviors merely for pleasure, accompanied by smiles and even laughter, and without the expectation of results characteristic of the circular reactions through which the child learns. It can be maintained that at this stage the reaction ceases to be an act of complete adaptation and merely gives rise to the pleasure of pure assimilation, assimilation which is simply functional: the *Funktionslust* of K. Dishier. Of course, the schemes due to circular reaction do not only result in games. Once acquired, they may equally well become parts of more complete adaptations. In other words, a schema is never essentially ludic or non-ludic, and its character as play depends on its context and on its actual functioning. But all schemes are capable of giving rise to pure assimilation, whose extreme form is play. The phenomenon is clear in the case of schemas such as those of phonation,

prehension (watching moving fingers, etc.), and certain visual schemas
(looking at things upside down, etc.)   **"**

Source: Piaget, J. (1976) 'Mastery play' and 'symbolic play',
in J. Bruner, A. Jolly and K. Sylva (eds) *Play – Its Role in
Development and Evolution*. Middlesex: Penguin, pp. 168–9

There are different types of play, each of which plays a part in child development. The main types are:

- Solitary play, which is a feature of early and later childhood. Solitary
  play involves children in playing alone without social contact. It can
  help children to begin to be independent and to persevere at tasks
  they may find difficult. Solitary play is a feature of Montessori education (Montessori, 1912) and capitalizes on the characteristic of early
  childhood, when children spend considerable amounts of time per-
  fecting a task.
- Parallel, or companionship play (Bruce, 2009), can lead from solitary
  play and is a feature of early childhood. Parallel play involves children
  in playing alongside each other, with little or no social interaction.
- Co-operative/collaborative play is a feature of middle and later childhood and involves children playing and interacting socially with each
  other; this requiring a degree of social development. Co-operation is
  an extension of parallel play and may involve only small amounts of
  social interaction. Collaboration on the other hand demands a higher
  level of social interaction so that the children are working towards
  one aim. Co-operation and collaboration can help children to develop
  an understanding of rules (both social and within games) and develop
  the skill of negotiation (Johnston and Nahmad-Williams, 2010), as
  well as the sense of responsibility (an important social attitude).
- Epistemic play occurs in children in early and middle childhood. It
  involves children using their existing knowledge in their play and
  can support the development of knowledge and understanding and
  language development.
- Exploratory play (Johnston, 2005) is where children use their senses to
  explore the world around them and supports cognitive development.
  Johnston (2005) advocates exploratory play for scientific development (understandings, skills and attitudes) for children in early and
  middle childhood and can lead to systematic investigations.
- Discovery play (DES, 1967; Johnston, 2004) is a feature of middle
  childhood and was advocated for primary education by the Plowden
  Report (DES, 1967). Through discovery, children learn about the
  world around them and develop cognitively, socially, emotionally
  and physically.

- Symbolic play (Piaget, 1976) starts in early childhood, but is a feature of middle and later childhood. It involves children substituting one object for another, pretending and imagining. Symbolic play can help children in overcoming emotional and social problems and support emotional social and cognitive development (Reed, 2007).
- Imaginative play can be seen throughout childhood and involves children in using their imaginations in their play. In imaginative play (Johnston and Nahmad-Williams, 2010) children can mix fact and fantasy; myth and reality. They can imagine objects, characters and events and so it can start with simple imaginings and lead to ludic play. Imaginative play can support creative and physical development.
- Ludic play (Piaget, 1976) is a characteristic of middle childhood, although it can be seen in younger and older children. Ludic play involves children in fantasy role play and supports creative development.
- Socio-dramatic play is a feature of middle childhood which develops from ludic play in younger children. Through socio-dramatic play, children engage in social interactions and explore and resolve personal and social issues, thus supporting social and emotional development and helping children to be more rounded citizens.

Piaget's ideas on symbolic play link the idea of play as a creative pasttime and cognitive development and are the focus of our next reading. The reading also indicates how observations of children can help us to understand the value of play.

66 Symbolic Play

The appearance or symbolism . . . is the crucial point in all the interpretations of the ludic function. Why is it that play becomes symbolic, instead of continuing to be mere sensory-motor exercise or intellectual experiment, and why should the enjoyment of movement, or activity for the fun of activity, which constitute a kind of practical make-believe, be completed at a given moment by imaginative make-believe? The reason is that among the attributes of assimilation for assimilation's sake is that of distortion, and therefore to the extent to which it is dissociated from immediate accommodation it is a source of symbolic make-believe. This explains why there is symbolism as soon as we leave the sensory-motor level for that of representational thought.

During the *fifth stage* (of the sensory-motor period) certain new elements will ensure the transition from the behaviours of stage IV to the ludic symbol of stage VI, and for that very reason will accentuate the ritualization we have just noted. In relation to the 'tertiary circular reactions' or 'experiments in order to see the result', it often happens that by chance, the child combines unrelated gestures without really trying to experiment, and subsequently repeats these gestures as a ritual and makes a motor game of them. But, in contrast to the combinations of stage VI, which are borrowed from the adapted schemes, these combinations are new and almost immediately have the character of play.

Observation 63. At 0; 10 J. put her nose close to her mother's cheek and then pressed it against it, which forced her to breathe much more loudly. This phenomenon at once interested her, but instead or merely repeating it or varying it so as to investigate it, she quickly complicated it for the fun of it: she drew back an inch or two, screwed up her nose, sniffed and breathed out alternately very hard (as if she were blowing her nose), then again thrust her nose against her mother's cheek, laughing heartily. These actions were repeated at least once a day for more than a month, as a ritual.

At I; 0 she was holding her hair with her right hand during her bath. Frequent relationships are formed between rituals and symbolism, the latter arising from the former as a result of progressive abstraction of the action. For instance, at about I; 3 J. learnt to balance on a curved piece of wood which she rocked with her feet, in a standing position. But at 1.4 she adopted the habit or walking on the ground with her legs apart, pretending to lose her balance, as if she were on the board. She laughed heartily and said 'Bimbam'.

At 1; 6 she herself swayed bits of wood or leaves and kept saying Bimbam and this term finally became a half-generic, half-symbolic schema referring to branches, hanging objects and even grasses.

Observation 65. In the case of L. 'make-believe' or the ludic symbol made its appearance at 1; 0, arising, as in the case of J., from the motor ritual. She was sitting in her cot when she unintentionally fell backwards. Then seeing a pillow, she got into the position for sleeping on her side, seizing the pillow with one hand and pressing it against her face (her ritual was different from J.'s). But instead of miming the action half seriously, she smiled broadly (she did not know she was being watched); her behaviour was then that of J. in observation 64. She remained in this position for a moment, then sat up delightedly. During the day she went through the process again a number of times, although she was no longer in her cot; first she smiled (this indication of the representational symbol is to be noted), then threw herself back, turned on her side, put her hands over her face as if she held a pillow (though there wasn't one) and remained motionless, with her eyes open, smiling quietly. The symbol was therefore established.

At 1; 3 she pretended to put a napkin-ring in her mouth, laughed, shook her head as if saying 'no' and removed it. This behaviour was an intermediate stage between ritual and symbol, but at I; 6 she pretended to eat and drink without having anything in her hand. At 1; 7 she pretended to drink out of a box and then held it to the mouths of all who were present. These last symbols had been prepared for during the preceding month or two by a progressive ritualization, the principal stages of which consisted in playing at drinking out of empty glasses and then repeating the action making noises with lips and throat.

These examples show the nature of the behaviours in which we have seen for the first time pretence or the feeling of 'make believe' characteristic of the ludic symbol as opposed to simple motor games. The child is using schemas which are familiar, and for the most part already ritualized games of the previous types: but (1) instead of using them in the presence of the objects to which they are usually applied, he assimilates to them new objectives unrelated to them from the point of view of effective adaptation; (2) these new objects, instead of resulting merely in an extension or the schema (as is the case in the generalization proper to intelligence), are used with no other purpose than that of allowing the subject to mime or evoke the schemas in question. It is the union of these two conditions – application of the schema to inadequate objects and evocation for pleasure – which in our opinion characterizes the beginning of pretence. For instance, as early as the fourth stage, the schema of going to sleep is already giving rise to ludic ritualizations, since in observation 62 J. reproduces it at the sight of her pillow. But there is then neither symbol nor consciousness of make-believe, since the child merely applies her usual movements to the pillow itself, i.e. to the normal stimulus of the behaviour. There certainly is play, insofar as the schema is only used for pleasure, but there is no symbolism. On the contrary, in observation 64 J. mimes sleep while she is holding a cloth, a coat collar, or even a donkey's tail, instead of a pillow, and in observation 65 L. does the same thing, pretending to be holding a pillow when her hands are empty. It can therefore no longer be said that the schema has been evoked by its usual stimulus, and we are forced to recognize that these objects merely serve as substitutes for the pillow, substitutes which become symbolic through the actions simulating sleep (actions which L's case go so far as pretence without any material aid). In a word, there is symbolism, and not only motor play, since there is pretence of assimilating an object to a schema and use of a schema without accommodation.

The connection between these 'symbolic schemata' or first ludic symbols end the deferred, representational imitation of this same sixth stage is clear. In both types of behavior we find a representational element whose existence is proved by the deferred character of the reaction. Deferred imitation of a new model takes place after the model has disappeared, and symbolic play reproduces a situation not directly related to the object which gives rise to it, the present object merely serving to evoke an absent one. As regards imitation, on the other hand, we find in the behaviours of 64 and 65 an element which might be considered imitative. In observation 64 J. imitates the actions she herself makes before going to sleep, or the actions of washing, eating and so on, and in observation 65 L. does the same. And yet, apart from the fact that this is only self-imitation, it is not purely imitative behavior, since the objects which are present (the fringes of the cloth, the coat collar, the donkey's tail used as the pillow, and L's box used as a plate, etc.) are merely assimilated, regardless of their objective character, to the objects which the imitated action usually accompanies (the pillow, the plate, etc.). There is therefore, and this is characteristic of symbolic play as opposed to mere motor play, both apparent imitation and ludic assimilation.   **99**

Source: Piaget, J. (1976) 'Mastery play' and 'symbolic play', in J. Bruner, A. Jolly and K. Sylva (eds) *Play – Its Role in Development and Evolution*. Middlesex: Penguin, pp. 54–9

Reflection

It is felt to be important (Hutt et al., 1988; Johnston and Nahmad-Williams, 2010) that children engage in a variety of different types of play to ensure balanced development. For example, if children engage in imaginative or ludic play but do not move on to socio-dramatic play or engage in symbolic, epistemic or exploratory play, they will not develop socially or cognitively.

Reflective tasks

EYFS:
- What type of play is characteristic of your practice?
- How can you balance the type of play you use in your setting?
- How can you develop play opportunities that encourage different types of play to support balanced learning and development?
- How can you support and extend development and learning through play?

KS1:
- Do you engage in one type of play more than others? Why might this be?
- How can you introduce other types of play? What might the advantages of this be?
- How might different learners benefit from play?

- How can adults support and extend development and learning through play?

KS2:
- Is play a feature of your practice at KS2? Explain why it is or is not.
- How might play benefit your children at KS2?
- How might you introduce elements of play into your planning?
- How do you think play can support more cognitive development in different subject areas?

Play in the curriculum

The Plowden Report (DES, 1967) recognized the importance of play in the primary curriculum.

> Play is the central activity in all nursery schools and in many infant schools. This sometimes leads to accusations that children are wasting their time in school: they should be "working". But this distinction between work and play is false, possibly throughout life, certainly in the primary school. Its essence lies in past notions of what is done in school hours (work) and what is done out of school (play). We know now that play – in the sense of "messing about" either with material objects or with other children, and of creating fantasies – is vital to children's learning and therefore vital in school. Adults who criticize teachers for allowing children to play are unaware that play is the principal means of learning in early childhood. It is the way through which children reconcile their inner lives with external reality. In play, children gradually develop concepts of causal relationships, the power to discriminate, to make judgments, to analyse and synthesise, to imagine and to formulate. Children become absorbed in their play and the satisfaction of bringing it to a satisfactory conclusion fixes habits of concentration which can be transferred to other learning.
>
> From infancy, children investigate the material world. Their interest is not wholly scientific but arises from a desire to control or use the things about them. Pleasure in "being a cause" seems to permeate children's earliest contact with materials. To destroy and construct involves learning the properties of things and in this way children can build up concepts of weight, height, size, volume and texture.
>
> Primitive materials such as sand, water, clay and wood attract young children and evoke concentration and inventiveness. Children are also stimulated by natural or manufactured materials of many shapes, colours

and textures. Their imagination seizes on particular facets of objects and leads them to invent as well as to create. All kinds of causal connections are discovered, illustrated and used. Children also use objects as symbols for things, feelings and experiences, for which they may lack words. A small girl may use a piece of material in slightly different ways to make herself into a bride, a queen or a nurse. When teachers enter into the play activity of children, they can help by watching the connections and relationships which children are making and by introducing, almost incidentally, the words for the concepts and feelings that are being expressed. Some symbolism is unconscious and may be the means by which children come to terms with actions or thoughts which are not acceptable to adults or are too frightening for the children themselves. In play are the roots of drama, expressive movement and art. In this way too children learn to understand other people. The earliest play of this kind probably emerges from play with materials. A child playing with a toy aeroplane can be seen to take the role of both the aeroplane and the pilot apparently simultaneously. All the important people of his world figure in this play: he imitates, he becomes, he symbolises. He works off aggression or compensates himself for lack of love by "being" one or other of the people who impinge on his life. By acting as he conceives they do, he tries to understand them. Since children tend to have inflexible roles thrust on them by adults, they need opportunities to explore different roles and to make a freer choice of their own. Early exploration of the actions, motives and feelings of themselves and of others is likely to be an important factor in the ability to form right relationships, which in its turn seems to be a crucial element in mental health. The difficulties of blind and deaf children whose play is restricted show how much play enriches the lives of ordinary children. Adults can help children in this form of play, and in their social development, by references to the thoughts, feelings and needs of other people. Through stories told to them, children enter into different ways of behaving and of looking at the world, and play new parts.

Just as adults relive experience in thought or words, so children play over and over the important happenings of their lives. The repetition is usually selective. Children who re-enact a painful scene repeatedly are not doing it to preserve the pain but to make it bearable and understandable. They incorporate those parts of the difficult situation which are endurable and add others as their courage and confidence grows. This is one of the ways in which they bring under control the feelings of frustration which must be experienced by those who are dependent on the will and love of adults. This kind of play can preserve self esteem by reducing unpleasant experiences to size, and reinforce confidence by dwelling on success.

Much of children's play is "cultural" play as opposed to the "natural" play of animals which mainly practises physical and survival skills. It often needs adult participation so that cultural facts and their significance can be communicated to children. The introduction into the classroom of objects for hospital play provides opportunities for coming to terms with one of the most common fears. Similarly the arrival of a new baby in the family, the death of someone important to the child, the invention of space rockets or new weapons may all call for the provision of materials for dramatic play which will help children to give expression to their feelings as a preliminary to understanding and controlling them. Sensitivity and observation are called for rather than intervention from the teacher. The knowledge of children gained from "active" observation is invaluable to teachers. It gives common ground for conversation and exchange of ideas which it is among the most important duties of teachers to initiate and foster.

A child's play at any given moment contains many elements. The layers of meaning may include a highly conscious organisation of the environment, exploration of physical and social relationships and an expression of the deepest levels of fantasy. Wide ranging and satisfying play is a means of learning, a powerful stimulus to learning, and a way to free learning from distortion by the emotions. Several writers have recently emphasised the importance of a period of play and exploration in new learning as, for example, in mathematics and science. Adults as well as children approach new learning in this way. **"**

Source: DES (1967) *Children and their Primary School: A Report of the Central Advisory Council for Education (England)* (vol. 1). London: HMSO, pp. 193–4

The Plowden Report (DES, 1967) recognized that play and discovery learning had a place in primary education and this was a characteristic of primary education in the 1960s and 1970s. In the 1980s, before the introduction of the national curriculum (now DfEE, 1999a), there were concerns that this pedagogical approach had led to primary classes, where children played without purpose or learning objectives and unsupported by adults. Of course, as the reading above shows, this was not the original view of the Plowden Report (DES, 1967). However, a critical report in the early 1990s (Alexander et al., 1992) followed by national strategies (DfEE, 1998; DfEE, 1999b), which advocated rigid pedagogical approaches, led to more structured learning in primary education. The story in early years education was significantly different and the Plowden Report influenced the development of the EYFS (DCSF, 2008), via a number of different versions, which strongly advocates play.

Play underpins the delivery of all the EYFS. Children must have opportunities to play indoors and outdoors. All early years providers must have access to an outdoor play area which can benefit the children. If a setting does not have direct access to an outdoor play area then they must make arrangements for daily opportunities for outdoor play in an appropriate nearby location. The EYFS CD-ROM also contains information suggesting innovative ways to engage children in outdoor play.

Play underpins all development and learning for young children. Most children play spontaneously, although some may need adult support, and it is through play that they develop intellectually, creatively, physically, socially and emotionally.

Providing well-planned experiences based on children's spontaneous play, both indoors and outdoors, is an important way in which practitioners support young children to learn with enjoyment and challenge. In playing, children behave in different ways: sometimes their play will be responsive or boisterous, sometimes they may describe and discuss what they are doing, sometimes they will be quiet and reflective as they play.

The role of the practitioner is crucial in:

- observing and reflecting on children's spontaneous play;
- building on this by planning and resourcing a challenging environment which:
  - supports and extends specific areas of children's learning;
  - extends and develops children's language and communication in their play.

Through play, in a secure but challenging environment with effective adult support, children can:

- explore, develop and represent learning experiences that help them to make sense of the world;
- practise and build up ideas, concepts and skills;
- learn how to understand the need for rules;
- take risks and make mistakes;
- think creatively and imaginatively;
- communicate with others as they investigate or solve problems.

(DCSF, 2008: 7–8)

It is pleasing to note that the part played by play approaches in primary education has been enhanced through reviews of the curriculum (Alexander, 2009; Rose, 2009), both incidentally led by academics who advocated the changes to a more structured approached in the 1990s (Alexander et al., 1992). Both reviews (Alexander, 2009; Rose, 2009) recommend that approaches used in the EYFS (DCSF, 2008) inform primary education.

Subject tasks

EYFS:
Plan some supported exploratory play to support learning outcomes for knowledge and understanding of the world. This could be exploring and sorting historical artefacts, a collection of natural objects, or exploratory water play, or sand play.

Observe and interact with the children and identify how the planned learning outcomes have been met.

Reflection

- How did the exploratory play support achievement of the learning outcomes?
- Was the play approach more successful than other, more structured learning approaches?
- How could you use exploratory play to achieve other learning outcomes?

KS1:
Set up a role-play area to develop children's ability to count and calculate. This may be a shop, where price lists can be created, multiple goods purchased and money can be exchanged for goods, or a building site, where numbers of bricks, length and height can be counted and calculated.

Observe and interact with the children and identify how the planned learning outcomes have been met.

Reflection

- How did the role play support and extend learning for different children at KS1?
- Was the play approach more successful than other, more structured learning approaches?
- How could you use role play in your classroom to achieve other learning outcomes?

KS2:
Set up a role-play day linked to learning outcomes in history and science. This may be a Victorian science day, where children can explore the way Victorians washed their clothes as compared to modern washing techniques, or wartime home, where home appliances, food and toys can be explored.

Observe and interact with the children and identify how the planned learning outcomes have been met.

Reflection

- How did the themed day motivate, support and extend learning in both areas for different children at KS2?
- Was the approach more successful than other, more structured learning approaches?
- How could you use themed play days in your classroom to achieve other learning outcomes?

The role of the teacher in play

When pedagogical approaches became more structured in the 1990s, the role of the teacher in the learning process changed from a creative facilitator to a didactic technician. With assessment based on narrow cognitive targets and teachers judged on their achievement of these narrow targets, teachers began to impart knowledge to children to ensure they could pass the next assessment stage. Indeed, some teachers have only ever taught in this way and so changes in light of the Rose (2009) and Cambridge Reviews (Alexander, 2009) are likely to be a big challenge.

The Plowden Report (DES, 1967: 242) identified the important role of the teacher in discovery and play by deciding the correct way to support individuals, assessing their level of need and ability, not letting them 'flounder too long or too helplessly' and supporting them by thoughtful questioning. For play approaches to be successful, the teacher needs to provide the correct mix of support, encouragement and time for the individual learners (Vygotsky, 1962, 1978; see also Chapter 1). This can be provided by the teacher working alongside the children, making suggestions, asking questions and/or modelling enquiry skills. In this way, children can be guided into new avenues of play, exploration and discovery and not 'over directed' (Johnston, 2004).

Impact tasks

Early career professional:
Plan some play activities in your setting/class and plan your involvement in the learning. Consider in particular:

- how you will introduce the play
- how you will interact/support/guide/model during the play
- what questions you will ask to encourage learning
- How you will evaluate your part in the learning.

Reflection

- What was the impact of your role on the children's learning?
- How did having less teacher control over the activity affect learning and behaviour?
- How can you develop your role to support and extend learning in other activities?

Later years professional:
Video yourself interacting with children during a play-based activity.

Reflection

- How did you interact/support/guide/model during the play?
- How did your interaction impact on the children's learning and behaviour?
- How can you develop your role to support and extend learning in other activities?

Professional leader:
Get each member of your staff to plan a play activity and consider the adult role in the learning. Consider in particular:

- how they will introduce the play
- how they will interact/support/guide/model during the play
- what questions they will ask to encourage learning
- how they will evaluate the adult role in the learning.

You may also video the activity so the adult role can be analysed more deeply.

Reflection

- How did the adult role impact on the children's learning and behaviour at different ages and ability levels?
- How can you develop your role to support and extend learning in other activities?
- What are the medium- and longer-term implications for practice in your setting/school?

References

Alexander, R. (ed.) (2009) *Children, their World, their Education: Final Report and Recommendations of the Cambridge Review*. London: Routledge.

Alexander, R., Rose, J. and Woodhead, C. (1992) *Curriculum Organisation and Classroom Practice in Primary Schools: A Discussion Paper*. London: Department of Education and Science (DES).

British Educational Research Association (BERA) Early Years Special Interest Group (2003) *Early Years Research: Pedagogy, Curriculum and Adult Roles, Training and Professionalism*. Southwell: BERA.

Bruce, T. (2009) *Early Childhood*, 2nd edn. London: Sage Publications.

Department for Children, Schools and Families (DCSF) (2008) *The Early Years Foundation Stage: Setting the Standard for Learning, Development and Care for Children from Birth to Five; Practice Guidance*. London: DCSF.

Department for Education and Science (DES) (1967) *Children and their Primary School: A Report of the Central Advisory Council for Education (England)* (vol. 1). London: Her Majesty's Stationery Office (HMSO).

Department for Education and Employment (DfEE) (1998) *The National Literacy Strategy*. London: DfEE.

—— (1999a) *The National Curriculum: Handbook for Teachers in England*. London: DfEE Qualifications and Curriculum Authority (QCA).

—— (1999b) *The National Numeracy Strategy*. London: DfEE.

Froebel, F. (1826) *On the Education of Man*. Keilhau, Leipzig: Wienbrach.

Hutt, C., Tyler, S., Hutt, J. and Christopherson, H. (eds) (1988) *Play, Exploration and Learning*. London: Routledge.

Johnston, J. (2004) The value of exploration and discovery, *Primary Science Review*, 85: 21–3.

Johnston, J. (2005) *Early Explorations in Science*, 2nd edn. Maidenhead: Open University Press.

Johnston, J. and Nahmad-Williams, L. (2010) Developing imagination and imaginative play, in A. Compton, J. Johnston, L. Nahmad-Williams and K. Taylor (2010) *Creative Development*. London: Continuum.

Montessori, M. (1912) *The Montessori Method*. London: Heinemann.

Piaget, J. (1976) 'Mastery play' and 'symbolic play', in J. Bruner, A. Jolly and K. Sylva (eds) *Play – Its Role in Development and Evolution*. Middlesex: Penguin.

Reed, S. (2007) The importance of symbolic play as a component of the early childhood curriculum, *Essays in Education*, vol. 19, Winter, 37–47. www.usca.edu/essays/vol192007/reed.pdf accessed 9/12/09.

Rose, J. (2009) *Independent Review of the Primary Curriculum: Final Report*. Nottingham: Department for Children, Families and Schools (DCFS).

Rousseau, J.-J. (1911) *Emile*. London: J. M. Dent & Sons.

Steiner, R. (1996) *The Education of the Child and Early Lectures on Education*. New York: Anthroposophic Press.

Vygotsky, L. (1962) *Thought and Language*. Cambridge, MA: The MIT Press.

Vygotsky, L. and Cole, M. (eds) (1978) *Mind in Society: The Development of Higher Psychological Processes*. Cambridge, MA: Harvard University Press.

8 Globalization

This chapter has two purposes. The first is to introduce you to the key concepts and current thinking about the nature of globalization in the early part of the twenty-first century. The second is to discuss some of the ways these might be interpreted and developed in the early years of primary education. One concern often expressed by people working with young children is that concepts of globalization are so vast and complex that they question whether these children are able to understand such issues. This perspective is introduced by David Hicks (2002) in the reading below which we use as a starting point for our thinking.

> ## ❝ Teaching about global issues
>
> Over the last twenty-five years, many educators have stressed the need for students to learn about global issues and have often taken this to be a relatively unproblematic area of pedagogy. An important Canadian study on the impact of teaching about such issues, however, suggests that the learning process may be much more complex than was previously assumed. This chapter reports on a research project that monitored student responses to learning about global futures and found much more going on beneath the surface than meets the eye. It would seem that strong cognitive, affective and existential responses need to be recognized and acknowledged as part of any journey towards personal and political change.
>
> Teaching about 'global issues' is shorthand for a variety of concerns that an increasing number of educators feel it important to deal with in schools and establishments of higher education. The issues studied range from those to do with the environment, development and human rights, to peace and conflict, race, gender, health and education. They may be part of existing courses in geography, social studies or humanities or take place under headings such as environmental education, global education and futures studies. All of these issues highlight major, maybe irresolvable,

problems about the human condition. They all involve much human pain and suffering (as well as joy and well-being) and also often impact disastrously on non-human species. Learning about global issues is thus potentially a traumatic activity, so what do students actually experience when they learn about them? And what responsibility do educators have to find out about this?

Facing global issues

Life at the beginning of the new century – whether personal or professional – is complex, chaotic, fragmented, exciting, challenging and stressful. The hazards of life under late modernity or post modernity have been well documented and provide the wider background to this study. Giddens writes:

> The crisis-prone nature of late modernity . . . has unsettling con-
> sequences in two respects: it fuels a general climate of uncertainty
> which an individual finds disturbing no matter how far he seeks to
> put it to the back of his mind; and it inevitably exposes everyone to
> a diversity of crisis situations . . . which may sometimes threaten
> the very core of self-identity.
>
> (Giddens 1991: 184)

This feeling of living on the edge, augmented by the local–global paradoxes and ambiguities of globalization, can lead to an underlying sense of personal insecurity which in turn triggers deeper existential anxieties. Beck (1998) highlights the dilemma of having to make decisions about risks about which we know nothing, and points out that society has become a laboratory where no one is prepared to take responsibility for the outcome of social, scientific and technological experiments.

It is not surprising, in the face of such disorientating change, that many people prefer not to know. 'Most people', says Walsh (1992: 63), 'experience great difficulty in acknowledging the true state of the world, its suffering and its peril. Repression and denial play major roles in this difficulty.' As in our personal lives, some problems are too much to bear so that we deny their very existence. Our defence mechanisms can thus lead to a 'psychic numbing' which denies the pain of the world and our part in producing it. By denying its existence we perpetuate it. Learning about global issues can never be solely a cognitive matter, although many educators may wish it to be. This is why the work of activist academics like Macy is of such importance. In outlining the theoretical underpinnings of her work, she writes:

> Our experience of pain for the world springs from our inter-
> connectedness with all beings, from which also arise our powers to
> act on their behalf. . . . Unlocking occurs when our pain for the
> world is not only intellectually validated, but experienced. . . .
> When we reconnect with life, by willingly enduring our pain for it,
> the mind retrieves its natural clarity.
>
> (Macy and Brown 1998: 59)

This echoes the argument of eco-psychologists like Roszak et al. (1995)
that much of the Angst of the late twentieth century is due to our being
cut off and alienated from the natural world in which humans have been
rooted for countless millennia.

For those interested in teaching about global issues, the crucial question is to what extent educators have addressed these matters. Certainly,
some of those involved in environmental education and futures research
have identified the distress and alienation that many young people feel
about the human condition. As adults, educators have had longer to live
with this awareness and may be better able to inure themselves to it.
Young people come to it with a freshness that makes it even more painful.
Whereas UK pupils are reasonably optimistic about their own futures, they
are pessimistic about global futures (Chapter 3), and Australian students
seem to be even more pessimistic (Hutchinson 1996; Eckersley 1999). In
their exploration of young people's environmental attitudes in Australia,
Connell et al. (1999)) found that environmental problems made them feel
frustrated, sad and pessimistic. Although scepticism and despair among
the young are sometimes belittled by adults, they might better be seen as
a valuable early warning system for present and future generations.

One of the most comprehensive examinations of the impact of learning about global issues are those carried out by Rogers (1994; 1998;
Rogers and Tough 1996). It was this study which provided the inspiration
for the research project described here. In her doctoral thesis, Rogers
examined in detail the impact on adult education students of a course
on global futures taught at the Ontario Institute for Studies in Education.
She was able to examine both the personal effect this had on students
and the complexities of the learning process itself. She notes:

> Coming to grips with the complexity of the world's problems,
> confronting uncertainty about the future, and critically examining
> deeply held worldviews may cause emotional and existential tur-
> moil. To try to cope with the onslaught of thoughts and feelings,
> people may resort to using defence mechanisms such as denial,
> suppression, intellectualisation or projection. Consequently, rather
> than being truly able to face the future, the protective defence

mechanisms may cause people to retreat or disconnect from reality. Thus paradoxically, the learning process may lead to paralysis rather than mobilising informed choice and action.

(Rogers and Tough 1996: 492–3)

As a result of interviewing course participants, Rogers observed that five, often overlapping, dimensions or stages of learning were involved (1996) as shown in the box below. From this detailed analysis of learning about global futures it can be seen that the endeavour is a complex, holistic and deeply personal one – it is far from being solely a cognitive endeavour. As a result of this investigation, Rogers developed the conceptual model of learning shown in Figure 10.1.

GLOBAL ISSUES: DIMENSIONS OF LEARNING

Cognitive *dimension*
The first stage involves learning new facts, ideas and concepts about the current global situation and its likely future consequences. This is traditionally considered to be the core of teaching about global issues. Some students, when faced with thinking about the future, thought it was 'out-of-touch' or 'airy fairy'. Being forced to step outside their usual spatial and temporal orientations sometimes lead to resistance. Students also felt cognitively overwhelmed, confused and pessimistic when faced with the complexities of the world's problems.

Affective *dimension*
Learning about global issues also involves an emotional response. This appears to occur when knowing shifts from being something intellectual and detached to a personal and connected knowing. Some students experienced a range of conflicting emotions, such as: elation/depression, hopefulness/hopelessness, fear/courage, sadness/happiness. Rogers and Tough (1996: 493) note: 'Grieving has been reported as a common response to learning about global threats to human survival and with respect to human processes of transition and change.' Most importantly, the emotional responses experienced by students need to be accepted and seen as part of a shared experience.

Existential *dimension*
Although rarely discussed in the literature, says Rogers, learning about global issues and possible futures can also lead to a deep soul-searching. For some students this involved a questioning of their values, life purposes, faith and ways of living. They wanted to 'find an answer', or to 'do something', but often found themselves searching without finding any

immediate answers. At this level they were being faced with a reconstruction of their own sense of self, something which often occurs when embarking on a quest for deeper meaning and purpose in life.

Empowerment *dimension*
If this upheaval of the soul can be satisfactorily resolved, students can begin to feel a sense of personal empowerment. This arises from a clearer **sense** of personal responsibility and a commitment to do something. It centres on individual resolution of the question, can one person make a difference? In order to feel empowered, students need to be able to envision positive scenarios for the future and to learn about success stories in which individuals and groups have clearly made a difference. There needs to be hope, humour and cautious optimism.

Action *dimension*
If the questions raised by the first four dimensions of learning have been satisfactorily resolved in some appropriate way for the student, then informed personal, social and political choices and action can occur. Some of the students Rogers interviewed reported that learning about global futures had eventually led to a significant reorientation of their lives, personally and/or professionally. Such major choices, she notes, also need to be acknowledged and supported as an outcome of the learning process. **99**

Source: Hicks, D. (2002) *Lessons for the Future: The Missing Dimension in Education*. London: Routledge, pp. 98–101

Reflection

This discussion by Hicks provides a useful starting point for our own analysis. The first issue is to actually stand back from the sometimes uncritical application make of the word 'global'. Perhaps as educators we need to be much more careful and precise in the use of the word. At the very least, be aware of the issues involved if you are to raise it in discussion or include it in school documents or teaching resources. This discussion applies of course both between adults and pupils. The second is to be aware of the scale of issues included in the term global. Hicks clearly indicates this early in his discussions. While we must not shy away from ideas on a global scale, we do need to be aware of how these may be interpreted by young people, while at the same time appreciating that perhaps they have a much broader global perspective than children even 20 years ago.

The second issue is the five dimensions of global learning offered by Hicks. Although the research by Rogers and Tough was based on adult perceptions, their findings may well have significance in the educational debates on younger people's understanding of a global dimension. Perhaps the strength of the five dimensions is that it can turn our focus away from learning about the world and more towards how children can be supported in the beginning to find their place in the world. At a practical level, you may wish to consider how the five dimensions may link with aspects of current educational ideas such as personal and social learning linking with the affective and empowerment dimensions.

Reflective tasks

EYFS:
- To what extent do you think the global dimension can realistically be incorporated into an EYFS curriculum?
- What levels of intellectual ability possessed by these young people could be developed through such engagement?

KS1:
- How might pupils' own knowledge and understanding of the world be used as starting points in developing a global dimension at this stage?
- What practical activities could be devised to help them understand geographical scales beyond their own first-hand experience?

KS2:
- How might current global issues be introduced and developed within this key stage?
- What aspects of working with controversial issues may need agreement across the school before embarking on such activities? An example might be 'what help, if any should we offer to people in disaster areas around the world, and why?'

Having considered one of the main questions asked about including a global dimension in education, we now turn to some of the current thinking and key concepts in globalization in order to help you place the teaching of it in a broader concept and to give you the confidence to justify the work you may develop with children.

It could be argued that human beings have been involved in a process of globalization from the first moment when they set out to explore the world and mix with groups of other people. The word can be found in literature dating back to the 1960s but it really became commonly used towards the end of the twentieth century. Academics are still debating what might be an accurate definition of globalization and there is certainly insufficient space in this chapter to come to any firm conclusions. Instead, let us consider two recent opinions of a possible definition. The first is from Anthony Giddens, former director of the London School of Economics, who suggests that globalization can thus be identified as the intensification of worldwide social relationships which link distant localities in such a way that local happenings are shaped by events occurring many miles away and vice versa. Another comes from Roland Robertson, Professor of Sociology at the University of Aberdeen, who argues that globalization as a concept refers both to the compression of the world and the intensification of consciousness of the world as a whole. It may be helpful to consider these in relation to your own compared to that of your great grandparents. Even back in their day, globalization was already well developed in terms of transport, communication systems and human movements. But perhaps the big difference between their experience and your experience of globalization today is the speed and complexity at which these linking processes are occurring and the considerable implications they can have.

Steger (2009) suggests that in fact four main mechanisms are at work in process of globalization in our world today. The first is that many new social relations are being created at great speed along with the multiplication of existing ones. The second is that our social, economic political and cultural relations are expanding and stretching. The third is that these are occurring at ever greater speed and intensification. The final mechanism Steger suggests is that the previous three are having a profound effect on individuals as they seek to make sense of their place in the world as they become ever more interlinked with it. Joining together these ideas Steger (2009: 15) offers his definition saying 'Globalization refers to the expansion and intensification of social relations and consciousness across world-time and world-space'.

To place this in a current context we briefly reflect on a few processes at work. The global financial markets have changed enormously over the past few months and because of the global scale and interrelationships at work, it becomes ever harder to predict what the future might hold. Concerns are expressed about the nuclear intentions of Iran: Missiles that can travel to distant destinations are a practical example of globalization at work. Swine flu is apparent in many places worldwide but we are very unsure as to how it may spread in the future. Although similar epidemics have occurred on a global scale in the past, it is hard to use them as predictive models for today precisely because the mechanisms identified by Steger are at work. It is the speed and complexity of the processes of globalization that make these events ever harder to manage and predict. Steger thus argues that it is this uncertainty that in turn affects our own human conscientiousness of being in the world.

Writers on globalization identify a number of dimensions that can help us to further understand the modem world. These are political, economic, cultural and ecological. We now briefly discuss these before moving on to their implications for the education of young people.

Political

If we look at the history of the world for the last few centuries, we see that we have organized space by the creation of nation states and the drawing of national boundaries to identify these territories. In the debate on globalizaton, one group of theorists argues that the nation state is in decline because so many processes of globalization totally ignore these traditional boundaries. Others suggest that some of the threats generated by processes of globalization may in fact fuel a growing identification of nation states as groups of people seek to manage and survive in a globalized world. An example of the decrease of the nation state can be found in the growing power of the European Union (EU) where various nation states have signed up to a notion that some activities should be based on mutual interest at the loss of state control. A current example of the reinforcement of the importance of the nation state is the notion that Britain should become much less reliant on the rest of the world for food and fuel supplies as we move towards a less and less secure world, where global demands on resources are rapidly increasing.

Those commentators who argue that the power of the nation state is in decline are referred to as 'hyperglobalizers'. They base their case that economic factors are now so globally at work that nations are not capable of operating in isolation. Their opponents say that those very economic processes are a direct result of nation states creating the economic mechanisms at work in the world today. An example might be the way in which many of these are dominated by mechanisms developed in specific nations. A real chicken and egg debate at a global scale! However, if we look at current issues such as migration, we see nation states exercising increased power to control movements of population. The heightened security measures on international travel further highlight the power of the nation state in controlling population movements. In addition, many states still have internal control over things such as education.

Scholte (2001) offers a model to help us understand where nation states fit into a globalizing world. In his model he lists the following things that may challenge the nature and existence of the nation state. Read through this list and relate it to news and other issues that are taking place at the time you are reading this chapter:

- nationalism
- troop movements
- surveillance by global governance agencies
- satellite communications
- diplomacy
- electronic money transfers
- migration

- transboundary pollution
- merchandise trade
- computer data flows.

Do you think we can consider Britain to be a nation state as an entity in itself in the light of your reflections on the above?

Another factor to consider in the politics of globalization is the number of international organizations that governments have set up. These include North Atlantic Treaty Organization (NATO), the United Nations (UN), Organization for Co-operation and Development (OECD) and the WTO. Membership of these is based on the notion of state membership and those in power control those who can and cannot belong. In contrast to these is the growing number of nongovernmental and voluntary organizations that transcend national boundaries. These include Oxfam, Save the Children and many more that you could list. All have their own way of contributing to political globalization.

Economics

In the previous section we considered the role of the nation state. It is interesting to reflect that between 1918–1939 the USA and Great Britain orchestrated various economic policies designed to protect their national economies. By the end of the Second World War the Bretton Woods economic conference established the International Monetary Fund (IMF) and what was to become the World Bank. Until the early 1970s national governments and these organizations controlled the flow of money around the world. During the 1970s there was a significant move towards neoliberal economic strategies in the global north. Neoliberalism is based on the idea that the market should be based on free competition where supply and demand balance each other and that free market economies would enable the fittest organizations and nations to rise to the top. You may well see parallels here with the discussions in the chapter on educational policy. The collapse of communism in the late 1980s also worked to support the growth of a neoliberal economic order.

Commentators identify three main mechanisms at work: internationalization of trade and finance, the growth of transnational corporations and finally the increased role of international economic organizations. The internationalization of trade and finance can be illustrated by a large increase in free trade around the world. This is based on the reduction of trade barriers, specialization, competition and the use of technology to support it. It also involves the liberalization of financial transactions. A very obvious example of these has been the recent developments and crises in the global economy where, for example, changes in the American mortgage industry had knock-on effects around the world. The power of transnational corporations is also having a significant economic effect on globalization. For example, Walmart and Mitsubishi are among the largest 200 transnational companies (TNCs) who create over half of the global industrial output. Some of these corporations match the economic power of nation states. For example, in 2007 Walmart stores had a revenue of $351,139 m while the GDP (gross domestic product) of Sweden was $354,115 m. This is sometimes described as 'corporate globalization'. It has also been linked to deregulation in the global labour market as corporations 'race for the bottom' to find the cheapest supplies of labour. Three major international economic institutions are the World Bank, the IMF and the World Trade Organization (WTO). They play crucial roles in making and policing the rules that control the world economy. Some commentators on globalization suggest that the richest nations of the north use them to promote their own interests at the expense of the poorer nations, basing their operations on neoliberal policies.

Culture

The Internet and other new technologies have played a major part in how we perceive culture within a global context. Values, ideas, traditions, beliefs and ideologies circulate the world with increasing speed and volume. Barber (2007) identifies the 'infotainment telesector' as a central player in the way our ideas are influenced and shaped by the media which is increasingly linked with the commercial world. In 2006, only eight transnational media corporations including names such as AOL/Time Warner controlled over two-thirds of the annual revenue brought in by the global communications industry. Some commentators argue that this is another global mechanism resulting in the decreased power and authority of the nation state, while others regard it as another form of the trend towards global 'Americanization'. A counter-argument is that such technologies open up for us a multi-cultural world that we can begin to respect and understand. This raises the interesting question of whether globalization is making people around the world more similar or different. However, Robertson (1992) argues that local and community cultural power can remain strong in such situations by re-enforcing those cultural values that a community holds to be of worth. All these global mechanisms operate through the use of language and much research on the globalization of languages takes place. Five main concepts have been identified by staff at the Globalization Research Center at the University of Hawaii. The first is that globally the number of languages in use is leading towards a unification of cultural forces. The second is that increased migration is affecting the distribution of languages around the world. The third is that the learning of foreign languages and increased tourism is spreading languages across national and cultural borders. The fourth is the impact of the Internet on languages and the domination of English within it. Finally, they identify the impact of international scientific publications as an important mechanism on the production and movement of knowledge across the globe. These issues are discussed further in the second part of this chapter examining the role of globalization in learning.

Ecology

Ecological discussion on globalization is perhaps the most powerful tool in understanding the key issues involved. Many of the main environmental processes affecting change in the world do not recognize national boundaries. In addition, the speed and intensity of these processes are rapidly growing in the early part of the twenty-first century. These processes make us increasingly aware that all humans are linked globally by the impacts they have on us as humans and the physical environment.

The huge increase in the global population is having a number of effects on the planet. The first is the rapidly growing demand for food. This is complicated by the fact that as nations become wealthier, they begin to demand more western styles of food, which in turn have an impact on how land is used and the quality of it, resulting from intensive farming methods. The majority of the global population now live in cities, which in turn places pressure on the amount of land available for food production. However, within this process it must be noted that a small proportion of the global population places the majority of demand on land and resources for food production. To find out more about the global distribution of these and many more processes, log on to 'Worldmapper' to study constantly updated information. Some of these maps could easily be used with older Key Stage 2 (KS2) pupils.

Transboundary pollution is now commonplace around the world. Greenhouse gasses are free to move within the atmosphere. Acid rain from power stations is moved around the earth by winds. Synthetic chemical such as CFCs are released in nations using 'advanced' technology and have impacts such as contributing to holes in the ozone layer. This process was identified in the 1970s and many of the developed countries producing CFCs have done much to reduce emissions. However, emerging economies are using such technology as they are often cheaper and simpler to run than the more complex but safer processes adopted by richer nations. The huge debate about climate change is a further example of the globalization of ecological issues. There is not space in this chapter for a detailed discussion of the issues. However, the Stern Report (2007) provides an informed, balanced and up-to-date review of key issues and debates.

While these various ecological processes are at work across the globe, the ability of people and nations to respond to them varies enormously. On the one hand, some nations are major creators of the problems and sometimes refuse to address the seriousness of the effects, the USA being an example of this. On the other hand, many poor nations who are largely not responsible for creating the problems are potentially at greatest risk. An example of this is how Bangladesh will be significantly affected by any increase in global sea level, but as a nation contributes very little to the process.

These four key areas are complex. The second part of this chapter discusses some of the ways in which they can be developed within the primary curriculum to introduce young people to global processes.

The global dimension in school

This section examines some of the key points to consider when developing a global dimension in your school. It is being written at a time when the final reports of the Rose and Alexander Reviews of the primary curriculum have been published along with the outlines given by Ed Balls in November 2009 as to what it will look like. However, there will be an election in 2010 and the final legal version of the primary curriculum for September 2011 has still, in that context, to be announced. Therefore, although Rose and Alexander both refer to a global dimension in the primary curriculum, this section focuses on key concepts of a global dimension which, hopefully, can underpin whatever version of the curriculum will go live in September 2011.

We start with the whole school. We would argue that little meaningful learning will take place in the classroom if the intrinsic values underpinning a global dimension are not apparent to everyone involved with the school as a whole. These are well summed up by Oxfam (2006) who consider education for global citizenship should 'develop critical thinking about complex global issues' and 'develop and express childrens' values and opinions. In order to achieve this, the school needs to provide a supportive context for learning in three ways:

1   It provides the knowledge, understanding, skills and values 'to make a positive contribution, both locally and globally'.
2   It involves children in their own learning through 'the use of a wide range of active and participatory learning methods'.
3   It encourages children to 'care about the planet' and 'to develop empathy with, and an active concern for others'.

(Pickford, 2009: 2)

The first statement relates to the cross-curricular nature of the primary curriculum. All current indications are that this is how teachers will be encouraged to plan and teach from 2011. This is a positive move for developing a global dimension because it required children to begin to understand how almost everything that happens on the planet is interconnected with other events and processes. A cross-curricular approach can provide the intellectual framework for helping pupils understand cause and effect, which as we saw in the first section of this chapter are fundamental to understanding globalization. The second statement requires us to provide a learning environment in which children actively engage in asking questions and evaluating information and ideas. If we adopt the opposite approach where we see global education as a way of telling children information about the world then we run a real risk of indoctrination or letting them accept information and ideas as fact, when in the real world very few, if any, global issues are black and white. An obvious example of this is the debate about the human influence on climate change. The final statement covers the global dimension at a full range of scales. On the one hand, pupils are introduced to ideas about how we might care for the planet. On the other hand, it roots action firmly into a concern for the welfare of others, whether they are immediate neighbours or on the other side of the globe. To have a truly successful approach to global learning, all aspects of the school need to promote it through these three ideas.

You may say that the paragraph above has many idealistic points. To counterbalance these we need to be aware of the much more utilitarian justifications for a global dimension that have been put foward in government documents in recent years. In 2004 the then DfES listed three goals for 'world-class education'; the first being 'equipping our children, young people and adults for life in a global society and work in a global economy' and gave practical reasons for this; for example, world travel and the integration of newcomers to the UK. Two further government publications (DFES, 2005, 2007) reinforced the need for a global dimension in education and tended to base their justification on practical, economic and life skill arguments. The challenge for schools is to find ways of developing a global dimension which, on the one hand, does prepare children for life in the twenty-first century, while at the same time providing them with the values and opinions to become active global citizens. We do not see a great problem here but it will require schools to plan carefully in order to provide pupils with active learning experiences which cover the full spectrum of objectives.

Reflective task

EYFS:
- Having developed your understanding of the key concepts of globalization, what do you feel you already do in your practice to introduce young children to living in their immediate and wider worlds?

KS1:

- What practical enquiries might pupils at KS1 develop in order to help take them beyond their immediate world?

KS2:

- By the time your pupils leave primary school, what skills, understanding and knowledge might you expect them to have relating to the global dimension of their education?

It is to be hoped, indeed expected, that the new primary curriculum will encourage teachers to design the structure and content much more along lines that are meaningful and relevant to pupils rather than the top-down, content-led approach which existed from 1988 with the introduction of science as the first national curriculum subject. However, being faced with a blank page can be just as daunting as an endless list of learning objectives and attainment targets. In 2005 the DfES produced a document containing eight concepts which may usefully support teachers to plan a global dimension into the whole curriculum. They could be developed into a planning grid to help map out experiences that will help pupils gain a global understanding of the world. Not all eight would necessarily be covered to the same extent each time global issues were planned, but rather they might act as a checklist to create balance, progression and continuity. Pickford (2009: 4) usefully sums them up as follows:

Global citizenship
Gaining the knowledge, skills and understanding of concepts and institutions necessary to become informed, active, responsible citizens

Conflict resolution
Understanding the nature of conflicts, their impact on development and why there is a need for their resolution and the promotion of harmony

Diversity
Understanding and respecting differences and relating these to our common humanity Human rights

Knowing about human rights including the UN Convention on the Rights of the Child Interdependence

Understanding how people, places, economies and environments are all inextricably interrelated, and that choices and events have repercussions on a global scale

Social justice
Understanding the importance of social justice as an element in both sustainable development and the improved welfare of all people

Sustainable development
Understanding the need to maintain and improve the quality of life now without damaging the planet for future generations

Values and perceptions
Developing a critical evaluation of representations of global issues and an appreciation of the effects these have on people's attitudes and values.

Hopefully, you will begin to see how these eight concepts relate back to the ideas discussed in the first part of this chapter. How might these look in practice?

Subject tasks

Early childhood professionals
Decide on something you do in your current good practice which could be developed into an activity to promote global understanding in your children. Study the eight concepts above and select those you think are relevant to your chosen activity. Note down the knowledge, skills and understanding you might hope to develop in introducing young children to the global dimension.

Later years professionals
Thinking of the pupils you currently work with, choose a current topic in the news and consider how you might use it to develop their broader global understanding. The Copenhagen Conference on climate change in 2009 ended with very limited progress having been made. It would be an opportunity for children to discuss what seems to have been agreed and the global impact it may or may not have. What resolutions and laws might they have passed if they had been delegates at the conference?

Professional leaders

Reflecting on those colleagues with whom you work, their expertise and broader interests, how might you build on these to enhance the opportunities for global education in your organization. This will involve a careful consideration of how subjects within the curriculum are organized and, where appropriate, integrated.

Conclusion

The study of globalization offers many opportunities for the development of cross-curricular activities that pupils can understand in practical ways, which are meaningful to their lives. The content of such studies will regularly change as new issues face us on a global scale. In many ways, this provides an excellent foundation for the development of a dynamic and meaningful curriculum.

References

Barber, B. (2007) *Consumed*. Norton & Company.

Department for Education and Skills (DfES) (2004) *Putting the World into World-class Education: An International Strategy for Education, Skills and Children's Services*. London: DfES.

———— (2005) *Developing the Global Dimension in the School Curriculum*. London: DfES.

———— (2007) *Sustainable Schools for Pupils, Communities and the Environment*. London: DfES.

Hicks, D. (2002) *Lessons for the Future: The Missing Dimension in Education*. London: Routledge.

Oxfam (2006) *Education for Global Citizenship: A Guide for Schools*. Oxford: Oxfam.

Pickford, T. (2009) *Get Global! A Practical Guide to Integrating the Global Dimension into the Primary Curriculum*. Stoke on Trent: Trentham Books.

Robertson, R. (1992) *Globalisation*. London: Sage Publications.

Scholte, J. (2001) The globalisation of world politics, in J. Bayliss and S. Smith (eds) *The Globalisation of World Politics*. Oxford: Oxford University Press.

Steger, M. (2009) *Globalisation: A Very Short Introduction*. Oxford: Oxford University Press.

Stern, N. (2007) *The Economics of Climate Change: The Stern Review*. Cambridge: Cambridge University Press.

9 Multicultural

The word multicultural has been in our vocabulary for a long time and there are many interpretations and definitions attached to it. It can also raise heated political debates as commentators consider the word to be value-laden in a variety of ways. The purpose of this chapter is not to come to any conclusions about these issues, but to highlight some current thinking and debate about what we may mean by multicultural and the implications it has for what we do, or indeed not do, in schools.

Working in initial teacher education, we like to discuss with students what we call the 'escalator of education' and the idea that students are stepping onto something that is already on the way upwards. We need to be aware of events and decisions from the past in order to understand the present and make informed decisions about the future. In 1967 the Labour Government published the Plowden Report entitled 'Children and their Primary Schools: A Report of the Central Advisory Council for Education (England)' (DES, 1967). The reading that follows is from Chapter 6 entitled 'Children of Immigrants'. As you read, note any content which you think still rings true today and any aspects which you feel have changed out of recognition in the first quarter of the twenty-first century.

> 66 183. These families, though handicapped by unfamiliarity with the English way of living, by their language and too often by poverty and cramped living conditions, are often drawn from the more enterprising citizens of their own country. Though the range of ability and temperament is wide, many children are intelligent and eager to learn. Indeed, this eagerness sometimes proves an embarrassment when it is for the disciplined book learning and formal instruction of their own culture and when the language barrier prevents the school explaining fully to parents the different way we go about education in England.
>
> 184. Although some immigrant children are at first upset by the English climate, they are usually well nourished and well clothed. When

their health is poor this is usually due to complaints which were common among working class people before the last war. Some special problems face local education authorities and others in areas with high concentrations of immigrants. Many immigrant children are at a disadvantage because of the poor educational background from which they have come. It is difficult to discriminate between the child who lacks intelligence and the child who is suffering from 'culture shock' or simply from inability to communicate. As a result, few immigrant children find places in selective schools. In one borough with nearly six per cent of immigrants in its school population, not a single child was selected for a grammar school in 1966. Children with high mathematical or technical ability are at a disadvantage because of their poor command of written English.

185. Teachers have generally not been trained during their courses at colleges of education to teach immigrant children. They, therefore, lack knowledge of the cultural traditions and family structure that lie behind the children's concepts and behaviour. Experienced teachers of immigrant children testify that they have found it of great help to know about family tradition and habits of worship, and about food, clothing and customs, which differ from ours. Unfortunately it is not easy to find authoritative books on these subjects suitable for teachers in training, and there has been a lack of in-service training courses.

186. A start has been made by the Association of Teachers of Pupils from Overseas, the British Caribbean Society and others, who are helping teachers to acquire background knowledge. The National Committee for Commonwealth Immigrants has begun the publication of a series of background booklets for teachers. The next step must be the inclusion in initial training courses for some teachers, and in some refresher courses, of discussion of the background of immigrant children. Local education authorities, where there are large numbers of immigrants, could hold induction courses for new teachers in these areas.

The Curriculum
187. The curriculum of the primary school with a substantial intake of immigrant children should take account of their previous environment, and prepare them for life in a different one. Their culture can enrich the school's geographical and historical studies and, if used imaginatively, can improve other children's appreciation of the newcomers besides enabling immigrant children to value their own culture and language. This is easier to achieve with older than with younger children. It is particularly important to introduce the younger children to their new environment. Visits to shops and factories, to the local fire station, to the library, the museum, and the country can provide a useful background to their school work.

Meanwhile, books used in schools should be re-examined. Some display out of date attitudes towards foreigners, coloured people, and even coloured dolls. Some are linguistically unsuitable, and some assume a social background incomprehensible to the newcomer.

188. Contacts with the home are especially important and, because of language difficulties, far from easy to establish. In one school, for example, 80 per cent of immigrant parents interviewed as compared with 20 per cent of the rest, did not know the name of their children's class teacher. The appointment of suitably trained immigrant teachers who would combine part-time teaching with welfare functions could be helpful. They could interpret the school's aims to immigrant parents and the parents' wishes and anxieties to the schools.

189. The education of the parents must not be neglected. Many of them are anxious to learn English, and to educate themselves in other ways. There is a possible role here for married women teachers willing to give up part of their time to teaching immigrant family groups in the afternoon or evening. They would require courses in teaching English as a foreign language.

190. It is absolutely essential to overcome the language barrier. This is less serious for a child entering the infant school. He rapidly acquires, both in the classroom and outside, a good command of the relatively limited number of words, phrases and sentences in common use among the other children. He can then learn to read with the rest, by normal methods. Immigrant children who arrive later in their school life have much greater problems. They need to learn a new language after the patterns and often the written forms of their own language have been thoroughly mastered. This calls for special techniques and materials and poses problems to which little research has been directed. It is necessary to distinguish between the non-English speaking Cypriot or Asian child and the West Indian who speaks a vernacular form of English, influenced to some extent by 'creole' English. It is a dialect form which, if not supplemented by a form nearer to 'received pronunciation', may place the speaker at a disadvantage in seeking employment and in ordinary social contacts. Techniques suitable for the child who goes home in the evening to a family speaking Urdu, or Greek, will not be suitable for the child whose parents speak a dialect of English which may be close to 'received pronunciation' or distant from it, depending on the island, or the social class, from which they come.

192. So far there has been very little opportunity for teachers to learn how to teach English to foreigners. The University of London Institute of Education has provided a few places; more are needed. No colleges of education have yet run courses, but we are told that seven plan to start this year. Some local education authorities are providing in-service

training. The University of Leeds Institute of Education, sponsored by the Schools Council, is preparing and testing materials for teaching English to children of immigrant families from Asia and Southern Europe.

193. When the concentration of non-English speaking children in a particular school reaches a level which seems to interfere with the opportunity for other children to learn, or with the teacher's ability to do justice to the immigrant children, there may be a demand for dispersal of the immigrants. The Secretary of State for Education and Science, in Circular 7/65, advised local authorities to avoid heavy concentrations of immigrants in particular schools: As the Circular points out, experienced teachers believe that a group containing up to one fifth of immigrant children can fit in a school with reasonable ease, but if the proportion goes beyond a third serious strains arise, and it may become difficult to prevent the proportion rising further. The Department's views are shared by many teachers and were reached only after the most serious study of the implications.

194. Yet some local education authorities after equally careful thought and a great deal of experience have preferred not to implement the Circular. One teacher of long experience in a notoriously deprived district has written: 'We have to accept that there are going to be schools in many of our cities with an intake largely coloured . . . Dispersal at the primary stage, except on a limited geographical basis, is administratively difficult and psychologically unsound'. This authority has preferred to trust to extra staffing and enrichment of the curriculum in smaller classes. Other authorities are trying a variety of solutions using partial dispersal, centres to which children go until they have some command of English, or a mixture of both. Whenever immigrant children are dispersed it must be done with great care and sensitivity. Children should be given special consideration on account of their language and other difficulties and not on account of their colour.

195. The Department of Education and Science have increased quotas of teachers for areas with substantial numbers of immigrants. Some authorities have been unable to fill these quotas, however, for the same reasons that they have been unable to staff the schools in their deprived areas. Our proposals for the priority areas (Chapter 5) may help to meet these staffing problems and our proposals for the training and recruitment of teachers' aides (Chapter 26) have a special relevance. The central government are already helping in other ways: the Local Government Bill now before Parliament provides for a new specific grant to those local authorities with concentrations of Commonwealth immigrants.

196. We have had evidence that volunteers in the year between sixth form and university have helped by being available to work with small groups of children, under the supervision of a trained teacher. We were

interested to learn that one authority plans to keep open some of its schools during the summer holidays for the continuous teaching of English to immigrant children so that they do not forget what they have learnt. There should be further experiment on these lines.

197. Remedial courses in spoken English are also needed for those immigrant teachers, especially from Asia, who, though in theory qualified to teach, find it impossible to obtain posts because their speech is inadequate. Holding university degrees and similar qualifications, they often cannot understand why they are not appointed as teachers. It is not easy to detect one's own speech peculiarities. Four remedial English courses are planned by the Department of Education and Science for 1966/67. All are heavily oversubscribed. There is a pressing need for an expansion of such courses which could also provide an introduction to English primary school methods and prepare some teachers for social work.

198. The purpose of the various measures we have discussed should be to eliminate, not perpetuate, the need for them. The time required to make the newcomers fully at home in the school and community will be an index of their success. The steps taken ought to be constantly reviewed as immigrant groups are absorbed into the native population. Special measures inevitably identify children as 'different' and their duration should be as brief as possible.

"

Source: DES (1967) *Children and their Primary Schools: A Report of the Central Advisory Council for Education* (England). London: Her Majesty's Stationery Office

Hopefully you found this text from the middle of the last century an interesting document to read in the light of issues currently facing education today. You will probably have noticed the use of particular language and the value-laden nature of much of it. One section is sub-headed 'Educational Problems' clearly indicating the authors' view that immigrant families brought problems which the education system had to solve. Assumptions are made about the living conditions many of the children were living in: while it may have been true for many, it is a huge generalization. Regarding the curriculum, the authors suggest that although teachers should take into account the pupils' previous backgrounds and experiences, their job was to 'prepare them for a life in a different one' (DES, 1967: 71). On the other hand they suggest that contact with the home is important, a view strongly agreed with today. They acknowledge that teachers need effective training to prepare them for working with classes having pupils from many parts of the world. Although the DfES require this to be included in initial teacher education, so many demands are placed on course time that even today this is rarely sufficient to prepare students for this demanding part of their professional work.

Reflection

The Plowden reading does help us to put current debates into an historical, social and political context. How might it help us reflect on our current position in education?

EYFS:
- How well do you not only know the cultural backgrounds of your pupils, but also how well do you understand the perspectives of their parents and carers?
- What further study might you need to undertake in order to have a secure knowledge and understanding of cultural questions as they apply to your professional life?

KS1:
- What influences may have already impacted on your pupils by this KS1 which have had an effect on how they perceive other cultures?
- What first-hand experience might you need to provide in order to maximize cultural understanding at this key stage? Plowden is very thin on this.

KS2:
- Plowden rather saw this aspect of primary education in a vacuum. How might you ensure their cultural understanding prepared them effectively for KS3 and the wider world?

The Plowden extract was chosen for this chapter as hopefully it helps to place in a broader context many of the issues arising today over the use of the term 'multicultural'. As mentioned earlier, the word has many powerful political interpretations. However, 'by the first decade of the 21st century there was no longer any official education policy or curriculum activity in British schools referred to as Multicultural education' (Tomlinson: 2009: 121).

Tomlinson also offers evidence to suggest that 'By the early 2000s the very notions of multiculturalism in a multicultural society were under sustained attack from a number of prominent political, media and other groups' (Tomlinson, 2009: 121). These groups based their attacks on the idea that multiculturalism was based on the notion that various groups in society would remain separate within a nation, but who were accepted in their own right. This in turn was seen to lead to segregation and therefore multiculturalism is seen as an enemy. Many official and political documents now refer to 'community cohesion' as a key way forward in addressing the issues facing society in England today. The 2004 Children Act prepared the way for *The Children's Plan* (DCSF, 2007) and the Every Child Matters Agenda. The 2006 Education Act stated that all schools had to promote inclusion and community cohesion. In 2004 the Training and Development Agency (TDA) launched the 'Multi-verse' website to support teachers to develop their understanding of ethnicity in their professional work. In 2005 the Community Cohesion Review Team was established and published a report on their findings including this clear focus of groups in society accepting and celebrating each other's values and tradition in an inclusive and co-operative manner.

> Very many of the definitions of cohesion and integration offered in the response to the Commission on Integration and Cohesion (Hereafter COIC) consultation spontaneously include a level of concern to distinguish integration from *assimilation*, stressing the importance for true cohesion of accepting – and celebrating – difference. Individual and group *identities* should not be endangered by the process of integration, but rather they should be enriched within both the incoming groups and the host nation. Cohesion implies a society in which differences of culture, race and faith are recognized and accommodated within an overall sense of identity, rather than a single identity, based on a uniform similarity.
>
> (CIC, 2007: 5)

None of the groups mentioned above focus on the notion of multiculturalism, rather they emphasize that the way forward is through individuals, groups, communities, faiths and religions working together to learn from each other and move forward in their thinking and not the liberalist approach of multiculturalism in which other ways of seeing the world are accepted but where the interested parties go their own ways.

This argument can sound convincing even if it is hard to picture how it might work in practice and through particular mechanisms. However, even back in 1981 James argued that British teachers 'need to ask how far multicultural education can be made a valid educational idea in a society whose institutions are not geared to be tolerant and pluralistic' (1981: 20).

One example of this which arises out of inconsistencies in government policy and rhetoric is the fact that the 2006 Education Act legally obliges local authorities to promote the mechanisms of parental choice of school and to advise on this and the transport facilities which enable it to happen. In other words, they have to actively support those parents who, for a variety of reasons, wealth, knowledge and class, aim to place their children in what they consider to be the best schools.

However, government in the latter years of the twentieth century was becoming aware of the need to address how our society may evolve in the future and in 1998 Jack Straw launched the Commission on the Future of Multi-Ethnic Britain. The Commission said that 'Our aim is to achieve a society which is not only comfortable with its differences but which rejoices in them' and added 'the government will lead the way. But working towards race equality remains the task for everyone in this country'. Later in this chapter we will assess the extent to which recommendations in the Rose Review echo these sentiments 10 years into the twenty-first century. The Parekh Report was published in 2000 and identified two main requirements for a multicultural society. The first is that the state must treat all citizens equally but with due recognition of cultural differences. The second is that a society must be cohesive (hang together) as well as being respectful of diversity. How might schools become a part of this process?

Impact task

Early career professional:
- What experiences have you had in your initial teacher education and the first part of your teaching career which you could identify as being examples of how these two requirements for a multicultural society have been positively promoted by what happens in school?

Think broadly about this: it is not just what goes on in the classroom, but what messages the school environment gives, the learning and teaching resources and the school policies, to name but a few.

Later year professional:
Looking back over your experience as a teacher, make a list of some significant activities, decisions and events that you have experienced which may have supported the two requirements identified by the Parekh Report. Include, but also think beyond, what happens in the classroom:

- What messages does the school environment give the people coming into school?
- Do the teaching resources reflect a nation which treats all equally and recognize cultural differences?
- Do school policies help society be cohesive and also respect diversity?

Professional leader:
Looking back over your time in positions of leadership, identify some decisions you have been party to which were opportunities to treat all equally and also recognize cultural differences. What decisions were opportunities to help

society become more cohesive and at the same time be respectful of diversity? Now, some of these decisions may have had implications beyond the school and give clear messages about how the school interprets equality and cohesiveness. An example of this might be the school policy regarding school uniform. It may have implications within the school for creating an ethos of equality where all pupils appear 'similar' but beyond the school there may be issues of social inequality from the perspective of parents and carers actually being able to afford the cost of school uniform. The uniform may give a public impression of a cohesive body of people who are the school. But it is also easy to see situations where the public display of a uniform may also give messages of superiority or inferiority, depending on how the wider public perceive that particular school. What sometimes appear to be a fairly unproblematic decision or policy might in fact have hidden messages for issues of cohesion, community and respect for diversity.

The Parekh Report (2000) suggests that cohesion, equality and diversity can be accommodated by a state using one of three models. One is a nationalist model that promotes a single national culture as defined by the state. Another is a liberal model based on a common political culture which is publically accepted but where autonomy is private life and cultural life is promoted. The third is a pluralist model where cultural diversity is valued and respected in the public realm. In the report it is described as the 'community of communities'. Government policy in recent years certainly seems to suggest that this is the model they have adopted to inform policy. An example of this is the 2006 Education and Inspections Act which specifically requires schools to have a clear policy on what they do to promote what Parekh calls a 'community of communities'. It also requires the Office for Standards in Education (Ofsted) to inspect for evidence of how a school actively promotes community cohesion: it identifies three areas for consideration: (1) teaching, learning and curriculum; (2) equity and excellence; and (3) engagement and ethos. We return to these later in this chapter.

So far we have examined the nature of multiculturalism with reference to sources rooted broadly within the realm of education. It can sometimes be helpful to examine an issue from other perspectives. In 2008 Ziauddin Sardar published a fascinating book entitled *Balti Britain: A Journey Through the British Asian Experience*. As a young boy in the 1960s, he came to Britain with his family. He draws on his own experience of living in a multi-ethnic society from an Asian perspective, but a particular strength of the book is how he integrates the thoughts and experiences of many other Asians within the many communities he visits and lives in.

Sardar begins his book with a discussion of the Asian experience in

Leicester. Currently, Leicester has become the first city in Britain to have a greater proportion of its population coming from nations other than Britain. He regards Leicester as an example of how people from multi-ethnic backgrounds can create what Parekh calls 'communities of communities'.

> Ethnic diversity appears to be the cornerstone of Leicester's prosperity and harmony, which means it is now seen as an ideal multicultural city, an example of how diversity works in an age of globalisation.
> (Sardar, 2008: 3)

When discussing what is now happening in Leicester, Sardar suggests that:

> Its success as a multicultural city is largely due to the business skills of its Asian community, and the fact that they eagerly represent themselves in all walks of life – including local politics.
> (Sardar, 2008: 3–4)

However, Sardar also accepts that no city or community can be 100 per cent perfect and that Leicester does have a range of community problems. Throughout the book Sardar is more concerned with how Asians in Britain are on a journey towards community cohesion than maintaining their diversity. He also argues that such success requires meaningful action and 'surely more than festivals and race relations committees' (2008: 6). There may be a message here for what we do in schools to promote community cohesion, to which we return later.

Sardar also provides an interesting perspective on the demise of multiculturalism and argues its demise can be traced back to the 2001 riots in Oldham, Burnley and Bradford which he believes in part has led to an anti-Muslim political culture. However, he also cites many examples of how Muslim communities are working in ways akin to the pluralist model described above. He concludes that:

> Conventional political theories, institutions, vocabulary and strategies we have developed over recent centuries in a homogeneous British state, dominated by a particular class, are not only inadequate but sometimes a Positive hindrance in dealing with the rapidly changing and complex diversity we find in contemporary Britain.
> (Sardar, 2008: 349)

It may be worth returning to this statement when considering the chapter on learning places. Sardar ends his book with the view that pluralistic, multicultural societies are just too complex to face the challenges of modern British society and that only by the complete accommodation of cultural diversity in all aspects of life can we progress.

The discussion so far has not looked at the context of where such changes in society may actually occur – the physical environment in which we all live. One year after the publication of Sardar's book, this physical and social environment was examined by Minton (2009). She argues that more and more space is becoming private and inaccessible to the majority as large organizations take more ownership and gated communities continue to grow, a situation controlled by extensive use of CCTV. She suggests that this leads to tension and social/community segregation. So, while we have many government acts and initiatives apparently aimed at promoting community cohesion, we perhaps need to consider how successful they can be, even with extensive support from those in communities, if they are trying to achieve such goals in an environment that first physically restricts such things happening and second in its design gives a clear message that some members of society do not wish such social changes to occur. It is a perspective worth raising because however much a school may agree with and wish to pursue the goals of community cohesion, and Ofsted enthusiastically looks forward to inspecting it, it will ultimately occur in the context of the physical environment within which the school is located and to which it is connected.

Minton (2009: 171) discusses the concept of trust in cities and argues that if a physical space includes a wide range of cultures, faiths, beliefs, classes (whatever that may mean), then it is likely that those with similarities will group together because as humans we tend to trust people more who are similar to ourselves. Putnam (2001) developed the idea of 'social capital' in which a wide range of community members who worked well together would develop a sense of community cohesion. New Labour certainly adopted many of his ideas, some of which of course may be identified in current policy. He suggests there may be two types of capital and this idea could be applied to thinking about your school in the context of the wider community. The first is 'bonding capital'. This is what we have when people with similar interests, beliefs and backgrounds develop social networks. An example could be a group of school choirs who decide to get together for a singing festival. His other type of capital is 'bridging capital'. This is developed when members of very different organizations get together to share interests, ideas, values and beliefs. A school example might be when a school deliberately decides to join up with signing groups entirely unconnected with schools; for example, a Barbers Shop band or a professional group of singers. We would argue that it is not just a question of making links with different groups of people. The two examples about still have music in common: it is more a question of how far a group is prepared to make contact with a group having less and less similarity. Therefore an extreme version of the above examples would be where your school choir joins with medical specialists interested in the way singing might improve the quality of life for elderly people.

However, sociologist Claude Fischer (2005) questions the empirical evidence for the existence of mechanisms which actually show how a wide range of groups do actually work together under certain conditions. Current government policy is trying to create those conditions and one wonders if the requirement for Ofsted to see if schools are actually working towards community cohesion is a way of forcing one area of society, the education system, to drive the policy forward. In other words, your community will be cohesive, even though you may not be sure you want it and the physical conditions may in fact make it very hard to achieve. So, the process of community cohesion becomes institutionalized, rather than spreading out from the members of the community itself.

Having considered some of the theoretical and political dimensions of the term 'multicultural', we now place these within the early years and primary school context at the start of the second decade of the twenty-first century. *The Independent Review of the Primary Curriculum: Final Report* (Rose Review) (DCSF, 2009) will be used as a basis for this discussion as it is the most recent document to emerge that is of direct relevance to the sector.

The frontispiece photograph of the Plowden Report (DES, 1967) includes seven non-white children, about a quarter of the total. The remaining 45 photographs in the report include only one non-white child. Compare this with the *Final Report* of the Rose Review: one in three of the children depicted on the cover are non-white. The rest of the document contains too many photographs to analyse for this purpose, but many of the photographs include children from a very wide range of ethnic backgrounds. Interestingly, while many teachers, assistants and carers are included in the photographs, all apart from two are white. The reader may make their own conclusions about the messages this may give about the nature of multi-ethnic Britain.

We have analysed the content of this *Final Report* in order to assess the way in which multiculturalism and community cohesion are a driving force within it. A justification for the structure being based on the six areas of learning is offered in the form of international comparisons where research found that:

> Most countries tend to structure the primary curriculum so as to facilitate a blend of subject teaching and cross-curricular studies. The analysis shows that it is possible to discern six widely accepted areas of learning.
>
> (DCSF, 2009: 18)

It goes on to make some rather general comments supporting the benefits of parents being fully involved in the education of their children. It provides evidence of links with other areas of policy by saying the revised curriculum is underpinned by the 2002 Education Act, the Children's Plan and Every Child Matters.

Language issues are central to a consideration to the multicultural and multi-ethnic debate. The section on languages says that 'schools should focus on teaching only one or two languages' (DCSF, 2009: 25). This does not appear to take into account the growing number of primary classrooms containing children who bring many languages into the school environment. However, it does accept that 'as a nation we are increasingly linguistically diverse . . . Nonetheless, the fact that English is a widely spoken world language continues to affect levels of motivation to learn another tongue. This makes it all the more important that we give every child the chance to learn another language, in order to gain insights into their own life and that of other around the world' (DCSF, 2009: 100). However, on pages 103–4 it tries to avoid upsetting both the Association of School and College Leaders (ASCL) who advocate a multilingual language awareness model, whereas the National Centre for Languages (CILT) does not support a multilingual language awareness model, it accepts that school should investigate and celebrate the range of languages brought to school by the pupils.

Subject task

EYFS:
Go to pages 156 and 157 of the (DCSF, 2009) report and you will see that languages are not included in the 'early' column. Read the content of the middle and later columns. Do you think that children in the EYFS should have some initial exposure to languages other than English? What messages does their omission give to children and parents whose first language is not English?

KS1:
The review suggests that the study of languages can develop intercultural understanding. Read the section M39–M41 on page 9 of the review (DCSF, 2009). How might you plan these three activities into other areas of the curriculum to ensure that they were experienced by children in a meaningful and relevant way?

KS2:
Which model would you choose for your school: the multilingual language awareness model or CILT's English and one other approach, but you can occasionally mention other languages do exist? Make a list of points to justify your decision. Even if your school already has a language policy, you may be revisiting it with the implementation of the Rose Review.

There is an interesting chart on page 34 of the DCSF *Final Report* which would be a document useful for you to study. Thinking back over the various concepts and issues we have discussed in this chapter, you may well find helpful links with the statements made in the chart, especially the bottom four boxes. For example, one bullet point says 'relate well to other and form good relationships' (DCSF, 2009: 34), while another says 'understand their own and others' cultures and traditions within the context of British heritage, and have a strong sense of their own place in the world'. This bullet point needs some discussion. Clearly, understanding a range of cultures matches some of the issues we have discussed and may help towards developing a cohesive community. But what is the reason for including the words 'within the context of British heritage'? Does this mean British heritage is at the centre of what we teach and other cultures are seen in context with it? Or, does it mean, as Sardar (2008) argues, that we have a wonderful opportunity in the curriculum to see how various cultures relate to each other, and make the point that any one culture is not worth more than any other. It is not the current curriculum model where British history is at the centre and other things link to it, rather that throughout history there have always been many connections between cultures. In Sardar's (2008) book, he gives the example of Britain's relationship with India. Traditionally, history has presented the idea of what Britain did for India but did not always recognize the enormous range of artistic, scientific, medical and philosophical expertise and talent that had already developed through time in the sub-continent. Currently, history is not always transparent about the problems caused by the British as they took over government of India. So, it may be that primary teachers need to engage and discuss together what they understand by the phrases used in the review and agree what it means for what they teach and how they teach it. The opportunities for curriculum development are discussed in Chapter 14.

In the 'Essentials for learning and life section' (DCSF, 2009: 148–9) the list of social skills would probably be accepted to be an important part of primary school life. As teachers become familiar with the recommendations, they need the confidence to interpret such statements in ways that will be relevant to their own pupils and the context of the school. The Rose recommendations are not lists of context that have to be covered, as it has been in the top-down model since 1988. It will now be up to teachers to take such statements and plan activities and discussions which enable such social skills to develop but in active and relevant ways. For example, if a current event in the news is being discussed with a geography focus, consider how it may be an opportunity to develop the 'negotiate' skills. It may be that the news item is based on a dispute over something: fish stock in the oceans would be a good starting point. What are the rules that control where nations can fish? Are they fair? Could the children improve on them and justify their decisions? This would immediately get them thinking about how we run the world and how we are all interconnected. Also, it would make the curriculum much more relevant as they can see how events beyond their immediate community impact on them.

Conclusion

This chapter began with an extract from the Plowden Report (DES, 1967). You may well now see many parallels between what it had to say about the 'children of immigrants' and our current thinking in a multi-ethic society. This chapter did not set out to provide the answers to what multiculturalism means in school. Rather, it offers some of the most recent thinking on multiculturalism from a range of viewpoints and asks you to consider what they mean in practical terms, as you take the opportunities provided by new curriculum guidelines and interpret them in your own school context. To place this in a broader picture we cite an article from the *Times Educational Supplement* (Stevens: 2009). Social science researchers in Spain have investigated the extent to which British children have become part of the Spanish community into which their parents have moved. A regional education adviser for the Benidorm area stated that British children:

> . . . carry a strong sense of English linguistic superiority and have this British view of Multiculturalism: 'Each to his own and each to his own god' he said. And they come here with this mentality, wanting to keep themselves to themselves, saying: 'If you keep out of my life, I'll keep out of yours' and they feel no obligation to integrate into our way of life.
>
> (Stevens, 2009: 16)

It is a thought-provoking set of statements and perhaps helps to told up a mirror to what may be happening in areas of Britain, because the article then goes on to explain how British children feel that Spanish schools and teachers do nothing to integrate them into school life or value what they bring to school in terms of previous achievement and talent and what is provided for them; for example, support in learning Spanish.

One of the authors of this book (John Halocha) has worked in initial teacher education since 1991 and is very aware that, through absolutely no fault of their own, we have perhaps two generations of teachers who have been told precisely what to do by government-led directives. You may remember those clocks you could buy for the classroom wall to make sure you kept to time in the literacy hour! Do we really think children learn like that? And what do they learn if the content and viewpoint of the curriculum is dominated by a British perspective? That perhaps is the challenge for teachers to take hold of, if we really are striving to achieve a sense of community and worth for all members of our own society and a recognition of the wonderful and diverse ways of seeing the world that we can share, as schools play their part in building a more cohesive community for the future.

References

Commission on Integration and Cohesion (CIC) (2007) *Themes, Messages and Challenges: A Final Analysis of Key Themes from the Public Consultation.* London: CIC.

Department for Children, Schools and Families (DCSF) (2007) *The Children's Plan: Building Brighter Futures.* London: The Stationery Office.

———— (2009) *Independent Review of the Primary Curriculum: Final Report.* Nottingham: DCSF.

DES (1967) *Children and their Primary Schools: A Report of the Central Advisory Council for Education (England).* London: Her Majesty's Stationery Office (HMSO).

Fischer, C. (2005) Bowling alone: What's the score? *Social Networks,* 27.

James, A. (1981) The 'multicultural' curriculum, in A. James and R. Jeffwate, *The School in a Multicultural Society.* London: Harper & Row.

Minton, A. (2009) *Ground Control: Fear and Happiness in the Twenty-first Century City.* London: Penguin.

Parekh Report (2000) *The Future of Multi-Ethnic Britain.* London: Profile Books.

Putnam, R. (2001) *Bowling Alone: The Collapse and Revival of American Community.* New York: Simon & Schuster.

Sardar, Z. (2008) *Balti Britain: A Journey Through the British Asian Experience.* London: Granta.

Stevens, J. (2009) *The Reign in Spain: Brit kids and their Isolationist Empire, Times Educational Supplement,* 21 August, pp. 16–17.

Tomlinson, S. (2009) Multicultural education in the UK, in J. Banks (ed.) *The Routledge International Companion to Multicultural Education.* Abingdon: Routledge.

10 The digital world

Introduction

For over a century technology has been seen as the way to improve education. Back in 1913 this was written in the *New York Dramatic Mirror*:

> Books will soon be obsolete in schools. Scholars will soon be instructed through the eye. It will be possible to teach every branch of human knowledge with the motion picture. Our school system will be completely changed in ten years.
>
> (Saettler, 1968: 98)

By the early 1960s electronic computers were establishing themselves in science, commerce and industry but were far too complex, large and expensive to be used in schools. At this time educationalists looked to programmed learning and teaching machines as a way of helping children to learn. You can see the parallel with computers: these machines needed programs and they were a machine, but nothing as complex as even the computers available at that time. Supporters and promoters of these teaching machines believed they would have a significant impact on how children learn and the nature of schools. Please refer the following reading from Trow (1963) and note any parallels to the arguments for and against using information and communication technology (ICT) in schools:

♮ **PROGRAMMED LEARNING AND TEACHING MACHINES**
The teaching machine is the only one of the mechanical inventions noted in Chapter III that was originally designed solely for educational purposes. It provides the necessary supplement to television and other audio-visual materials in that it makes the student an active participant in learning instead of a passive recipient. It requires them to respond successively

to many questions, and it furnishes feedback on the correctness of their responses.

Many kinds of machines have been invented and are on the market, some sixty or so companies already have them to sell, ranging from simple devices in which the program sheets are inserted and moved up by hand, including more complex inventions that have levers or knobs to move the program sheets or microfilm, and that show the answers and also record mistakes, to highly complex electronic devices with taped comments on them that admonish the student in an avuncular fashion. Several hundred thousand have already been sold and the trade anticipates a 50 million dollar business in ten years. Others are not so enthusiastic, like the mother who exclaimed, "A machine to teach my child? Not on your life! A child needs human warmth." By the same token she would not want her child to learn from books. Some have asked somewhat fearfully whether the machine will replace the teacher. Stated in this way, this is a foolish question although some intelligent men have attempted to answer it. Some say yes, that teachers who fear they will be replaced probably should be. They go on to describe the possibilities of electronically operated computers. Some, perhaps to reassure the profession, say no, that it will only relieve the teacher of the onerous task of drilling pupils and leave him more time for real teaching. Neither of these answers is an honest one because the meaning of the question is not clear. What is meant by "the teacher"? For almost everyone it suggests the stereotype previously mentioned. The teacher–the classroom stereotype, it can confidently be predicted, will be less frequent in actuality than it is at present.

And what is meant by "replace"? Rewording the question clarifies it. Will machines do many of the things teachers now do? The answer here is an unqualified affirmative, even with the addition – and do them better. The typewriter and printing press, the adding machine and computer are faster and more accurate than human scribes and accountants. But does this mean that machines will replace school personnel? Obviously not. There will no doubt be fewer "general practitioners" and more people who are specialists whether or not they are called teachers. We already have curriculum specialists, audio-visualists, school librarians, visiting teachers, counselors, and school psychologists, to say nothing of the subject matter specialists. Others may be expected to develop.

And so far as the machines are concerned, they are not so important as the programs they carry. Actually, programs do not have to be presented by machines at all. They can be printed in books, so-called programmed texts. The question as to which is the more satisfactory way to present a program, by machine or textbook, has not been satisfactorily answered. Machines are probably more attractive to children, perhaps because of their so-called toy appeal. They are convenient to use because frequent page turning is eliminated. Furthermore, on most machines it is not so easy for the student to read the answers provided before writing them down, and the overt manipulation of the shift mechanism theoretically is an aid to reinforcement, although this is not borne out by experiments. The use of microfilm gives promise of reducing the sheer bulk of paper now used in machines and programmed textbooks alike, and it is likewise favored for recording student errors and for connection with other devices including tape and film.

On the other hand, machines are expensive and mechanical difficulties arise, thus adding maintenance costs. Program sheets do not fit equally well into different types of machines and the paper may tear. Mature students may prefer the book form, since this is what they are used to, or, when the novelty has worn off, may not care to fool around with a machine. For short supplementary programs, the textbook format is likely to be all that is needed. Although much attention has been given to the design of different kinds of machines, whatever the method of presentation, it is important that the program be good. For it serves a dual function, that of a tutor who asks questions in a kind of Socratic fashion to lead the student step-by-step to further knowledge and understanding, and also that of the workbook which perhaps quizzes the student more systematically and calls for written answers. But it does these things more effectively than classroom teacher and workbook. "The teacher" cannot possibly give individual attention to the oral and written answers of all the pupils in a class, nor are his questions or those in the workbook likely to be so carefully prepared and sequentially arranged as are the self-instructional programs.   **99**

So, what might we learn from this? The first parallel you may have noticed was the use of the term 'active participant in learning'. But the content in the programs was provided for the pupils and the responses to questions were of necessity very limited and the programs were of a linear nature, rather like some of the early drill and practice 'educational' programs of the 1980s. In passing you may also have noted the phrase 'admonish the student in an avuncular fashion'. It could be argued that some present-day computer operating systems have hardly moved forward on this front in nearly 45 years! Trow (1963) then predicts the advent of electronically operated computers becoming available in the classroom and raises the question of whether they will replace teachers. He then makes a perceptive prediction that 'The teacher in the classroom stereotype, it can be confidently predicted, will be less frequent in actuality than it is at present' (1963: 91). The huge advances made in computer technology could indeed have transformed classrooms by the end of the first decade of the twenty-first century. But think for a minute of the educational context in which you work.

Reflection

EYFS:

- What impact does ICT already have on the lives of your pupils beyond school? How do you know?
- To what extent do you think ICT should be a part of the EYFS environment? Why?

KS1:

- How do you think ICT in school may have had a positive impact on your pupils as they enter this key stage?
- Is ICT used as a teaching tool or a learning environment?

KS2:

- Do your older pupils think ICT experiences in school are less interesting and relevant than those they engage in out of school?
- How often and why do you use pupils' external interest in ICT within the school environment?

To what extent is the physical environment and the teaching methods employed different to what would have been happening there 10 or 20 years ago? More important, has ICT actually transformed the learning and teaching process to any significant degree? Trow (1963) suggests that the quality of programs is the key factor in the use of machines in the learning and teaching process. He is clearly correct here. However, the problem today is that we are overloaded with programs of various types that in theory may have educational applications. Google Earth is a fantastic program, but how much do we really know about how it can develop learning and teaching? Indeed, we use it in school, but how much of its potential has not been realized simply because, as busy professionals, we do not have the time to explore and reflect? At the end of one paragraph Trow makes an almost throw-away remark which he believes needs more thought in today's world of powerful computers and complex software. He says 'For short supplementary programs, the textbook format is likely to be all that is needed' (Trow, 1963: 92). Here the word program means a sequence of teaching, rather like we would say short-term plan today. He is suggesting that for some types of learning, machines may not be the best way forward. We raise this now for reflection as we will discuss the implications when we analyse the Rose Review (DCSF, 2009) in terms of what it says about ICT in the curriculum. Finally, Trow (1963) argues that the Socratic method of teaching allows learners to make the most of learning opportunities and that well-programmed machines can help the pupil learn by asking carefully structured questions. The Socratic approach is based on the idea that the most effective teacher asks questions for pupils to discuss, argue and engage with, rather than being the provider of facts, knowledge, information and right answers. The technology of the 1960s' teaching machines certainly did not have that capacity, but some of the most recent technology may have some potential for learners to think about and mould their learning in more active ways.

Today's digital world

ICT is the answer to everything

It is almost a cliché that ICT is embedded in so much of what happens in the world today. A study of the website www.nextgenerationlearning.org.uk makes fascinating reading. It is a government campaign led by the British Educational Communications and Technology Agency (BECTA) to promote the use of ICT in schools and in particular to inform parents and carers of the benefits of doing this. While there is some useful content, we would like to stand back and think a little more critically about the current push for ICT as a key driving force in education. The government argues that ICT is essential if we are to be key global players, whether that is in finance, trade, media, tourism, environmental management, and so on. The website presents ICT as the main way forward for success as individuals, communities and as a nation. If we adopt this notion and promote it to both pupils and parents, might we be presenting a rather distorted view of the world? An obvious example of the uncritical use of ICT is travellers who unquestioningly use satellite navigation systems to move around. Many people who get into difficulties with this technology do so because they are not fully aware of actually how it works and the limitations it has.

The other issue is that they may well not know how such technology relates to other skills and knowledge that are crucial for making effective use of it. For example, a standard Global Positioning System (GPS) stuck on a car windscreen produces lines which represent roads, rivers, and so on. Any more detail on such a screen would first create information overload and second the size of the screen makes such details impossible to read. A traditional paper map shows your position in relation to many more features and once trained to read a map the user can gain far more complex information to both help them to their destination and understand the surrounding landscape. The point for education is that any ICT used in school needs to be used alongside other related technologies such as maps, books, photographs, and so on to enable the pupil to understand the advantages and disadvantages of the technology and, even more important, how it relates to other understanding, skills and knowledge. Another example of this is how mobile phones offer users the opportunity to record moving images. When you look at those produced by those around us and on You Tube, most examples are almost unintelligible and meaningless. The reason is that the phone user has no understanding of the very simple techniques they could use to make a film. We are not suggesting that they use Hollywood-style film-making techniques; rather, the basics needed to make an effective record of an event or communicate something to other people. Once they have this, the technology then frees them up to be as creative as they wish.

The use of ICT is unproblematic

The final report of the Rose Review (DSCF, 2009) includes a very large number of references as to how ICT can be used across the curriculum to enhance all aspects of learning. Examples of these are analysed later in this chapter. Reading the whole of the *Final Report* leaves the reader with a sense that ICT is projected as an all-good, all-singing and dancing facility that is always useful. We would like to challenge that notion because if schools take on many of the examples provided in the *Final Report* we may be in danger of producing a generation of pupils who unthinkingly fall into a mindset that sees ICT as unproblematic in all walks of life. Nowhere in the *Final Report* is there a mention that pupils should question and challenge the nature of ICT, its implications and the social and moral repercussions in the world in which they will continue to live. It is always promoted as a useful tool for solving problems, design, finding information, and so on. The examples below have been chosen to enable you as a professional to assess the extent to which you are aware of the questions we need to ask about how society is being drawn unquestioningly into a world dominated by ICT and one in which people may not be aware that ICT is the driving force behind such trend and developments.

There are more than 4.2 million CCTV cameras in Britain giving us one for every 14 people (Hyperlink, 2006). This has arisen through the use of ICT to create communication systems and the intelligence in the cameras themselves. For a few years there have been cameras in London that are able to lip-read the people on whom they are focused. Until recently, the technology has made cameras large and obvious. Next time you are out, take time to look upwards. You will rarely see something the size of a shoebox anymore; instead, you will see a small black sphere on the top of a pole. You will not even know which way the lens is pointing. How long will it be before CCTV cameras are so small we will not even know we are being watched? Is this the type of society you wish to live in or indeed that future world your pupils will inhabit? One of the authors of this book (John Halocha) recently visited colleagues in Germany and asked why he saw hardly any CCTV cameras in public places. The reply came back 'the German people would not allow that to happen'. We leave you to reflect on that remark. Face recognition is now commonplace in CCTV cameras and the police argue it is an effective tool in tracking criminals. You could follow up that idea, but they also record the faces of many innocent people.

Private letters sent through the post remain private and strict laws control any right to open them. But how many of us now communicate in that way? Once we have sent an email we have very little way of knowing who can open and read it. Software is available to scan emails and search for words and phrases. The government would like to implement a scheme where all private emails are centrally stored for a certain period of time. This would certainly make an interesting debate with pupils and draw on many of the language and social skills recommended in the Rose Review.

Fewer and fewer organizations now accept bank cheques as a means of payment. They are about as private as a letter sent through the post so your spending patterns remain private. It is very hard to make electronic connections through them, but as soon as you pay by card or over the Internet, all your details are recorded. An example that has been around a long time is the supermarket loyalty card. You can pay by bank card and only your card number can be recorded, but link that to your address and the opportunities are endless. That is why loyalty cards were introduced; nothing at all to do with giving you savings and special offers: information is power. It also enables a database based on your postcode to be created of your personal purchases. That does not sound a problem until we introduce the idea that increasingly databases can be connected. How far in the future will it be before your insurance company will have access to your eating habits in order to assess your potential health risk to them? It sounds far-fetched but imagine how the concept of the Internet would have sounded the same to the public 40 years ago.

Finally, the word 'digital' is now in regular use in our language and is promoted as offering something better and more advanced. A current example is the switch-over to digital TV. We have no choice. Analogue transmitters are being phased out. FM radio transmissions may also be closed and replaced with digital radio. Digital broadcasting is promoted as being 'better' than analogue. However, this is not always the case. Digital radio does offer less interference and potentially more choice of stations. The actual sound quality is questionable simply because much of the original data from the sound is compressed digitally so in fact the detail of the sound is less than that of analogue, reducing our overall experience of the original. Again, this would be an interesting theme to follow with your pupils as a linked study with history and music, especially if you have access to some 'old' technology. To offer a balanced debate, you could then give the example that we can now hear digitally remastered recording of originals made way back in the twentieth century. The author recently bought a CD of Elgar conducting his own music. The quality of the remastered recording is very good and enables us to compare his interpretation of the work with that of today's conductors.

With a little research you will be able to find examples to use in school of how information technology is affecting and controlling our lives: ask the person at your supermarket checkout if the speed of them scanning bar codes is being monitored and whether there is a minimum speed at which they have to work.

Finally, it is worth noting that one of the key features of the new primary curriculum stated in the *Independent Review of the Primary Curriculum: Final Report* is the need to:

> Strengthen the teaching and learning of information and communication technology (ICT) to enable children to be independent and confident users of technology by the end of primary education.
>
> (DCSF, 2009: 12)

It does not ask pupils to be critical and informed users of ICT. Placing this statement in the context of the earlier discussion about the need for them also to be critical and aware users of ICT, consider the following.

Subject task

EYFS:
Many young children will arrive with you already confident in the use of various forms of ICT in the home and the wider world. Some, however, for a variety of reasons, will have far more limited experience, knowledge and confidence.

- How will you identify this?
- What activities might you and your colleagues develop in order to build up these aspects of their learning?
- How will you justify your choice of activities?

KS1:
The *Independent Review* overloads you with examples of how ICT may be across the six areas of learning. How might you go about working with colleagues to ensure progression and continuity in pupils' experience of ICT across the curriculum?

KS2:
Thinking back to our discussion of the need to be critical and aware of issues surrounding the use of ICT in our digital world, what opportunities might there be in your curriculum to raise these issues in ways that will be relevant and meaningful to children?

The digital world of the Rose Review

At the front of the *Independent Review of the Primary Curriculum: Final Report* there is a covering letter from Sir Jim Rose to the Secretary of State. In it he says:

> Our best primary schools already demonstrate that, far from narrow-ing learning, these priorities – literacy, numeracy, ICT skills and personal development – are crucial for enabling children to access a broad and balanced curriculum.
>
> (DCSF, 2009: 3)

This is the first clear message of the proposed status of ICT within a revised primary curriculum. It is seen as one of four key priorities around which every-thing else is based. But the message is changed on page 22 where it states under Recommendation 8 sub-heading 'Literacy, numeracy and ICT' that 'literacy, numeracy and ICT should form the new core of the primary curriculum' (DCSF, 2009: 22). Personal development has been left out of this 'core' but it is included on the following page with a heading of the same status that is used for this quote. Finally, under the sub-heading 'Personal development' the report writer returns to the view on page three that 'personal development together with literacy, numeracy and ICT constitute the essentials for learning and life' (DCSF, 2009: 23). It begs the question as to the need for Recommenda-tions 8 and 13 being written separately. Does each of the four areas have equal status and how will school implement these recommendations?

The debate about the status of ICT in the new primary curriculum is con-tinued on page 30. Under the sub-heading 'Continuing support for a National Curriculum', the report states:

> No respondents to this review suggested, as the recent report by the Children, Schools and Families Committee recommended, that schools should only be required to follow the curriculum for English, mathematics, science and ICT.
>
> (DCSF, 2009: 30)

This is a very interesting point for a number of reasons. The first is that various official bodies are not in agreement over what should and should not be in a new primary curriculum. The second is that the Children, Schools and Families (CSF) committee do not include personal development as a required part of the curriculum. The word 'required' is important whatever group have the final say over the content of the curriculum. It ends up being based on the Rose Review that the area of numeracy, literacy, ICT and personal development will prevail. Office for Standards in Education (British) (Ofsted) will then have a framework on which to inspect schools. What is not specified is the proportion of time allocated to each. This would of course be hard to define if schools do become more cross-curricular and then it will be a question of deciding how much literacy, numeracy, ICT and personal development constitutes a bottom line for fulfilling the school's obligation to deliver the legal curriculum.

On page 45 the Final Report (DCSF, 2009) includes a chart mapping curriculum progression between the stages of 0–5 years, 5–11 years and 11–14 years. Information and communication technology (ICT) is recognized as a subject in the 5–11 and 11–14 columns but does not appear in the 0–5 years column. However, if you then look at Annex B between pages 148–200 you will find frequent references to the application of ICT under the 'Early' column heading. The interpretation of this will require discussion within the context in which you work.

Finally, in the 'Essentials for learning and life' section, the thinking behind ICT in the primary curriculum is taken a little further. It is interesting to analyse the words used to justify ICT:

> In all branches of knowledge, all professions and all vocations, the effective use of new technologies will be vital. Children not only need to learn to use specific devices and applications, they also need to understand the fundamental concepts of safe and critical use. The review therefore calls for an understanding of technology to be taught and ingrained in curriculum design and delivery.
>
> (DCSF, 2009: 71)

The message is clear that ICT is a powerful driving force with an almost inevitable existence in a digital world. But the word 'critical' is also included: if that means a debate about some of the issues surrounding the increasing use of ICT as discussed earlier in the chapter, then here is some justification for those points. 'Ingrained' is a strong word and the final section discusses some of the ways in which this might happen across the curriculum.

The digital world across the curriculum

Annex B: Programmes of learning in the Final Report (DCSF, 2009) contains many references to ICT and examples of how it might be used within the primary curriculum. In this section we look at a range of these where the application of ICT seems to be a strength in developing an area.

The annex begins with a section headed 'Essentials for learning and life'. Under ICT capability it states that children should learn how to:

1   Find and select information;

2 Create, manipulate and process information;
3 Collaborate, communicate and share information;
4 Refine and improve their work.

The focus also requires children to 'become independent and discerning users of technology, recognising opportunities and risks and using strategies to stay safe' (DCSF, 2009: 148). Clearly, there are references here to the safety of children when using ICT, such as concerns of access to certain websites and contact with strangers. The word 'discerning' could mean both the critical choice of hardware, software or information; for example, evaluating whether or not a particular website contains the information they really need. It could also echo back to earlier discussions about social and moral implications of how ICT is used by individual, groups and organizations within society.

As we discuss some of the cross-curricular examples of ICT, reflect on the following in relation to your current stage of professional development.

Subject example of ICT

A detailed example of how ICT is ingrained into the curriculum is the 'English and communication – writing' section of the 'Understanding English, communication and languages' area of learning. In the 'Early' column two examples of ICT are given. The first is 'to plan, discuss and review their work in order to improve it including using ICT where appropriate'. This seems to be a perfectly reasonable statement. It raises some practical questions. One is at what point do you stop asking pupils to use a specific piece of technology and rely on their judgement as to what is actually most appropriate? Another is the availability of ICT resources for a particular activity. Until all pupils have unlimited access to resources there will always be an issue of who can and who cannot use it. At this early stage there is also the question of deciding when and where specific skills will be developed. Does access to word-processing at this stage encourage pupils to write rather than the use of traditional pencil and paper?

The second example suggests pupils 'communicate with known audiences using ICT where appropriate' (DCSF, 2009: 155). Two points arise. The first is the acknowledgement that pupils of this age need to be introduced to the idea that when we communicate we need to think about our audience. The second revolves around the word 'known'. Safety is clearly being addressed here and the footnotes suggest using the school website to communicate with parents and carers. This is clearly a good example of how writing can be made relevant to pupils.

In the middle column it is suggested pupils 'share ideas and collaborate with others remotely using ICT' (DCSF, 2009: 155). The explanatory text gives the example of using videoconferencing and webcams to achieve. The use of most recent and advanced technologies is often given in many of the explanatory texts. Clearly, pupils need to use the latest technology and may consider school to be out of date if they do not. The author remembers pupils still having to use dot matrix printers in school when many of them said they had the next generation of printers at home. However, in the real world schools may not have the very latest technology or sufficient for the needs of larger groups. Making an audio CD or DVD and actually sending it to the other audience will allow them to develop most of the skills they would use in videoconferencing and webcams, apart perhaps from the social skill of quickly having to analyse how your audience is reacting and what your response will be. Again, this can be turned to advantage if some pupils correspond using audio CD and DVD while others use live link-ups. These groups can then compare their experiences and consider the advantages and disadvantages of each. It is therefore a question of adapting the examples in the explanatory texts to achieve maximum learning with the facilities you have available.

In the Later Years column three examples of the use of ICT are given. The first is 'to plan, create, and review their work, knowing when and how to improve it including the use of ICT' (DCSF, 2009: 155). This statement is not really problematic and represents current good practice. The second statement asks pupils 'to synthesise ideas using ICT by combining a variety of information from different sources' (p. 155). Again, it is now well recognized that ICT enable us effectively, easily and creatively to choose, integrate and sort written sources into a complete and new text. To be a fully effective statement it needs to be linked to the notion that while pupils are doing this, they are also using critical facilities to assess the relevance of content. The final example states that pupils should 'communicate and collaborate with others remotely and in locations beyond the school by selecting and using appropriate ICT' (p. 155). This is a good example of how such English statements which include an ICT possibility can be used to help plan cross-curricular activities. An example would be the geographical study of another place beyond the school. Having this specific reason will make the English communication activity more relevant to pupils and give a sense of purpose and development. The explanatory text for this statement is clearly trying to enable progression and continuity by saying these links could be with 'unknown audiences', but in the geography example there may well be good reason for such communications to be built up with audiences that pupils get to know increasingly well as mutual trust builds up.

Impact task

Early career professional:
Plan an English activity which requires the use of some aspect of ICT to support and enhance the learning of English while at the same time further developing pupils' ICT skills.

- What specific English objectives are you trying to achieve?
- What specific ICT objectives are you trying to achieve?
- What support might you be looking for in order to answer these questions effectively?

Later years professional:
Plan a sequence of related English activities which provide opportunities for all four of the ICT essentials for learning and life to be incorporated in appropriate ways.

- To what extent can pupils be encouraged to identify opportunities to use ICT rather than be told they are to use certain hardware and/or software?
- What practical classroom implications would you have to consider in managing this sequence in the learning environment?

Professional leader:
Looking across the whole of your school curriculum, devise a method you might use to collect and collate information in an effective yet simple way in order to provide evidence to Ofsted on how ICT is integrated.

- Without undue burden on teachers, how would you collect and record the information?
- What criteria might you use to analyse your findings?
- How might you evaluate the progression and continuity within ICT both across age phases and between the areas of learning?

The future of digital worlds

In the first part of this chapter we considered how some official sources see ICT as unproblematic and an essential way forward for progress to be made. We then considered some of the social, moral and ethical issues relating to how ICT is being developed and used. These were placed within the context of recommendations by the Rose Review. The final stage is to consider how children see ICT and its application in school.

Although children will come to school with various degrees of skill, confidence and interest in ICT, very few will have limited experiences. Tied into these experiences may be a whole set of values related to how they interact with technology. The following paragraph gives just a few examples to begin you thinking about the broader context in which we need to place ICT in school.

The author's current research interests include the way in which geography is represented on broadcast television. One concept that comes from media theory is that of 'Homo Zappiens' where TV viewers increasingly zap between channels because they have developed an understanding of programme structure which enables them to piece together the various parts they watch and keep in touch with the plot. What implications does this have for the way we learn, retention spans, and so on? Research into parenting shows how digital media are used to entertain and occupy children, rather than through active engagement with them. Might this affect pupils approach to using ICT in a proactive way, which is certainly how it is portrayed in curriculum documents and reports? Children with access to latest technology are going to quickly evaluate what the school can offer in terms of a digital world and react accordingly. Can schools respond to the growing range of equipment that children are aware of? If ICT resources are limited in schools' and pupils' experience bouncing between traditional facilities such as writing with pen and paper and word-processing but have learnt the skills of using word-procession to craft a piece of work, how will they react if the majority of time they are using a less flexible tool? During the author's visits to schools he often see pupils taken off a piece of ICT equipment so it can be shared between more of them. How do they assess this in the light of what they experience at home when they may well have almost unrestricted time to use ICT to achieve something? An example of this was recently talking to a pupil about some research he had done at home on shipping around the world. It was impressive and he clearly understood a whole range of issues. Does this raise questions about the future interface between home and school and the possible outmoded concept of 'homework'? Does this word need bringing into the twenty-first century where there is a more seamless notion of learning and enquiry both in and beyond school?

Currently, the government's ICT plans have just been published in the form of the 'Digital Britain' report. The government proposes a £300 m Home Access programme which will connect low-income families by providing computers for the home along with a nation much improved broadband network. This is intended to support both child and adult learners. By the end of 2010 we will know how this initiative has developed and be able to assess the implications it may have for schools and the wider community. It is an example of how our digital world may develop and could have valuable implications for the way we apply ICT both within and beyond the school.

References

Department for Children, Schools and Families (DCSF) (2009) *Independent Review of the Primary Curriculum: Final Report*. Nottingham: DCSF.

Hyperlink (2006) *How we are being watched*. Available online at www.bbc.co.uk (accessed 27 August 2009).

Saettler, P. (1968) *A History of Instructional Technology*. New York: McGraw-Hill.

Trow, W. (1963) *Teacher and Technology*. New York: Appleton-Century-Crofts.

PART 3
Changing practice and professionalism

11 Working together

The importance of different agencies involved in child care and education working together, is not a new phenomena. Froebel (1889: 230–1) wrote the following in his book *The Education of Man:*

> In the family the child grows up to boyhood and pupilage; there-fore, the school must link itself to the family. The union of the school and of life, of domestic and scholastic life, is the first and indispensable requisite of a perfect human education of this period. The union of family and school life is the indispensable requisite of the education of this period, if men, indeed, are ever to free themselves from the oppressive burden and emptiness of merely extraneously communicated knowledge heaped up in memory; if they would ever rise to the joy and vigour of a knowledge of the inner nature and essence of things, to a living knowledge of things – a knowledge which like a sound, vigorous tree, like a family or gener-ation full of the joy and consciousness of life, is spontaneously developed from within; if they would cease at last to play in word and deed with the valueless shadows of things, and to go through life in a mask.
>
> It would prove a boon to our children and a blessing to coming generations if we could but come to see that we possess a great oppres-sive load of extraneous and merely external information and culture, that we foolishly seek to increase this from day to day, and that we are very poor in inner knowledge, in information evolved from our own soul and grown up with it.
>
> We should at last cease making a vain display of the thoughts, the knowledge, and even the feelings of others. We should no longer seek the highest glory of our education and of our schools in efforts to garnish the minds of our children with foreign knowledge and skill.

The importance of working together

The importance of the family, carers and educators working together is well represented in theory (e.g. Bronfenbrenner, 1995; see also Chapter 1, Social development and Figure 1.1) and policy (DfES, 2004; DCSF, 2008a). For example, one of the four themes that underpin the Early Years Foundation Stage (EYFS) (DCSF, 2008a) recognize the importance of adult–child relationships; Positive Relationships recognize that children learn to be strong and independent from a base of loving and secure relationships with parents and/or a key person. The *Every Child Matters* agenda (DfES, 2004) led to the development of integrated services to provide

> a hub within the community for parents and providers of childcare services for children of all ages. Their integrated approach will:
> - provide holistic support for children's development;
> - support families with young children;
> - facilitate the return to work of parents who are currently unemployed;
> - offer a base for childminder networks and a link to other day care provision, out of school clubs and extended schools.
>
> (Sure Start, 2004: 9)

The aim was for professionals to work in partnership with:

- local training and education providers;
- Jobcentre Plus, especially Jobcentre Plus Childcare Partnership Managers;
- Children's Information Services;
- local schools, extended schools and out-of-school activities;
- health service providers, including Primary Care Trusts (PCTs).

(Sure Start, 2004: 9)

This can be challenging for everyone in the partnership but it is important to have shared values and visions, clearly defined roles and responsibilities as well as a collective responsibility for the development of children and mutual trust, respect and support (Bolam et al., 2005). There also needs to be a system of evaluation to ensure good practice, which in turn should be praised and celebrated. Parents and the outside community should also be involved in the partnership. This is important because worried parents and carers can adversely affect the children in their emotional, social and cognitive development and also because parents and carers have in-depth knowledge of their children and also special knowledge which they can bring to the partnership. In addition, since much of the child's time is spent at home, parents and carers can support development outside of care and education. Professional dialogue is of vital importance (Bolam et al., 2005) when working together, as can the use of support mechanisms, such as mentors or 'critical friends', home–school liaison.

When we work effectively together, we can begin to develop learning communities, which involve

> a slight shift in attention from an obsession with outcome, which calls for a simplistic focus on cause and effect, to attention to how people learn to think, act and change their environments. That adjusted focus permits an exploration of how people develop the wherewithal to deal with new knowledge, whether that knowledge is simply new to them or is a new development in the community of practice in which they are participating.
>
> (Edwards et al., 2002: 120)

Learning communities involve groups of professionals, children, families and the wider community developing and learning together, socially emotionally, physically and cognitively (Alexander, 2009) and have 'a capacity for effective problem-solving and reflective revision of previously held ideas. In such a community, the agentic action of both teachers and learners' (and others in the learning community, 'is directed primarily towards as better understanding of an outcome (Edwards et al., 2002: 121).

Reflection

Learning communities are not new suggestions (e.g. Ruddock and McIntyre, 2007), although the tendency is to focus on children's views (DCSF, 2009) and children working with professionals, although the reality is less persuasive than the rhetoric, and effective learning communities are often not fully evident in schools. The Cambridge Review (Alexander, 2009) advocates a wider learning community that includes families and the wider community (see Bronfenbrenner, 1995; see Chapter 1, Figure 1.1).

Reflective tasks

EYFS:
- Who are the groups/individuals who make up your learning community?

- Which groups identify specific challenges to integrated working and the development of an effective learning community? Explain your reasoning.
- How can you improve working relationships with all groups and overcome the identified challenges?

KS1:

- Should the learning community be different for formal schooling at KS1? Explain your reasoning.
- How can you develop the learning community at KS1?
- What specific challenges are there to development of an effective learning community? How can you overcome these challenges?

KS2:

- What roles and responsibilities should professionals, children, families and the wider community play in the learning community at KS2? Explain your reasoning.
- How does involving specific groups create challenges for you at KS2?
- How can you overcome these challenges to develop an effective learning community?

Parent, professionals and children working together

Families are important partners in the learning community, as children spend more time in their families than in settings and schools (DFES, 2004; DCSF, 2008a). The early years recognizes the importance of involving parents and usually have different strategies to involve parents, starting before the children are admitted to the setting/school, with visits, newsletters, parent sessions, and so on. Sometimes these strategies imply passivity on the part of the parents (Vincent, 2000) and there is a distinct power relationship that some parents find uncomfortable. Sometimes parents can support the school learning community by fund-raising and parent–teacher associations. Some of these are parent-led and have no teacher involvement and others may be instructed on what to do and how to do it by teachers or learners themselves, as defined by parent partnerships in which parents confirm that they will support the setting and professionals in their endeavours. In this way, despite being less passive parental individuality, responsibility, expertise and initiative are not recognized. Less often, parents are fully active partners with rights and responsibilities in the learning community (Vincent, 2000).

Professionals often find the relationship with parents difficult, although they do recognize the importance of good working relationships, especially when they are parents themselves. Putting the ideas into practice can be much more difficult and it cannot be assumed that professionals have the skills or expertise to develop good working relationships with families and the wider community. Success relies on all partners being on an equal basis and seeing themselves as equal partners. Features of good home–school partnerships include:

- home visits and visits to settings from an early age (mother and toddler sessions, pre-school playgroups, crèches, and so on)
- book and toy loan schemes so parents can support a range of developments and learning in the home environment
- sessions where children and their families can learn together during the school day or as special evening events
- parental information sessions, where professionals and children share learning. These often take the form of class assemblies
- family newsletters.

To be truly effective the working relationship needs to be on an equal basis, have shared responsibilities and involve two-way communication and consultation. This will enable an effective partnership to help meet the *Every Child Matters* agenda (DfES, 2004). If parents are concerned about the care or education children are receiving and if they do not feel part of the learning community, this can have an adverse effect on their children and adversely affect their emotional, social and cognitive development (see Chapters 1 'Social development', 2 'Emotional development' and 4 'Cognitive development'). The arguments for improved parental and child involvement in the learning community is strong. Children who are unsettled at school for any reason will have worried parents and this will adversely affect the learning outcomes. Parents and carers and children know more about their abilities, achievements and challenges than any professional can and so can, and should, be more involved in making decisions about learning pathways/routes. This may involve an honest dialogue about the children's achievements and partnership to help children meet their challenges. Parents and children may also have experiences and expertise that they can share with others, so facilitating partnerships that change the traditional roles, responsibilities and power relationships.

Reflection

The Education Act 2002 identified that professionals should consult with parents and more widely regarding the provision of extended childcare, homework, sport and creative arts clubs. Many of the suggestions tend to be clear about idealized rhetoric and less clear about practical applications. The *Every Child Matters Outcomes Framework* (DCSF, 2008b) is clear on the strategic developments that are needed, but less clear on specifics for the professional having to put it into practice.

Reflective tasks

EYFS:
- How are you and your setting addressing the *Every Child Matters Outcomes Framework* (DCSF, 2008b) and developing the learning community?
- What short-, medium- and long-term initiatives can you introduce in your setting to develop the learning community?
- How can you evaluate the success of the introduction of your initiatives?

KS1:
- How does the *Every Child Matters Outcomes Framework* (DCSF, 2008b) relate to your work in KS1?
- How can you build on the work of the EYFS to develop a learning community in your school?
- How could you evaluate new initiatives to develop a learning community?

KS2:
- How do you see your place in the learning community at KS2?
- How can you work more effectively with professionals, parents and children to develop a more effective learning community?
- How could you evaluate the effectiveness of your learning community at KS2?

Impact tasks

Level 3
Identify how successful your setting is in working effectively and professionally within the setting and the wider community.

- What groups or individuals do you need to work more effectively with?

- How can you and the staff in your setting work together to develop professional working relationships?

Produce a development plan to improve your professional working relationships, identifying the short-, medium- and long-term actions you can make. Keep a record of your plans, achievements and challenges and review the plan after a period of time.

Early career professional:
Plan how you can develop an initiative (as above) to develop the learning community in your professional context. This may involve improving your working relationships with one of the following groups, class teachers, teaching assistants, setting heads and managers, college tutors, learning mentors, parents and children.

Keep a record of how successful you are in developing your professional relationships.

Reflection

- How effective was the development of your relationships?
- What were the challenges you faced and how did you overcome them?
- How did the initiative impact on learning in your setting/school?

Later years professional:
Make a list of all the groups and individuals you work with on a daily, weekly or an occasional basis and who should be part of the learning community in your setting/school. Identify those who you need to work with more effectively. Plan for how you can do this in the short and medium term and how you can evaluate the impact on children's learning.

Reflection

- How did the development of working relationships impact on children's learning in the short and medium term?
- How did you overcome the challenges you faced?
- How might you develop working relationships in the longer term?

Professional leader:
Audit the different working relationships in your setting/school and prioritize development in the short, medium and longer term. Plan an initiative to secure/ develop relationships. This may involve children working with professionals

more effectively in their own learning, or professionals and parents communicating and working together more effectively.

Reflection

- How effective was the development in supporting/developing relationships?
- How did you overcome the challenges that you faced?
- What is the impact on learning and teaching in your setting/school?

Working together through transitions

Transitions are difficult at any time of life and require good working relationships to ensure that children's learning is not adversely affected. First transitions involve children leaving the care of their families and being cared for and supported by others. This can be stressful for children and affect their emotional (Bowlby, 2007) and social development (Palmer, 2006), although there are benefits for language development and socialization (EPPE, 2003). There are many different practices in the EYFS (DCSF, 2008a) to support transitions, such as full parental involvement, parent–child play sessions at the start and/or end of the day, home visits, and so on. Some early settings are designed to be similar to the home environment so children see them as extensions of home (and indeed some children are cared for in the homes of child-minders). Research into early transitions (Sanders et al., 2005) has indicated that parents want to know how to support their children and this involves information about transitions, so they can prepare their children for the next stage in their educational development. They also want to meet their children's teachers before transitions and discuss their anxieties. Since parents are well placed to make transitions smooth, it seems foolish not to capitalize on this and involve parents specifically in transitions.

Transitions are equally important at other stages of childhood and even adulthood. *Every Child Matters* (DfES, 2003: 19–22) recognizes this.

> When children enter primary school, children from poorer backgrounds start to fall behind children from higher income families. As Figure 3 shows, children from a poor background with a high developmental score at 22 months have fallen behind by the age of 10, compared to children from higher socio-economic groups but with a low developmental score at 22 months.

Although experience during the early years is important, life chances continue to be forged throughout children's lives. Problems can build up cumulatively over time reinforcing disadvantage, as Figure 4 shows.

A critical transition is from primary to secondary school and the onset of puberty. As Figure 5 shows, the gap in educational achievement between higher and lower socio-economic groups opens up starkly in the first years of secondary school from 11 to 14.

Policy challenges

The implications of this analysis are that there needs to be:

- **better prevention.** We need to tackle the key drivers of poor outcomes, including poverty, poor childcare and early years education, poor schooling and lack of access to health services. By mainstreaming preventative approaches, such as those developed through Sure Start, we ought to reduce the numbers of children requiring more intensive support. Support needs to be provided throughout the lifecycle, with increasing attention focused on two critical periods: the early years, and the beginning of secondary school as children experience puberty. Services need to focus particularly on addressing inequalities across gender and ethnicity.

- **a stronger focus on parenting and families.** We need to pay more attention to the critical relationships between children and their families and provide them with better support. We should recognise the vital role played by fathers as well as mothers. When children cannot remain with their birth parents, we need to ensure that they can develop stable, loving relationships with carers.

- **earlier intervention.** We need a greater focus on ensuring children at risk are identified earlier. We need to be able to share information to identify children who require additional support, and provide a tailored service that safeguards them from abuse and neglect, and enables them to fulfil their potential.

To deliver these reforms, we need to address two underlying challenges, highlighted by the Victoria Climbié Inquiry Report, and other studies:

- **weak accountability and poor integration.** Our existing system for supporting children and young people who are beginning to experience difficulties is often poorly co-ordinated and accountability is unclear. This means that information is not shared between agencies so that warning signs are not recognised and acted upon. Some children are assessed many times by different agencies and despite this may get no services. Children may experience a range of professionals involved in their lives but little continuity and consistency of support. Organisations may disagree over who should pay for meeting a child's needs because their problems cut across organisational boundaries. Fragmentation locally is often driven by conflicting messages and competing priorities from central Government.

- **workforce reform.** We need to do more to ensure working with children is seen as an attractive career, and improve skills and inter-professional relationships. Many of those who work with children and young people in vital frontline roles feel undervalued, and in some cases under siege. Problems are most acute in social work, where there is an 11 percent vacancy rate nationally (as high as 40–50 percent in some London boroughs). Some professionals working with children have no routine training in child development, child protection or domestic violence issues and frontline staff often lack awareness of specialist issues like mental health, special educational needs and substance misuse.

Reflection

Reflect on the transitions that exist in your setting school:

- transitions from one stage of development and learning to another
- transitions between home and setting/school
- transitions between classes
- transitions between settings/schools, on moving house
- transitions between lessons, activities
- transitions from work/activities and play-time or home-time
- other transitions.

Reflective tasks

EYFS:
- How do different children cope with the challenges of transition in your setting?

- How do you work with parents/carers, children and other professionals to ease transitions?
- How could you work more effectively with others to ease transitions?

KS1:

- What are the significant transition challenges for children at KS1?
- How do these transitions affect children?
- How can you work with others (children, parents/carers and other professionals) to support transitions?

KS2:

- How are transitions different for children at KS2?
- How can transitions affect different groups of children?
- How can you work with others (children, parents/carers and other professionals) to support transitions?

Parents recognize the importance and want to work together with professionals to support their children in transitions (Primary National Strategy, 2006). Parents and carers want their children to be settled and happy, to be supported in their development and learning, but not pressured to grow up at a rate that is not suitable for them. Parents and carers want to be involved in the wider life of their child, becoming involved with professionals and other parents.

Settings that have effective working relationships with parents, have consulted with them, welcomed them, shared with them and involved them fully are more likely to have children who move smoothly through the care and educational system and have fewer developmental problems. Bia Sena, Foundation Stage Coordinator at the British School, Rio de Janeiro (Johnston et al., 2007) has identified some early barriers to smooth transitions, including the classroom environment (furniture type and size and grouping of furniture), the move from play-based, child-centred pedagogical approaches to more adult-led cognitive approaches and the changing role and value of the role of parents.

Poor transitions have a health implication on children, as a longitudinal survey of 105 children due to start their first year of formal schooling has indicated (Turner-Cobb, 2006). This has shown that children's levels of cortisol (produced by the adrenal glands and referred to as the 'stress hormone' were higher than expected before starting school, increased further at transition, and reduced significantly at follow-up. More extroverted children and those socially isolated during the first six months of school were more affected by transitions. Children with higher cortisol levels at transition were less likely to become ill and those who tended to be shy at transition were more likely to become ill during the following six months.

Impact tasks

Consider how you can ease stress for children by easing transition. Prepare an action plan for some changes that will ease transition over a period of at least one term. Your action plan should identify:

- the overall aim
- what impact you expect for you, the children, the setting/school, parents/carers, and other professionals
- success criteria, which should be specific, measurable and realistic given the timescale
- what resources and staff are involved
- what are the sources of challenge and support at different stages
- how you will review progress review
- if there are any ethical considerations
- how and when you will evaluate the impact.

Early career professional:
This should be a small change in your practice, such as easing transition into the setting/school at the beginning of the day with a shared play session, easing transition between activities, by giving children more freedom to move from one activity to another, or making children responsible for managing their tasks/ activities during part of the day (deciding what activity they should do), or easing transition between break/play times/end of the day and more formal activities.

Later years professional:
This could be a bigger change in practice, such as initiating a family play session (for the youngest children), a family learning day, or getting children to keep a diary of their concerns and feelings about transition (for older children).

Professional leader:
The action plan could involve liaison between classes in your setting/school or with feeder school(s). It could involve the development of a topic/theme to span the transition between classes/settings, organizing a visit to the next class/school, or setting up groups of professionals, children and parents/carers to advise support transition.

Reflection

- How well did you achieve the planned success criteria?
- What was the impact on different individuals?
- What were the challenges you faced? How did you overcome these?
- How could you continue to work with others to ease transitions?

Subject tasks

These are tasks that could form part of the actions planned above.

EYFS:
Organize a family play session, so that parents, children and professionals can play games together. These may be board games that involve rules, 'turn-taking', this supporting social and cognitive development, or physical games, that, additionally, support physical development.

Carry out the session and evaluate according to preplanned success criteria.

Reflection

- How well did the activity meet the success criteria?
- How did the session impact on different partners and support the 'working together' agenda?
- How does the evaluation inform future initiatives to support transition and the 'working together' agenda?

KS1:
Arrange to teach the class that feeds into yours. This could be on a subject/theme/topic that spans the transition between the two classes or that you have a particular expertise in and can follow up when the children move to your class. Before you teach the session, find out how the class is organized, what teaching and learning approaches are used and what class rules there and decide how you can help the children move from this organization and rules to your own, or if you should change your approaches and rules to accommodate the children who are moving to your class.

Carry out the session and evaluate according to preplanned success criteria.

Reflection

- How well did the activity meet your success criteria?
- How did the session impact on the children during the transition period (approximately half a term before and after transition)?
- How did you modify your approaches to accommodate the children? How can you work together with the other class teachers to aid transition for all concerned (children, parents, professionals)?

KS2:
Organize some team teaching with another class that feeds into/or that your class feeds into. This could be on a specific topic or theme, such as a local environment (geography, science) project comparing a local park, with the seaside, or a historical theme, such as the Romans. This may involve a visit where both classes and teachers can work towards the planned learning outcomes together.

Carry out the activities and evaluate according to preplanned success criteria.

Reflection

- How well did the activities meet your success criteria?
- How did the activities impact on the children's transition and help you develop your practice?
- How can you work with other professionals and children to ease transition for groups of children?

References

Alexander, R. (ed.) (2009) *Children, their World, their Education: Final Report and Recommendations of the Cambridge Review*. London: Routledge.

Bolam, R., McMahon, A., Stoll, L., Thomas, S. and Wallace, M. (2005) *Creating and Sustaining Effective Professional Learning Communities Research Brief RB637*. Annesley: Department for Education and Skills (DfES).

Bowlby, R. (2007) Babies and toddlers in non-parental daycare can avoid stress and anxiety if they develop a lasting secondary attachment bond with one carer who is consistently accessible to them, *Attachment & Human Development*, 9(4): 3017–19.

Bronfenbrenner, U. (1995) The bioecological model from a life course perspective: reflections of a participant observer, in P. Moen, G. H. Elder, Jnr. & K. Lűscher (eds) *Examining Lives in Context*. Washington, DC: American Psychological Association, pp. 599–618.

Department for Children, Schools and Families (DCSF) (2008a) *The Early Years Foundation Stage: Setting the Standard for Learning, Development and Care for Children from Birth to Five; Practice Guidance*. London: DCSF.

Department for Children, Schools and Families (DCSF) (2008b) *Every Child Matters Outcomes Framework*. Annesley, Notts: DCSF.

Department for Children, Schools and Families (DCSF) (2009) *Pupil Voice*. Available online at www.standards.dfes.gov.uk/research/themes/pupil_voice/?digest=all (accessed 11 December 2009).

Department for Education and Skills (DfES) (2003) *Every Child Matters*. Norwich: The Stationery Office.

Department for Education and Skills (DfES) (2004) *Every Child Matters: Change for Children*. London: DfES.

Edwards, A., Gilroy, P. and Hartley, D. (2002) *Rethinking Teacher Education: Collaborative Responses to Uncertainty*. London: RoutledgeFalmer.

Effective Provision of Pre-school Education (EPPE) (2003) *Measuring the Impact of Pre-School on Children's Social/behavioural Development over the Pre-School Period*, The EPPE Project Technical Paper 8b, London: Institute of Education.

Froebel, F. (1889) *The Education of Man*. New York: D. Appleton.

Johnston, J., Halocha, J. and Chater, M. (2007) *Developing Teaching Skills in the Primary School*. Maidenhead: Open University Press.

Palmer, S. (2006) *Toxic Childhood. How the Modern World is Damaging Our Children and What We Can Do About It*. London: Orion.

Primary National Strategy (2006) *Seamless Transitions: Supporting Continuity in Young Children'S Learning*. Norwich: Sure Start Department for Education and Skills (DfES).

Ruddock, J. and McIntyre, D. (2007) *Improving Learning Through Consulting Pupils*. London: Routledge.

Sanders, D., White, G., Burge, B., Sharp, C., Eames, A., McEune, R. and Grayson, H. (2005) *A Study of the Transition from the Foundation Stage to Key Stage 1*. London: Sure Start.

Sure Start (2004) *Working Together: A Sure Start Guide to the Childcare and Early Education Field*. Annesley: Department for Education and Skills (DFES).

Turner-Cobb, J.M. (2006) *The Social Experience of Transition to School: Learning and Health Outcomes*. Swindon: Economic and Social Research Council (ESRC).

Vincent, C. (2000) *Including Parents? Education, Citizenship and Parental Agency*. Buckingham: Open University Press.

12 Professionals

Introduction

We begin this chapter with a reading from Freire's (1970) book entitled *Pedagogy of the Oppressed*. You can probably already guess from the title the general theme of Freire's argument about education: since mass education has been adopted those doing the teaching have oppressed and controlled those being taught. This is what he says:

> 66 A careful analysis of the teacher–student relationship at any level, inside or outside the school, reveals its fundamentally narrative character. This relationship involves a narrating subject (the teacher) and patient, listening objects (the students). The contents, whether values or empirical dimensions of reality, tend in the process of being narrated to become lifeless and petrified. Education is suffering from narration sickness.
>
> The teacher talks about reality as if it were motionless, static, compartmentalized and predictable. Or else he expounds on a topic completely alien to the existential experience of the students. His task is to 'fill' the students with the contents of his narration – contents which are detached from reality, disconnected from the totality that engendered them and could give them significance. Words are emptied of their concreteness and become a hollow, alienated and alienating verbosity.
>
> The outstanding characteristic of this narrative education, then, is the sonority of words, not their transforming power. 'Four times four is sixteen; the capital of Para is Belem.' The student records, memorizes and repeats these phrases without perceiving what four times four really means, or realizing the true significance of 'capital' in the affirmation 'the capital of Para is Belem,' that is, what Belem means for Para and what Para means for Brazil.
>
> Narration (with the teacher as narrator) leads the students to memorize mechanically the narrated content. Worse still, it turns them into

'containers', into receptacles to be filled by the teacher. The more completely he fills the receptacles, the better a teacher he is. The more meekly the receptacles permit themselves to be filled, the better students they are.

Education thus becomes an act of depositing, in which the students are the depositories and the teacher is the depositor. Instead of communicating, the teacher issues communiqués and 'makes deposits' which the students patiently receive, memorize, and repeat. This is the 'banking' concept of education, in which the scope of action allowed to the students extends only as far as receiving, filing, and storing the deposits. They do, it is true, have the opportunity to become collectors or cataloguers of the things they store. But in the last analysis, it is men themselves who are filed away through the lack of creativity, transformation, and knowledge in this (at best) misguided system. For apart from inquiry, apart from the praxis, men cannot be truly human. Knowledge emerges only through invention and re-invention, through the restless, impatient, continuing, hopeful inquiry men pursue in the world, with the world, and with each other.

In the banking concept of education, knowledge is a gift bestowed by those who consider themselves knowledgeable upon those whom they consider to know nothing. Projecting an absolute ignorance onto others, a characteristic of the ideology of oppression, negates education and knowledge as processes of inquiry. The teacher presents himself to his students as their necessary opposite; by considering their ignorance absolute, he justifies his own existence. The students, alienated like the slave in the Hegelian dialectic, accept their ignorance as justifying the teacher's existence – but, unlike the slave, they never discover that they educate the teacher.

The *raison d'être* of libertarian education, on the other hand, lies in its drive towards reconciliation. Education must begin with the solution of the teacher–student contradiction, by reconciling the poles of the contradiction so that both are simultaneously teachers and students.

This solution is not (nor can it be) found in the banking concept. On the contrary, banking education maintains and even stimulates the contradiction through the following attitudes and practices, which mirror oppressive society as a whole:

1.   The teacher teaches and the students are taught.
2.   The teacher knows everything and the students know nothing.
3.   The teacher thinks and the students are thought about.
4.   The teacher talks and the students listen – meekly.
5.   The teacher disciplines and the students are disciplined.
6.   The teacher chooses and enforces his choice, and the students comply.

7. The teacher acts and the students have the illusion of acting through the action of the teacher.
8. The teacher chooses the programme content, and the students (who were not consulted) adapt to it.
9. The teacher confuses the authority of knowledge with his own professional authority, which he sets in opposition to the freedom of the students.
10. The teacher is the subject of the learning process, while the pupils are mere objects.

It is not surprising that the banking concept of education regards men as adaptable, manageable beings. The more students work at storing the deposits entrusted to them, the less they develop the critical consciousness which would result from their intervention in the world as transformers of that world. The more completely they accept the passive role imposed on them, the more they tend simply to adapt to the world as it is and to the fragmented view of reality deposited in them.

The capacity of banking education to minimize or annul the students' creative power and to stimulate their credulity serves the interests of the oppressors, who care neither to have the world revealed nor to see it transformed. The oppressors use their 'humanitarianism' to preserve a profitable situation. Thus they react almost instinctively against any experiment in education which stimulates the critical faculties and is not content with a partial view of reality but is always seeking out the ties which link one point to another and one problem to another.   **99**

(Freire, 1970: 45–7)

There is clearly a politically driven argument here and it is also set in the context of education back in the 1960s. However, this reading has been chosen to encourage you to rethink the key elements of what it is to be a professional in education in the second decade of the twenty-first century within the context of the British educational system.

Reflection

EYFS:
*   Might it still be possible to identify any aspects of teaching and learning in EYFS that Freire could identify today?
*   Are there any messages in the Freire reading that still have relevance today as they impact on childrens' first experience of the educational system?

KS1:
- Are there times as pupils get older when aspects of the banking system of education might be effectively employed?
- To what extent do you think parents and carers still think schools do or should work on the banking concept of education?

KS2:
- By the time your pupils leave primary school, how independent are they of the need for teacher guidance in learning?
- How has your study of the above reading helped you reflect on your own philosophy of teaching and learning?

Freire's case is based on the notion of power being a key mechanism in the process of mass education in which many people are employed. Perhaps it may be helpful to break this into two parts for a consideration of our current situation. The first is the notion of power in terms of political control over the educational system. Chapter 13, 'Policy', goes into much detail to analyse how this power has and still is being used to control much of what we do in the education of younger children. A current example would be the so-called 'independent' Rose Review of the primary curriculum. Most people are now very aware that the whole process was steered by the government and Rose had very little real independence about what his review could actually recommend: he had been told the basic framework by his political masters and now teachers will be expected to translate his recommendations into a workable curriculum. Again, the broader issues in this are discussed in the chapter examining curriculum. Second, the notion of power may also be thought of in today's context more in the way referred to by Freire: the power relation between those doing the educating and those being educated. While many readers would probably hope the educational context in which they work does not have the harshness, almost brutality, described by Freire, perhaps we can sometimes be lulled into a false sense of well-being simply because of the familiarity of what we do in our work.

A current example would be the way in which the vast majority of young people in English schools are still taught literacy and numeracy in the morning and leave the other subjects until the afternoon. Teachers, heads and governors all come up with very convincing reasons why this should be, but essentially they are based on the notion that at the end of the day schools are assessed and placed in league tables, which actually have very little to do with real learning. So, the power can be traced back to the government who pass the task to gain certain results to the teachers who in turn create learning environments they think will help to achieve these. So maybe Freire's ideas still hold today, but in the English context need to be extended out to the notion of political control over the education system.

Currently, we have the recommendations of the Rose Review and some commentators suggest that the ways in which schools could implement its recommendations may actually change little of current curriculum organization and structure because those professionals involved will still be looking over their shoulders to the SATS results and the Office for Standards in Education (British) (Ofsted) inspection reports on them. In contrast, the Scottish government has recently introduced the 'Curriculum for Excellence' into early and primary education. It has many similarities with the recommendations of the Rose Review. The big difference in Scotland is that testing has been largely removed in this age range and their inspectors have new and less restrictive guidelines on what they should be inspecting. In many ways this might be seen as a very clever move by the Scottish government because it takes away from their education professionals any possible excuses for not implementing the new 'Curriculum for Excellence'. Sometimes, it can be very interesting to reflect on how education is organized in other national contexts in order to hold up a mirror to our own experiences in order to avoid the possibility of taking too much for granted: there is more than one way to brush a badger.

The remaining sections of this chapter critically examines how educational professionals operate and one way to set the context is to consider another politically taken-for-granted foundation, namely the Professional Standards for Teachers in England which came into effect in September 2007. The government argued that their introduction would provide coherence in professional and occupational standards for everyone involved in the educational workforce. It may be helpful to have these documents to hand for the impact tasks below. They may be found at www.tda.gov.uldteachers/professionalstandards.aspx.

Impact tasks

Early career professional:
To what extent do you think the recommendations of the Standards actually have an effect on your daily professional life? Are they having any real impact on how you may be shaping your career for the future?

Later year professional:
You will probably have begun your professional career in education before the introduction of the Standards. List the ways in which your approach to professionalism has been adapted by having to take the Standards into account as

your career is now progressing. Do you think the Standards have clarified your role as a professional?

Professional leader:
Has the introduction of the Professional Standards made your role easier or harder as you support those who work for you? What improvements would you like to see and why should they be amended at any time in the future?

The Professional Standards are probably going to be central to the professional lives of those working in educational contexts during the shelf life of this book. If the broader issue of how educational professional duties have evolved since the introduction of the Education Reform Act (ERA) in 1988 interests you, Gates (2003) provides a very detailed analysis of the process leading up to the introduction of the current Standards.

Initial teacher education

Since 1991 the government has legally required us to ensure that those preparing to teach reach certain professional levels of performance before being awarded qualified teacher status. Today, these are based on 'professional attributes, professional knowledge and understanding, and professional skills' just like the other levels through which educational professionals may progress. In a sense our students are being conditioned into accepting these three interrelated sections without question in defining what it is to be an effective professional. However, Patrick et al. argue that expecting student teachers to accept these ideas of professionalism in order to qualify creates:

> . . . a specific and simplistic conception of professionalism: firstly, that the professional is one who is competent and develops excellence only in respect of measurable pre-defined standards; and secondly, that professional skills can be described readily, defined meaningfully and delivered through simple transfer (with values, attitudes, knowledge and understanding being classes as subsets of general teaching skills).
> (2003: 240)

They also suggest that this content of the Professional Standards then controls the way in which continuing professional development (CPD) becomes a mainly functional process rather than a reflective professional one. Many readers will in some way, depending on their role in education, have contact with students in initial teacher education. You may be directly involved in the assessment of their progress in achieving the Standards. While they currently have to legally achieve them, it may be worth reflecting on what opportunities you provide for them to think beyond the Standards into what other qualities not formally made explicit or assessed are also required to truly develop a professional attitude and performance in educational contexts. One example from the author's own experience is the notion that professional understanding needs to be based on research evidence. It is very hard to read a Standard leading to qualified teacher status (QTS) which actually makes this explicit. However, education is one profession where very little policy and practice is based on valid and reliable research unlike, for example, the medical profession. As discussed in Chapter 13 on 'Policy', much of what educationalists are expected to do is based on political decisions which are rarely founded on relevant research. One way in which the author attempts to encourage this more researched-based approach to learning and teaching is to encourage his geography specialist students to undertake research in educational contexts and then write them up as articles for relevant professional geographical journals. In addition to helping them to develop a more critical approach to their professional practice, it also increases their personal confidence that they can indeed get ideas published as beginning professionals and at the same time increase their credibility for employment as having been published, something that very few students achieve before qualifying. Such critical writing also encourages them to reflect on the actual impact they can have on a largely prescribed curriculum.

> Although the platform is only espoused theory, writing it usually begins a reflective process of greater depth. Writing itself has the potential to be a powerfully reflective process.
>
> (Osterman and Kottkamp, 1993: 880)

The curriculum

Alexander (2010: 449) states that:

> Compelled to comply with government prescriptions for curriculum and, to a large extent, pedagogy, teachers have warned that their creativity, imagination, expertise and confidence have all been constrained.

This has largely taken place since 1987 with the introduction of the national curriculum and the huge number of directives placed on primary education with the government objective stated as being to raise standards. All readers will have their own personal views and experience of this protracted process.

Currently, we have the published recommendations of both the government-controlled 'independent' review of the curriculum from Rose (DCSF, 2009) and the final report and recommendations of the Cambridge Primary Review (Alexander, 2010). If educational professionals are truly to engage with this process of change in the curriculum along with the notion that now the curriculum should not be seen as something prescribed and then changed *en masse* after a certain period of time, they need support to enable them to engage in the reflective debates that will allow informed decisions to be made. However, the Rose Review (DCSF, 2009: 21) perhaps underestimates this process by recommending that:

> In line with arrangements for implementing the new secondary curriculum, the DCSF should provide primary schools with one extra training day in 2010 to enable the workforce in each school to understand the new primary curriculum and start planning how it will work in their school.

The reader is left to decide whether this demonstrates the government's total lack of understanding of the size and nature of the process involved on the ground, or a reflection of the notion that all the thinking has been done for education professionals. This is stated in the report and now it simply has to be implemented in schools. It begs the question of actually what professional role educators should play in the development of a curriculum. Rose gives the impression that the curriculum they have created should be taken by educators and be made to be responsive to the needs of pupils and the communities served by each school or learning organization. This is an important point that must not be missed both in the preparation for implementation in 2011 but also beyond as the curriculum is regularly reviewed and amended in the light of professional reflection by all those involved in the education process. However, it will require a new mindset on the part of all those involved. Since 1987 the national curriculum has come to be regarded as something set in stone by legislation and occasionally changed by government directives. An example of this was how the English and mathematics national curricula was introduced in 1988 and in 1998 when they were largely replaced with the literacy and numeracy strategies. These were not statutory as such but the pressure on schools to adopt them was considerable.

Professionals now need to develop that sense of control and ownership over the curriculum that will enable them to do what the government expects in terms of Every Child Matters and in terms of professional responsibility which the workforce already has in the way that the majority of its members work, to ensure that pupils develop positive values towards learning and achieve their full potential in all aspects of development. Webb and Vulliamy (2006) suggest that one current and strong perception of what educational professionals perceive to be central to their professionalism is 'the ability to motivate and develop children's learning and to boost their confidence and self image' (2006: 126). But in order to achieve this, the professionals involved need ownership and understanding of the type of curriculum they will use to enable it to happen.

The ideas about how professionals may actually be involved in reflective curriculum development should be read in order to consider the following impact tasks, appropriate to your role.

Subject tasks

Early career professional:
Not having been influenced by factors affecting previous curriculum changes, what skills and perspectives might you wish to offer the collaborative process of curriculum development in your educational setting? What might you need to be aware of in order for your ideas to be considered?

Later year professional:
Thinking back to curriculum development or implementation activities in which you have been involved, what professional opportunities would you now wish to have in order that you and your colleagues take control and ownership of the changes you will be developing?

Professional leader:
How might you support colleagues in developing the confidence to take professional ownership of curriculum change by moving beyond the various experiences they may have had at previous times of change?

Perhaps the first point to consider regarding professional engagement in curriculum development is having the ability to think beyond previous experiences and understand that things can be very different. This may be illustrated by the time in the late 1990s when 'curriculum consultants' were busy rushing into schools telling teachers exactly how they were to implement the strategies. Many teachers could identify the flaws in the strategies but did not challenge them. Relating this to the Rose recommendations and their future adaptation in the years ahead, perhaps one professional approach may be to see them as starting points but to use your own expertise and experience to adapt them to the needs of your pupils. For example, the area of 'Understanding physical development, health and well-being' offers many examples of how teachers can plan for its content to be covered. However, it specifically does not suggest that out-of-classroom activities and fieldwork could be excellent tools for promoting aspects of this area of learning. It is opportunities like this, thinking beyond the recommendations of the report and coming up with your own solutions, that could bring the curriculum to life.

To be fair, the Rose Review does list and make clear what schools do control in terms of curriculum planning. A key professional skill will be in not taking for granted what is current practice but asking how might it be improved for the future? One example is to question whether English and mathematics should always occur in the morning in future. This issue might be resolved in those schools where very carefully planned cross-curricular studies will begin to blur the borders between subjects *as* pupils begin to be introduced to thinking in a linked and cross-curricular way. Rose (DCSF, 2009) lists the following processes which may benefit from professional scrutiny in order to identify new ways of developing the curriculum:

- teaching methods and pedagogy;
- teaching content additional to the statutory National Curriculum;
- how the curriculum is organised and described, for example as subjects, topics or themes;
- the distribution of the curriculum across each key stage;
- the daily timetable, i.e. start and finish times of the day, break and lunchtimes;
- the teaching hours per week (providing that they are at or above, the recommended minimum);
- the time allocated to each subject and the length of each lesson;
- the organisation of teaching groups, for example by age, ability or otherwise;
- how the curriculum caters for inclusion and differentiation, for example for children with specific learning difficulties;
- the resources for learning; and assessment for learning, and assessments and tests other than for national reporting.

(DCSF, 2009: 39)

Communities of professionals

Perhaps one of the benefits of the many changes that are occurring in English primary education is the ethos of professional and related people working more closely together as the various workforce reforms began to become the norm after 2004 in learning organizations. Fullan (1999: 27) suggests that:

Vitality springs from experiencing conflict and tension in systems which also incorporate anxiety-containing supportive relationships.

Collaborative cultures are innovative not just because they provide support, but also because they recognize the value of disonance inside and outside the organization.

Indeed, this was recognized by Ofsted (2007) following research into the increasing range of people who were working in schools and other learning organizations. What they were less convinced about was how all this increased activity was being supported and monitored by members of the school leadership teams. This is perhaps a relevant point because many of these contributions may have specific impacts in where they originate from but the potential for further development is often not realized. Taking an illustration from the author's experience of supervising initial teacher education students in schools where, for example, a head teacher is astute enough to note some specific talents a student may have, the more proactive will think creatively and, while not putting their main reason for being in school at stake, will give the student opportunities to share that talent in other parts of the school. This of course in turn boosts the student's morale and confidence is seen as being valued by other professional colleagues.

In order to make these professional connections even more effective, we perhaps need to reconsider some of the traditional roles people have in educational settings. Again, using an example from the author's experience in many schools, it is traditionally the mentor/class teacher who takes the leading role in supporting students on school experience. It is not common, but where it does occur, much professional development can take place when other members of the school community become actively involved in the school experience process. The author has seen excellent examples of where teaching assistants become involved in discussion with students about their progress on school placement. Everyone feels more valued and indeed the three-way learning reflection can be intense.

Ethics and professionalism

An issue that is rarely discussed in the current educational climate is the relationship between ethics and the nature of professionalism. Indeed, it is hard to find them clearly articulated in the Professional Standards for Teachers in England. Yet perhaps an underlying set of values and principles may be the foundation on which all the more mechanical and technical aspects of professionalism listed in the Standards needs to be based. They do require teachers to provide a safe and secure environment, but do professional ethics need to go much deeper than this physical nature of the learning environment? There is not space in this chapter to discuss in depth the ways in which effective learning communities can be developed through greater professional interaction. However, Sullivan and Glanz (2006) suggest many practical ways in which strategies for leadership, learning and collaboration may be used to develop more reflective and connected learning environments.

Ethics and professionalism

An issue that is rarely discussed in the current educational climate is the relationship between ethics and the nature of professionalism. Indeed, it is hard to find them clearly articulated in the Professional Standards for Teachers in England. Yet perhaps an underlying set of values and principles may be the foundation on which all the more mechanical and technical aspects of professionalism listed in the Standards needs to be based. They do require teachers to provide a safe and secure environment, but do professional ethics need to go much deeper than this physical nature of the learning environment?

Buzzelli and Johnson (2002: 156) suggest that teachers do have a moral sense within their professional working lives and 'inherently know that teaching is a moral activity'. In contrast, Campbell (2005) perhaps offers a more realistic perspective in saying that:

> I would argue, by slight comparison, that only some teachers *know* this (in the sense of possessing ethical knowledge), and, of them, some are more aware than others of how their moral agency role influences the specific aspects of their practice and behaviour.
>
> (2005: 117)

The author would tend to agree with Campbell, having visited students in many schools around the country since 1991. This is in no way meant to suggest that teachers of younger pupils do not have morals and values which influence their professional practice. It is more that the immense external pressures placed on them since the late 1980s have had a number of effects: one is that they have been placed in a context where other people, mainly politicians, have set the ground rules as to what education is all about. Chapter 13, 'Policy', provides more details on the subject. This has created an environment where many education professionals have come to the conclusion that there is little they can do about the context in which they work because in reality they have very little power to influence education policy. Leading on from this, it has caused a situation where teachers are so involved with managing their daily professional activities that they do not have time to stand back and reflect on the moral aspects of their practice. This may be illustrated by an example from a recent school visit made by the author:

A commercial organization had been contacting schools to promote a method of encouraging extended writing to move on from the very limited opportunities pupils had for extended writing in the heyday of the literacy strategy. It involved buying CDs of music from them which were meant to be played for an hour in which time pupils wrote creatively. The student in question had a reception class. She had been instructed by the teacher that this approach to writing was a 'whole school policy' and all classes had to do it. Teachers were meant to leave the pupils to their writing. It does not take much understanding of reception pupils to realize just how little this process benefited their writing development at that age. The ethos of that particular school was very much a 'whole school policy' approach to everything they did. The author and student felt very uncomfortable in the classroom for those lessons because the pupils were being put under stress knowing that they could do nothing else within the hour. This example is given because it raises some moral issues which in many ways relate back to the reading by Freire provided at the beginning of this chapter. Freire might argue that those writing lessons in the twenty-first century were also an example of the 'pedagogy of the oppressed'. But the oppression was not only on the pupils, but also the teacher who in a very tactful way explained to the student that she had very personal reservations about using the method with her age of pupils, but senior management had made it clear all teachers had to use the package. The teacher in question was clearly a highly skilled and experienced professional who was being restricted from using her judgement as to what learning and teaching methods were most appropriate for her pupils. As a teacher educator I was also involved in the moral dilemma of the situation. The student clearly had views on the situation and we were able to discuss them in private. As a new entrant to the profession she learnt from this experience that, while she was in the school to learn, she was also right in exercising her moral judgement as a professional to realize that she was not seeing good practice and indeed many of the pupils were being put under stress during the lesson because they knew they could not achieve the extended writing expected of them. The author's position on this was that while he could not openly criticize the school's policy, he could engage the student in a critical debate on what we had observed in which she was encouraged to discuss and justify her own views on the situation, which hopefully helped her to deepen her sense of some of the moral issues involved in a profession where children are entrusted to us to make the best use of their time in school.

In some ways the example above of professional morals at work in practice may be related to professional development. It might be hoped that the introduction of such a whole school policy resulted from whole staff discussion and analysis of why such a writing policy was to be introduced. When discussing CPD for teachers in a British context in the twenty-first century, Lock (2006: 665) suggests that:

> (a) one-shot and one-size-fits-all workshops; (b) use of the transmission model from experts to teachers; (c) failure to address school-specific differences; (d) just-in-case training; and (e) system-wide presentations that do not provide sufficient time to learn new strategies to meet the reality of their own classroom.

Indeed, Pickering et al. (2007) ague that for education professionals to really understand the morals and impact of their practice, they need to analyse it through becoming involved in CPD which is not a top-down model but one which focuses on shared practice, collaborative CPD and scholarly reflection on practice.

Professional well-being

This chapter on professionals will conclude with an issue which makes no appearance in the Professional Standards for Teachers in England: professional well-being. It is deliberately included here because the official line on Professional Standards makes no reference to professionals needing to be aware of their own well-being in order to be effective and motivated practitioners. Indeed, the only reference to well-being in the government's Professional Standards (TDA: 2007) refers to pupils by stating that 'The term well-being refers to the rights of the children and young people (as set out, and consulted on, in the *Every Child Matters Green Paper* and subsequently set out in the Children Act 2004)'. Indeed, a careful reading of the language used in the section on how the Standards will be used clearly gives a message that teachers need to be managed for example 'In all these cases, performance management is the key process'. No mention is made of supporting professionals at a more personal level in order to improve their performance and quality of life. But the author would argue that education professionals do need to have a perspective on well-being as most official sources simply focus on the children and performance at a range of scales. This whole issue has been discussed by Holmes (2005) who states that they can promote true improvements in the quality of life that we experience; and, as concepts, well-being and quality of life cannot be separated. For this reason, stress in the teaching profession is one of life's ironies: perhaps greater than we have ever appreciated.

She suggests that you may approach your own assessment of your well-being by breaking it up into four categories:

- Physical well-being;
- Emotional well-being;
- Mental and intellectual well-being;
- Spiritual well-being.

(Holmes, 2005: 3)

In addition, she suggests that in considering the above, they also need to be viewed holistically as they are all related in ways specific to each individual. A personal example would be that currently the author's physical well-being is not up to standard because too much time is being spent at the computer. On the other hand, there is a sense of intellectual well-being as the writing of my chapters in this book is drawing to an end and I have learnt much during the process.

If this brief introduction to professional well-being interests you, the following websites provide more practical information and ideas:

- www.worklifesupport.com
- www.hvec.org.ulc/hvecmain/sections
- www.thegrid.org.uldwellbeing/herts/risk_assessment

The last site is run by Hertfordshire County Council for its education professional and offers information and ideas for all educational professionals to discuss and evaluate their well-being in practice. No amount of discussion or analysis of educational professionals will be of much use if they themselves are not able to reflect and act on their understanding of their personal well-being.

References

Alexander, R. (ed.) (2010) *Children, the World, their Education*. London: Routledge.

Buzzelli, C. and Johnson, B. (2002) *The Moral Dimensions of Teaching: Language, Power and the Culture of Classroom Interaction*. London: Routledge Palmer.

Campbell, E. (2005) Challenges in fostering ethical knowledge as professionalism within schools as teaching communities, *Journal of Educational Change*, 6(3): 207–26.

Department for Children, Schools and Families (DCSF) (2009) *Independent Review of the Primary Curriculum: Final Report*. Nottingham: DCSF.

Freire, P. (1970) *Pedagogy of the Oppressed*. Harmondsworth: Penguin.

Fullan, M. (1999) *Changing Forces: The Sequel*. London: Falmer.

Gates, N. (2003) *Teachers' Professional Duties and Teachers' Legal Liabilities and Responsibilities*. Hatfield: University of Hertfordshire.

Holmes, E. (2005) *Teacher Well-being: Looking After Yourself in the Classroom*. London: Routledge Falmer.

Lock, J. (2006) A new image: online communities to facilitate teacher professional development, *Journal of Technology and Teacher Education*, 14(4): 663–78.

Ofsted (2007) *Reforming and Developing the School Workforce*. London: Ofsted.

Osterman, K. and Kottkamp, R. (1993) *Reflective Practice for Educators: Improving Schooling through Professional Development*. Thousand Oaks, CA: Corwin.

Patrick, F., Forde, C. and McPhee, A. (2003) Challenging the 'new professionalism': from managerialism to pedagogy? *Journal of In-Service Education*, 29(2): 237–53.

Pickering, J., Daly, C. and Pachler, N. (eds) (2007) *New Designs for Teachers' Professional Learning*. London: Institute of Education University of London.

Sullivan, S. and Glanz, J. (2006) *Building Effective Learning Communities*. Thousand Oaks, CA: Corwin.

tda.gov.ultheachers/professionalstandards.aspx.

Webb, R. and Vulliamy, G. (2006) *Coming Full Circle? The Impact of New Labour's Education Policies on Primary School Teachers' Work*. London: Association of Teachers and Lecturers.

13 Policy

The purpose of this chapter is to give you an opportunity to stand back from the demands and pressures of your everyday experience of education and to critically reflect on the underlying policies which inform and direct it. In order to place these in context, we first need to consider some broader issues and will do this by discussing the key points from this reading by Whitty (2002).

> 66 There has been a growing emphasis on market forces in state education in many parts of the world where education has hitherto been treated as a public service. Alongside, and potentially in place of, collective provision by public bodies with a responsibility to cater for the needs of the whole population, there are increasing numbers of quasi-autonomous schools with devolved budgets competing for individual clients in the market-place. Increasingly, education is being treated as a private good rather than a public responsibility. While calling, in response to these developments, for a reassertion of citizen rights alongside consumer rights in education, I also suggest that changes in the nature of contemporary societies require the development of new conceptions of citizenship and new forms of representation through which citizen rights can be expressed. Although, as we have seen, the celebration of diversity and choice among individuals with unequal access to cultural and material resources is likely to inhibit rather than enhance their chances of emancipation, new modes of collectivism do need to be developed that pay more attention to the legitimate aspirations of individuals from all social backgrounds.

The Neoliberal Agenda
For the neoliberal politicians who dominated educational policy-making in Britain and elsewhere in the 1980s and 1990s, social affairs are best organised according to the 'general principle of consumer sovereignty', which holds that each individual is the best judge of his or her needs and wants, and of what is in their best interests. The preference for introducing

market mechanisms into education, partly from a predilection for freedom of choice as a good in itself, is also grounded in the belief that competition produces improvements in the quality of services on offer which in turn enhance the wealth-producing potential of the economy, thereby bringing about gains for the least well-off as well as for the socially advantaged.

In so far as it is accepted at all that markets have losers (even victims) as well as winners, the provision of a minimum safety net rather than universal benefits is seen as the best way to protect the weak without removing incentives or creating a universal dependency culture. But it is also sometimes claimed that the market will actually enhance social justice even for the least well-off, by placing real choice in the hands of those trapped in neighbourhood comprehensives in the inner city rather than, as before, having a system where only the wealthy or the knowing could get choice of school by moving house even if they could not afford to go private. In a strictly economic sense, these quasi-market policies cannot be regarded as privatisation of the education system, but they do require public sector institutions to operate more like private sector ones and families to treat educational decisions in a similar way to other decisions about private consumption.

Such reforms have been widely criticised from the Left, because they seem to embody a commitment to creating, not a more equal society but one that is more 'acceptably' unequal. There is no aspiration towards a rough equality of educational outcomes between different social class and ethnic groups, it being argued that such a target has brought about a 'levelling down' of achievement, and has been pursued at the expense of individual freedom. To those on the Left, it seems that individual rights are being privileged at the expense of the notion of a just social order (Connell, 1993).

However, although such reforms can be seen as a typical New Right crusade to stimulate market forces at the expense of 'producer interests', that is only one way of looking at it. Part of their wider appeal lies in a declared intention to encourage the growth of different types of school, responsive to the needs of particular communities and interest groups. This argument is especially appealing when it is linked with the claim that diversity in types of schooling does not necessarily mean hierarchy and, in this context, the new policies have gained some adherents among disadvantaged groups. They also link to concepts of multiple identities and radical pluralism and can seem more attractive than unidimensional notions of comprehensive schooling and, indeed, unidimensional notions of citizenship.

Thus, the espousal of choice and diversity in education seems superficially to resonate with notions of an open, democratic society as well as with a market ideology. Put in those terms, the new policies have a potential appeal far beyond the coteries or the New Right and have to be taken seriously by those professing a commitment to social justice. The multiple accenting of recent reforms was particularly marked in the Picot Report in New Zealand (Grace, 1991; Gordon, 1992). In Britain, the reforms were always mainly associated with a New Right agenda and the ambiguities there related as much to tensions between neoliberal and neoconservative voices as to the effects of any lingering social democratic equity agenda. However, according to Roger Dale (1994), some of the tensions might also be attributed to an emergent neo-Schumpeterian agenda evident in a recent British White Paper on economic competitiveness and influenced by policies pursued in many of the economies of the Pacific Rim.

Meanwhile, the American commentators Chubb and Moe (1992), whose work was mentioned in Chapter 3, have identified the neoliberal aspects of the British approach as 'a lesson in school reform' that other countries should follow. The rhetoric of the Conservative government's 'five great themes' – quality, diversity, parental choice, school autonomy and accountability (DFE, 1992a) – is already familiar in many other countries with different political regimes (Whitty and Edwards, 1998; Whitty, Power and Halpin, 1998). Such policies have so far been most marked in the Anglophone world, especially Britain, the USA, New Zealand and parts of Australia, but there is some evidence that their appeal has been spreading. Despite popular resistance to increased state aid to private schools in France, there has been a growing interest in deregulating schooling in various European countries. A paper by Manfred Weiss (1993) suggested that 'pluralism, decentralisation, deregulation, greater diversity and parent empowerment' were being mooted as new guiding principles in education policy in corporatist Germany. Even Taiwan, one of the 'tiger economies' of the Pacific Rim which hitherto has had a highly directed and centralist education system, has made some tentative moves in the same direction, while parts of Japan are now experimenting with school choice (Green, 2001).

Making Sense of the Reforms
In the final chapter of our book on *Specialisation and Choice in Urban Education* (Whitty et al., 1993), Tony Edwards, Sharon Gewirtz and I considered how far the British reforms might be part of a movement that is much broader and deeper than the particular set of policies that had come to be termed 'Thatcherism'. In particular, we considered how far these shifts in the nature of education policy reflected broader changes in the nature of advanced industrial societies, that is the extent to which they could be seen as a response to shifts in the economy, or more specifically patterns of production and consumption, often described as post-Fordism,

and how far they might be an expression of broader social changes that are sometimes taken to signal the existence of a 'postmodern' age.

Firstly, we noted that some observers suggest that the reforms can be understood in terms of the transportation of changing modes of regulation from the sphere of production into other arenas, such as schooling and welfare services. They have pointed to a correspondence between the establishment of markets in welfare and a shift in the economy away from Fordism towards a post-Fordist mode of accumulation which 'places a lower value on mass individual and collective consumption and creates pressures for a more differentiated production and distribution of health, education, transport and housing' (Jessup et al., 1987). Various commentators, such as Stephen Ball, have claimed to see in new forms of schooling a shift from the 'Fordist' school of the era of mass production to the 'post-Fordist school' (Ball, 1990). The emergence of new and specialised sorts of school may be the educational equivalent of the rise of flexible specialisation driven by the imperatives of differentiated consumption, and taking the place of the old assembly-line world of mass production. These 'post-Fordist schools' are designed 'not only to produce the post-Fordist, multi-skilled, innovative worker but to behave in post-Fordist ways themselves; moving away from mass production and mass markets to niche markets and "flexible specialization" . . . a post-Fordist mind-set is thus having implications in schools for management styles, curriculum, pedagogy and assessment' (Kenway, 1993: 115). So, it is argued, the new policies not only reflect such changes, they help to foster and legitimate them.

However, we said that there were problems about assuming a straightforward correspondence between education and production, as well as with the notion of post-Fordism as an entirely new regime of accumulation. We therefore urged caution about concluding that we were experiencing a wholesale move away from a mass-produced welfare system towards a flexible, individualised and customised post-Fordist one. In the field of education, it is certainly difficult to establish a sharp distinction between mass and market systems. The so-called 'comprehensive system' in Britain was never as homogeneous as the concept of mass produced welfare suggests. Indeed, it was always a system differentiated by class and ability. We therefore felt that neo-Fordism was a more appropriate term for the recent changes than post-Fordism which implied something entirely distinctive. We suggested, however, that we might actually be witnessing an intensification of social differences and a celebration of them in a new rhetoric of legitimation. In the new rhetoric, choice, specialisation and diversity replace the previous language of common and comprehensive schooling. (Whitty, 2002: 79–82) **99**

Source: Whitty, G. (2002) *Making Sense of Education Policy*.
London: Sage Publications

The first point made in the reading asks us to consider whether any version of current education policy which can be based along a continuum between consumer rights and citizen rights now needs to be viewed more in the light of fundamental changes in society in order to reposition education in relation to the state and the individual.

Reflection

EYFS:

- As their children begin school, to what extent do you think parents and carers view education as the development of a person or for preparing them to contribute to society?
- Recent education policy in England has placed increased pressure on getting children to start the education process at an earlier and earlier age. What are the positive and negative aspects of this process?

KS1:

- The 2011 curriculum marks the start of modern foreign languages as a requirement. How might this be introduced while minimizing curriculum overload?
- Government thinking about educational choice is appearing (June 2010). To what extent may your planning be affected by possible government policy?

KS2:

- What impact might government policies beyond education have on older children in primary schools?
- Why might this be occurring?

In order to understand how we have reached the current state of educational policy in England, Bell (2007) identifies four stages which he argues English education policy has gone through since 1960. We briefly examine these in order to help understand how they have influenced where we find ourselves today.

Background to current education policy

Bell suggests that the Social Democratic Phase ran from 1960 to 1973. Based on the 1944 Education Act, education policy was based on the notion that it existed to reduce inequalities in all aspects of society. Policy would be developed by the teaching profession and politicians with the purpose that 'all children should have an equal opportunity of acquiring intelligence, and of developing their talents and abilities to the full' (Boyle, 1963: 1). The Plowden Report (HMSO, 1967) promoted teacher autonomy to support child-centred primary education and enquiry learning and an integrated curriculum developed by teachers and pupils. By the 1970s the economic climate had worsened and commentators were suggesting that this was a result of declining standards in schools, leading to what Bell (2007) calls the Resources Constrained Phase 1973–87. Perhaps one of the most significant of these commentaries was made by Callaghan (1976) where he questioned whether or not schools were producing future workers with sufficient skills to enable the nation to survive in the economic and technical climate of the age. It illustrates the beginning of a move to view education as a process in society to support the development of the state, rather in the previous phase which focused on the development of equality for the individual. In order to achieve results attention began to be focused on school management and the effective use of resources (money) in the education system. It also signalled a move away from education professional and politicians working together towards power being held almost entirely by the politicians in terms of decision-making.

Bell argues that between 1988 and 1996 education policy was in the Market Phase. This was based on quality, diversity, choice, autonomy and accountability. By now you are probably beginning to feel familiar with the thinking of this era as much still remains in the education system. It was based on the belief that market forces were the best way to control the education system by offering individuals freedom of choice to select the best products (schools) available to them. The Targets Phase (1997 onwards) began in 1997 when New Labour came to power. While much policy of the previous phase continues in similar forms (e.g. SATs), Blair's Third Way was an attempt to acknowledge changes in society by developing policies that addressed social welfare and he placed education at the centre of this change in direction. The policy focus in this phase is on delivering excellence and this is achieved by effective head teachers who are central to the government's strategy. Alongside this developed a government-controlled curriculum in the form of various revisions to the national curriculum and the literacy and numeracy strategies. This must now all sound very familiar to you. In terms of primary education we are currently at an interesting stage of policy-making as the new government (May 2010) impacts on the system. Before analysing this report in the context of education policy, we consider some key issues surrounding decision-making in education policy.

Key issues in education policy

The first area we examine is to consider what the role of education might be in the current and future social, political, moral and economic climate both of the nation and in a global context. Back in 1693 John Locke argued for the rights of the child and for them to be able to grow up in natural ways. By 1802 we see government taking an active interest in the education of the population with the Health and Morals of Apprentices Act which made the teaching of reading, writing and arithmetic compulsory for apprentices in their first four years of apprenticeship, along with religious teaching. A study of the remaining history of education in this country reveals an ever-increasing involvement of the state in the creation of educational organizations, the curriculum and how its effectiveness is monitored. A slightly greater focus of the child at the centre of education occured after the 1944 Education Act and lasted until the early 1970s. The overall historical picture is of adults telling children what will happen to them in school. McGuinn (2002) suggests that the reason we have not really made extensive leaps forward with education policy is that:

> The root of the problem . . . is that our education system is based upon force. Education is imposed by the powerful (adults) upon the weak (children). We take all our young people – each of whom is a complex mixture of different abilities, needs, personalities and learning styles – and we force them, by law, through what is in effect a 'one-size-fits-all' education system. Why do we do this?
>
> (McGuinn, 2002: 107)

Reflective task

EYFS:
In recent years government policy in this country has been to formalize the education process at ever younger and younger ages. In many other European nations, children do not start formal school until the age of six or seven. Their pre-school opportunities are often very informal. It is interesting to note how the *Final Report* of the Rose Review (2009) carefully avoids publishing the ages at which pupils go to school in those countries where it is significantly later than in England (DCSF, 2009: 126), presumably to avoid the opportunity for reflection and debate about our national policy. What are the benefits and disadvantages of having such formalization of education at an increasingly young age in this country?

KS1:
National testing at the end of KS1 has been dominated by SATs for many years. Numerous education professionals, parents and carers, and other interested parties questioned their validity and purpose but they remained statutory. Why do you think the public voice against KS1 SATs remained ineffective for so long and what might this tell us about recent educational policy?

KS2:
A careful reading of the new government's education statements (May 2010) states that it returns to teachers the power to decide how the primary curriculum is organized along a continuum from discrete subject to a more integrated approach. It also says that teachers will have much more control over its content based on their understanding of pupils and the context in which they work. What other factors at work processes in the education system may support or restrict this actually taking place at KS2? What reason would you offer this?

Hopefully your engagement with your chosen task above has helped you to think beyond our taken-for-granted approach to education policy. Clearly, McGuinn wants us to consider how far some of the problems in the education system may be a result of children being forced to jump through the various hoops and mechanisms imposed on them. We do not think he is arguing for children to take control of the education system; rather, that as education professionals we organize schools to enable children to feel ownership of what they are doing and can see the reason for it. Clearly, many teachers are already doing this so far as the system allows them to. Perhaps we need a little more confidence to challenge the policies imposed on us. If we do not, perhaps in a century of rapid change and development, we may find that the current education system becomes more and more alienated from children and society as its relevance and purpose is increasingly hard to justify. Some would argue that ICT offers many opportunities to change this situation and you may like to consider the point having read Chapter 10, 'The digital world'.

Ball (2007) develops the notion that some fundamental changes may need to be made in our education policies if a formal system of state education is to remain a viable option in the future. He suggests that the question is:

> not just about new organisational forms or 'worker incentives' or re-articulated professional ethics; they are about access to and the distribution of educational opportunity in terms of race, class, gender and physical ability.
>
> (Ball, 2007: 45–6)

By 'organizational forms' Ball is talking about the physical organization of education; for example;, the design of school environments. He would include the structure of the curriculum and other factors such as the whole nature of the assessment system in education. 'Worker incentives' would be the relevance of education to pupils, the way in which the system apparently selects and prepares pupils for different opportunities in their lives and a justification for what the system does; for example, the current government push for information and communication technology (ICT) as a necessity for personal and national survival and growth. 'Professional ethics' means the arguments and beliefs we offer to justify what we do. This might include teachers who believe in spending much time on making the learning environment as attractive and stimulating as possible. The author (John Halocha) spent many enjoyable hours in the classroom doing just that and believed it was important. However, in recent years he has visited many primary classrooms across Europe and has seen children learning in far less attractive environments. He did see high standards in terms of, for example, mathematical ability and the vast majority of these schools seemed very happy places. So, we do also need to question what we often take for granted. Sometimes professional ethics are closely linked to education policy; for example, those head teachers who see results and league tables as the driving force and reason for the school to exist.

Another dimension we need to examine is the social context in which education policy operates. Bell (2007) suggested that in Britain today we live in an 'audit society' and a 'performative society'. This not only applies to education, as can be seen in the current questioning of huge bonuses for some city bank employees (audit society) while at the same time people wanting interest rates to perform as well as possible for their savings (performance society). There are perhaps two fundamental questions regarding the notion of the audit society and education. The first is why do we need to audit the education system and the second is how does this impact on the education of children? Clearly, a lot of money is spent on the education system and there is a case for ensuring it is spent in the best way. But what is the best way? It would be interesting to know how much the government has spent on curriculum change in primary schools since the 1998 Education Reform Act. Has this spending actually improved pupil learning and how do we measure it? Current policy is to take SATs for granted and say they serve that purpose.

In terms of a performative society is education's role to ensure that both individuals and the state gain as much as possible from it? Does this mean that the system has to ensure future citizens have the necessary skills for the future? Does it mean that these skills will be used to ensure the nation's well-being at a global level? But these questions also require us to ask if we know what skills will be required in the future. Many of the children educated in the 1960s and 1970s within a Plowden (1967) ethos are still at work. Plowden made no mention of their need for advanced ICT skills in our world today because its authors had no idea of how technology would develop. Are we today actually any better equipped and informed to know what children in particular and society in general will need in five, twenty or fifty years time? We suspect not. Might that then suggest we should be educating for the present? Would this make education more relevant? Does education policy need to be more reactive to current needs rather than providing us with huge national curricula we are told are the way forward for years into the future? What type of education policy and system can offer a meaningful education for the individual while at the same time support the nation within a global context? Do we need to refocus on the child as suggested earlier?

Bell (2007) suggests that we need to consider much more deeply the external and internal values of education. What do we mean by accountability? To whom and why? Bell offers the phrase 'communicative rationality' as a sociological starting point. This is not one where politicians provide a top-down version of education but one in which all members of society are engaged in the debate about the purpose and content of education. He offers the tool of 'reflexive questioning of achievement' through which mutual accountability is the discourse for both agreeing on what is important in education and how it is judged. The growth in the use of reflective journals in many walks of life and professions might be an example of this idea in practice. The content of the journal is negotiated and justified by the writer and evaluated by an assessor through a reflexive questioning of achievement. If the author applies this to his own university workplace, he can see many opportunities for such an approach. However, the formal internal and external assessment policies currently taken for granted in higher education would impose considerable obstacles in its implementation. The idea can also work at a more global level.

Currently, universities across the European Union (EU), through the mechanism of the 'Bolognia' process, are slowly working towards a situation where students will be able to study in various universities across Europe in order to gain their qualifications. Does such a policy in higher education actually enable the purpose of higher education to be more easily identified or might it impose even greater mechanisms through which students will have to navigate in order to gain qualifications? We already have student mobility in higher education across Europe and the author's experience is that while academic study provides students with alternative perspectives on learning and knowledge, one of the greatest benefits is increased social awareness and understanding of cultures across Europe. Ball's 'mutual accountability' might have even more worth within a social context than a purely educational one.

O'Neill (2002) develops this further through the notion of professional accountability within an educational context where policy decisions are not made currently through central government, but by professionals who are accountable within society at large. He argues that 'the social capital of active duties-orientated citizenship' (2002: 209) would be the mechanism through which educational professions would operate to ensure transparency, responsibility and responsiveness to the community at large. In order to understand this notion it may be helpful to apply it within another professional context.

The health service has many parallels with the education system in Britain. It has been led by policies of the market, freedom of choice and competition between organizations. It is also highly results driven in its accountability mechanisms. The politics behind the policies were to give the patient choice and transparency within a high-quality system. The big difference goes back to the point made earlier in the chapter: children are legally forced to attend school, patients are not forced to attend a doctor's surgery or hospital. Defending the NHS at a time of considerable debate in the USA as to what form of health service should be available to Americans, Darzi and Kibasi (2009) state that:

> Under our NHS constitution, patients have a legal right to choice of provider. That means any provider – public, private or not-for-profit. By April 2010 our NHS will be the first health system in the world to systematically measure and openly publish the quality of care achieved by every clinical department in every hospital. It means patients will be able to make meaningful, informed choices on what is best for them and their family. Some of this data is already published.

There appears to be professional support for a system that does measure the performance of fellow practitioners and far from being a threat, it is actually seen as good for patient choice. The deeper question perhaps goes back to O'Neills' (2002) point of professional accountability. He would argue that the accountability measures are actually created and administered by the educational professionals rather than central government, but the quote above comes from two highly respected British medical academics who appear to support a system largely created and monitored by central government. Perhaps as educationalists, we need further debate on the relationship between ourselves, government and the communities within which we work as to the balance of power in who actually decides educational policy. This is effectively summed up by Whitty (2002: 92) who says:

> We now have to ask what are the appropriate constituencies through which to express community interests in the new millennium? What forms of democracy can express the complexity of contemporary communities?

Policy in action

The Rose Review was abandoned by politicians in April 2010. Jim Rose was asked by the Secretary of State for Education to conduct a thorough review of the primary curriculum but a careful reading of his original letter included a clear steer from the government. In contrast, the Alexander Review was totally independent of government. It is another case of top-down policy-making in education. It is interesting to note that primary teachers had been asking for significant changes but the government had to be seen to be in control by actually setting up the Review. In this sense, students of the history of education in the future will have two interesting reports to analyse along with the impacts they will have on education. The aim of this section is to analyse the *Final Report* (DCSF, 2009) from the perspective of what it might tell us about government education policy, both explicitly and implicitly, as a recent case study of government policy thinking.

The letter accompanying the Report sent by Rose to the Secretary of State is a fascinating place to begin. His brief was to review the primary curriculum but not national assessment procedures, not financing of education, not the environments in which children and teachers actually work. In this sense it demonstrates how policy-makers either do not or will not understand or admit that one aspect of the educational system cannot be radically reworked without an acceptance that other parts of the system also have to change. Rose states (DCSF, 2009: 4) 'The review is about the curriculum rather than the whole of primary education'. It does not acknowledge that unless the current national testing arrangements are changed, then many head teachers will be reluctant to adapt the curriculum in ways which may accept their school results and position in the league tables. He escapes the issue by agreeing that assessment does 'intersect with the curriculum' (DCSF, 2009:4). Rather than merely intersect, it might be considered to be central to the curriculum today. The language in his letter is amazing in places. He says:

> The remit of the review is to tackle several stubborn obstacles in the way of securing the best curriculum for primary children. One such obstacle is that there is too much prescribed content on the current curriculum.
>
> (DCSF, 2009: 4)

It is almost suggesting that the curriculum itself is being stubborn, rather than admitting government policies of the last 20 years have been the main cause of curriculum overload. What does the main body of the Report tell us about policy?

Throughout the Report the language used suggests that much professional and informed judgement has been used in deciding the content. Indeed, a wide range of people and organizations were offered an opportunity to respond and some organizations were represented on the Editorial Expert Group. But the language fails to acknowledge that at the end of the day the report represents a policy whereby central government still controls the key elements of the curriculum.

> Difficult decisions had to be taken by this review about what constitutes the **essential** knowledge, skills and understanding that all children ages 5–11 should be taught as part of a national entitlement, as opposed to what is **desirable**.
>
> (DCSF, 2009: 14, author's emphasis)

The essential knowledge is still decided and controlled by central policy. Indeed, the ability to decide on what is essential and what is desirable seems to lay with government-appointed reviewers and report writers. In addition, it also infers from the Report writers know what will be essential in the future.

As educationists, we are all quite aware of the way in which subjects are given status by the order in which they are listed in documents, in the amount of space and where they are allocated in the school timetable, the subject budgets and how they may be perceived by the wider community. The Review continues this tradition. On page 17 (DCSF, 2009) the six recommended areas of learning are listed beginning with English and ending with the arts. There is no reason why at this point in the Report the six areas could not have been listed alphabetically, but instead the writers have used every opportunity throughout the Report to reinforce the perceived hierarchy of importance of the six areas. What was once applied to the hierarchical listing of traditional subjects has been transferred to the new six areas of learning: it is a clear statement of policy decisions and preferences.

Since 1988 primary education has been dominated by a target and goals-driven policy informed by an intensive range of centrally imposed assessment strategies. Little appears to have changed when you read on page 18 that

> The existing National Curriculum level descriptors have been reviewed to make sure they are in step with the progress expected of primary children of all abilities.
>
> (DCSF, 2009: 18)

Surely, one would have hoped they were written with the above in mind in the first place. If not, then teachers may have been using a very insecure assessment tool for many years. The more fundamental point is that a tool from a previous policy is being slightly adapted to inform a new curriculum which perhaps deserves a new way of looking at progression and assessment based more on the current needs of community rather than the results and shaming culture of the late 1980s.

A further example of the continued assumption that education professions need constant guidance from a central source comes on page 19 where it is stated that the DCSF (2009) and Qualifications and Curriculum Authority (QCA) will offer comprehensive packages because it patronizingly says schools will need a 'significant amount of support to aid planning' (DCSF, 2009: 19). This is in stark contrast to the authors' own subject association who are offering support based on the perceived needs of teachers at local level and working alongside them in the development of new and relevant resources. Between pages 22–24 there are nine statements suggesting that central organizations such as QCA, DCSF and British Educational Communications and Technology Agency (BECTA) should provide teachers with support and guidance on how to implement the new curriculum. It appears that once again professionals' own experience, ability, enthusiasm and judgement will be swamped with more centrally offered advice.

A final point regarding policy in relation to the Review relates to issues discussed in Chapter 9 where we considered the deeper debates surrounding how individuals and communities understand the concept of a nation and ways in which they belong. These underlying issues are passed over with little regard when it is stated that the review envisages:

> . . . the curriculum as a construct derived from what we as a nation value most highly for our children. For the purposes of this review, therefore, the curriculum is taken to mean that which our society deems to be the worthwhile knowledge, skills and understanding that primary-aged children should gain at school.
>
> (DCSF, 2009: 28)

If the writers genuinely believe they have managed to do that, it is indeed an amazing achievement. We end this chapter with a selection of impact tasks related to the above DCSF statement.

Impact tasks

Early career professional:
What examples have you experienced either in your own education or in teaching that have made you question the ability of a curriculum to be a representative reflection of what a nation actually thinks is worth learning? What may have been the underlying tensions of policy that created this situation?

Later year professional:
Thinking about the children you currently teach, what needs do they have which cannot alone be reflected in and met through a state-articulated curriculum? What strategies have you found effective in managing this situation?

Professional leader:
Rank the pressures and demands placed on you by external factors that influence your decisions regarding the curriculum you are prepared to accept responsibility for in your organization? What ideas and issues discussed in this chapter may support you in rethinking the curriculum as something that evolves for the pupils rather than reflecting central policy decisions in education?

Conclusion

State policy has influenced education since the early nineteenth century. It is based on a fundamental belief that what and how people learn should in some way be decided and monitored by someone or some organization other than themselves. As we move well into the twenty-first century, it may be worth asking whether this is a model of education that is both appropriate for the social, cultural, economic and moral needs of individuals and to what extent it will prepare learners who are growing up in an ever more complex and uncertain world.

References

Ball, S. (2007) Big policies/small world, in B. Lingard and J. Osga (eds) *The Routledge Falmer Reader in Education Policy and Politics*. London: Routledge Falmer.

Bell, L. (2007) *Perspectives on Educational Management and Leadership*. London: Continuum.

Boyle, E. (1963) *The Newsom Report*. London: Her Majesty's Stationery Office (HMSO).

Callaghan, J. (1976) Towards a national debate: text of the Prime Minister's Ruskin speech, *Education*, 22 October, pp. 332–3.

Darzi, A. and Kibasi, T. (2009) In defence of Britain's health system, *The Washington Post*, Monday 17 August.

Department for Children, Schools and Families (DCSF) (2009) *Independent Review of the Primary Curriculum: Final Report*. Nottingham: DCSF.

Her Majesty's Stationery Office (HMSO) (1967) *Children and their Primary Schools*. London: HMSO.

Locke, J. (1693) *Some Thoughts Concerning Education*.

McGuinn, N. (2002) Response to 'Policy, Practice and Principles', in I. Davies, I. Gregory and N. McGuinn (eds) *Key Debates in Education*. London: Continuum.

O'Neill, O. (2002) *A Question of Trust* (The BBC Reith Lectures). Cambridge: Cambridge University Press.

Whitty, G. (2002) *Making Sense of Education Policy*. London: Sage Publications.

14 The curriculum

A new government is now in power (June, 2010). Rather than attempt to predict the future developments in curriculum, this chapter first reflects on an earlier major curriculum development project, the Plowden Report (HMSO, 1967), through the chosen reading below. This will be related to broad current issues surrounding the primary curriculum. We then discuss six key terms in curriculum discourse as identified by Alexander (2010) as a possible framework for your own discussions on curriculum development within your own specific educational context.

The reading from the Plowden Report (HMSO, 1967) has been chosen because of the fascinating insights it offers us into what was officially considered effective primary curriculum practice in the late 1960s. Unless you trained to teach at the same time as the author (John Halocha) in the early 1970s, you may well be unfamiliar with the Report. However, it had an immense impact on practice in primary education until the introduction of the national curriculum in 1988. As you read it, consider how much practice has changed with all the government directives of the last 20 years.

> **❝ The Time table**
>
> 536. These beliefs about how children learn have practical implications for the time table and the curriculum. One idea now widespread is embodied in the expression 'free day' and another, associated with it, is the 'integrated curriculum'. The strongest influence making for the free day has been the conviction of some teachers and other educationalists that it is through play that young children learn. Nursery schools began by devoting half an hour to free play. This is still done by many kindergartens which we visited abroad. Now the whole day is spent on various forms of play, though groups of children may break away to enjoy stories or music with an adult. Infant schools usually give at least an hour a day to play, though it may be called by many different names. If teachers encourage overlap between what is done in periods of self chosen activity

and in the times allocated, for example, to reading and to writing, a good learning situation will probably result. Children who are not yet ready to read can go on playing and building up vocabulary while other children are reading. Play can lead naturally to reading and writing associated with it. Children do not flit from activity to activity in their anxiety to make use of materials not available at other times of the day. Some infant schools are now confident enough in the value of self chosen activity to give the whole day to it, except for times which are used for stories, poetry, movement, and music – and even these may be voluntary, particularly for the younger children. The tendency is spreading in junior schools. Children may plan when to do work assigned to them and also have time in which to follow personal or group interests of their own choice. In a few infant and junior schools the day is still divided into a succession of short periods. In the great majority, we are glad to say, there are longer periods and these can be adjusted at the teacher's discretion.

537. These changes represent a revolution from the type of time table implied by the forms completed by schools for local education authorities until quite recently. Heads were expected to show exactly what each class was doing during every minute of the week and to provide a summary showing the total number of minutes to be spent on each subject. In extreme cases, the curriculum was divided into spelling, dictation, grammar, exercises, composition, recitation, reading, handwriting, tables and mental arithmetic. It is obvious that this arrangement was not suited to what was known of the nature of children, of the classification of subject matter, or of the art of teaching. Children's interest varies in length according to personality, age and circumstances, and it is folly either to interrupt it when it is intense, or to flog it when it has declined. The teacher can best judge when to make a change and the moment of change may not be the same for each child in the class. In many schools, as we have said, children plan much of their work. Yet the teacher must constantly ensure a balance within the day or week both for the class and for individuals. He must see that time is profitably spent and give guidance on its use. In the last resort, the teacher's relationship with his pupils, his openness to their suggestions and their trust in him are far more important than the nominal degree of freedom in the time table.

Flexibility in the Curriculum
538. The extent to which subject matter ought to be classified and the headings under which the classification is made will vary with the age of the children, with the demands made by the structure of the subject matter which is being studied, and with the circumstances of the school.

Any practice which predetermines the pattern and imposes it upon all is to be condemned. Some teachers find it helpful in maintaining a balance in individual and class work to think in terms of broad areas of the curriculum such as language, science and mathematics, environmental study and the expressive arts. No pattern can be perfect since many subjects fall into one category or another according to the aspect which is being studied. For young children, the broadest of divisions is suitable. For children from 9 to 12, more subject divisions can be expected, though experience in secondary schools has shown that teaching of rigidly defined subjects, often by specialist teachers, is far from suitable for the oldest children who will be in the middle schools. This is one of our reasons for suggesting a change in the age of transfer to secondary education.

539. There is little place for the type of scheme which sets down exactly what ground should be covered and what skill should be acquired by each class in the school. Yet to put nothing in its place may be to leave some teachers prisoners of tradition and to make difficulties for newcomers to a staff who are left to pick up, little by little, the ethos of a school. The best solution seems to be to provide brief schemes for the school as a whole: outlines of aims in various areas of the curriculum, the sequence of development which can be expected in children and the methods through which work can be soundly based and progress accelerated. It is also useful to have a record of experiences, topics, books, poems and music which have been found to succeed with children of different ages, and for attention to be drawn to notable experimental work. In good schools, schemes are often subject to a process of accretion which may make them so long that few teachers have time to read them. It is better for them to be sifted and revised, for matter to be dropped as well as added. Individual members of staff, with such help as the head and others can give, will need to plan in more detail the work of their particular classes. Often it will develop in an unexpected direction. A brief report on the topics, literature and so forth which have absorbed children during the course of the year will be necessary for teachers who take them later in their school career.

540. The idea of flexibility has found expression in a number of practices, all of them designed to make good use of the interest and curiosity of children, to minimise the notion of subject matter being rigidly compartmental, and to allow the teacher to adopt a consultative, guiding, stimulating role rather than a purely didactic one. The oldest of these methods is the 'project'. Some topic, such as 'transport' is chosen, ideally by the children, but frequently by the teacher. The topic cuts across the boundaries of subjects and is treated as its nature requires without reference to subjects as such. At its best the method leads to the use of

books of reference, to individual work and to active participation in learning. Unfortunately it is no guarantee of this and the appearance of text books of projects, which achieved at one time considerable popularity, is proof of how completely a good idea can be misunderstood.

541. A variation on the project, originally associated with the infant school but often better suited to older children, is 'the centre of interest'. It begins with a topic which is of such inherent interest and variety as to make it possible and reasonable to make much of the work of the class revolve round it for a period of a week, a month or a term or even longer. Experience has shown that it is artificial to try to link most of the work of a class to one centre of interest. It has become more common to have several interests – topic is now the usual word – going at once. Much of the work may be individual, falling under broad subject headings. One topic for the time being can involve both group and class interest, and may splinter off into all kinds of individual work.

542. When a class of seven year olds notice the birds that come to the bird table outside the classroom window, they may decide, after discussion with their teacher, to make their own aviary. They will set to with a will, and paint the birds in flight, make models of them in clay or papier mâché, write stories and poems about them and look up reference books to find out more about their habits. Children are not assimilating inert ideas but are wholly involved in thinking, feeling and doing. The slow and the bright share a common experience and each takes from it what he can at his own level. There is no attempt to put reading and writing into separate compartments; both serve a wider purpose, and artificial barriers do not fragment the learning experience. A top junior class became interested in the problem of measuring the area of an awkwardly shaped field at the back of the school. The problem stimulated much learning about surveying and triangles. From surveying, interest passed to navigation; for the more difficult aspects of the work, co-operation between members of staff as well as pupils was needed. For one boy, the work on navigation took the form of a story of encounters of pirate ships and men-of-war, and involved a great deal of calculation, history, geography and English. Integration is not only a question of allowing time for interests which do not fit under subject headings; it is as much a matter of seeing the different dimensions of subject work and of using the forms of observation and communication which are most suitable to a given sequence of learning. 99

(HMSO, 1967: 197–9)

Many issues are raised that are still very pertinent today. The first is what the notion of a timetable was. In the decades leading up to the 1960s there had been monitoring of how long was spent teaching various subjects. However, by the 1960s the prevailing focus was on the child as a learner rather than the content and structure of a curriculum imposed on the child from outside. The impression given in the reading is one of the child being at the centre of the learning process and the sensitive teacher being there to guide and support them, while at the same time ensuring they had a balance of experiences. Another interesting point is the notion of a timetable. Instead of it being seen as fixed blocks of time for specific subjects, one gets a sense of the school day/week/year being a flexible opportunity to arrange for children to have appropriate blocks of time for various parts of their learning. This can sound ideal, but what happened in practice in the 1970s and 1980s was that, while it was carefully adopted in many schools, with effective broad planning, assessment and record-keeping, in others it led to a random range of experiences which with minimal progression and sometimes limited challenge, even though the Report itself stated 'the teacher must constantly ensure a balance within the day or week' (HMSO, 1967: 198). Her Majesty's Inspectorate (HMI) identified some of these pitfalls from the mid-1980s and this led to various publications such as the 1989 publication on the teaching and learning of history and geography (HMI, 1989).

Plowden also raises the ever-present issue of the extent specific subjects should be identified within the curriculum and timetable or whether terms such as 'topics' or 'centres of interest' are more appropriate, following the notion that the real world is not made up of water-tight compartments of knowledge, skill and understanding that academic subjects can suggest. Plowden argues that broad schemes should be brief enough to provide a structure into which the teacher and pupils can build the detail of learning experiences. This is very different to the 1,024 specific objectives of the 1997 literacy strategy. The reading concludes with the notion that integration allows aspects of subjects to be selected and studied together in order to better understand the aspect of learning taking place at any one time. Time has been taken to tease out these messages from Plowden because many readers work in an educational context where such ideas on the curriculum process, content and structure are currently very different.

Reflection

EYFS:
- What are the advantages and disadvantages of young people beginning their learning at ever younger ages?
- Based on your personal experience, in what ways would you like to see the current design of the EYFS adapted to improve learning for our youngest children?

KS1:
- To what extent is your planning joining, where appropriate, subjects from across the curriculum?
- Is citizenship a separate subject or a way of life in your school?

KS2:
- By the time pupils leave primary school, to what extent do you think they understand how specific subjects such as geography actually contribute to their learning?
- How far do formal tests results affect the way in which your school's curriculum is organized and taught?

While Plowden gives us a window into primary education in the later part of the twentieth century, the *Cambridge Primary Review* (Alexander, 2010) used a huge amount of research data to build a picture of the current state of primary education in the first decade of the twenty-first century. Based on a critical analysis of this data within the political, cultural and social context of England, it also proposes a new primary curriculum which 'addresses and seeks to resolve the problems of present and past arrangements' (Alexander, 2010: 275). This review contains a tremendous amount of detailed discussion and analysis of curriculum issues. Alexander states:

> It is essential to get the structure, balance and content of the primary curriculum right. It is no less essential to ensure that schools have the time and expertise to ensure that it is coherently planned and well taught. Neither of these things will happen until we sort out three essential terms in curriculum discourse. These terms are *subjects, knowledge* and *skill*. To these . . . we add the contingent terms *discipline, curriculum* and *timetable*.
>
> (Alexander, 2010: 245)

Issues surrounding these six terms are now discussed in order to offer a possible framework for you to think about curriculum design in your own educational context.

Impact task

The task below may be undertaken by early career professionals, later year professional and professional leaders. Ideally, a comparison and sharing of the ideas you note down might form a starting point to curriculum development activities within your organization.

Divide a large piece of paper into six equal sections and write one of the following words in each box: subjects, knowledge, skill, discipline, curriculum, timetable. Write down your definition of each word in terms of curriculum. In the next section, we discuss some of the issues surrounding these words using ideas from the Alexander Review as starting points.

Subjects

To many readers the word 'subject' will be closely linked with a national curriculum interpretation and presentation of what it is. This has been the prevalent educational world since 1988. Alexander (2010: 206–13) provides a useful range of tables to show the subject content of past and present curricula in England. The Rose Review has grouped these subjects into areas of learning. Some people argue that this will weaken children's understanding of what they are learning because they may not have clear labels. There are also subject supporters who simply want to ensure the subject does not disappear from public conscientiousness. The author can understand this point, being a strong champion of geography at all levels of learning. However, he would also argue that real geographical understanding cannot happen in isolation from other subjects. For example, we need mathematical ability in order to read map scales, grid references and the data contained within them. Two key issues may be raised: the first is the extent to which educators have a clear knowledge and understanding of each of the subjects they are teaching, or at the very least, access to colleagues who can support them in this. The second is an awareness that if subjects are subsumed into areas of learning, the identity of the specific knowledge, skill and understanding contained in them are used in planning a broad and balanced curriculum.

Again, taking an example from geography, if children do experience a wide range of geographical activities in primary school, but do not have the opportunity to consider the moral dimensions of geographical understanding, they have only experienced a part of what it is to have geographical understanding. An example of moral geographical understanding could be critically thinking about how we share the resources we have in the world and why we do what we do. This could easily be planned into science work on water, where a clear geographical issue might also be explored in a meaningful way. We do need to consider this visibility of subjects if we are to move into a curriculum planning world where areas of learning are the main building blocks: the author has experience of examples from the German system of primary education where what geography exists is subsumed within their area of learning called 'social studies', depending which region of Germany you are looking at. In many instances their teachers say that in reality this means that pupils experience very little geography in the primary years. This issue of pupil's overall experience of subjects goes beyond primary education. Many of them will not study geography after the age of 14 under current structures at KS3 and KS4. This therefore places an even greater need to ensure that a broad and balanced range of geographical learning takes place in the Early Years Foundation Stage (EYFS) and primary years.

Knowledge

Reflective curriculum development needs a careful review and analysis of what we think knowledge is. It may be helpful to consider possible definitions of knowledge on a continuum. At one end it is facts of whatever type make up the subject or area of learning under consideration. In English we know what a verb is. In history we know the Second World War began in 1939. We can then begin the move along this continuum by interpreting knowledge in more complex ways. Part-way along, we can know how to use verbs in various types of writing in which we are involved, perhaps using information and communication technology (ICT) to support writing knowledge. Also, in history we can know which countries were involved in the Second World War in 1939 and where they are located, thus joining knowledge of other subjects. Towards the other end of the continuum, we might know how to analyse and discuss various forms of literature and writing where our basic knowledge of what a verb is takes us into much more complex understandings of the writing and reading process. Likewise in history at this end of the continuum, we know how to access sources of historical data and interpret them in a variety of ways: we will know that different nations had very different interpretations of how and why the Second World War began. All this is knowledge, but at very different levels of complexity.

This brief discussion of knowledge also needs to be placed within our current and future social, cultural and technological contexts. A case can be made that with new and rapidly changing forms of technology, we do not really need much knowledge, as long as we know how to access it, but is this really helping pupils to develop as full and rounded human beings? The author knows how to find information in atlases and on Google Earth, but he also has an ever-growing mental map of the world at a range of scales which he carries in his head (knowledge) in order to survive and adapt. That will still be there when the atlas is left at home or the Sat Nav has broken down. Finally, it may also be worth considering some of the hidden curriculum messages which are transmitted to pupils in terms of what knowledge actually is. About half of a child's time at school will be spent on English and mathematics. All the other subjects have to be covered in the remaining time, yet each one of them has a huge subject discipline behind them where knowledge and ideas are constantly growing and changing. Are we actually being fair to our pupils to present such a distorted view of the field of human understanding and, indeed, is there an issue of equality of opportunity here in that maybe we do not sufficiently provide them with experiences that may one day encourage them to explore a subject in much more depth?

Skills

Alexander (2010: 249) cites a number of government and other organizations which have come up with various lists of skills they believe children should acquire through the curriculum in schools. For example, the Rose Review lists four new core 'skills for learning and life – literacy, numeracy, ICT and personal development'. The reader is left to reflect on this range of essential skills Qualifications and Curriculum Authority (QCA) is promoting. But what do we really mean by a skill because so often they are included in curriculum planning materials? *The Oxford English Dictionary* defines a skill as the 'ability to do something (especially manual or physical) well; proficiency, expertness, dexterity . . . acquired through practice and learning'.

Subject task

EYFS:
Think back over some recent professional activities you have been engaged in with young children. List the skills they have developed to a high level for their own age and ability. How have these been expressed in curriculum terms?

KS1:
Think back over some recent professional activities you have been engaged in with KS1 children. List a range of skills that you have planned for them to acquire but which they have found particularly challenging. Why do you think this was and how might you reconsider future teaching and learning strategies?

KS2:
Locate a current curriculum document you use with your pupils. Identify a range of skills which are included to be taught or further developed. List any other skills you think should be added or removed in any future development of your KS2 curriculum?

It is easy to be prepossessed by the numerous lists of skills that can be found in official documents relating to the primary curriculum: very often these are addressing particular agendas that various organizations wish to place on the curriculum. However, Hargreaves (2004) offers a list not generated from a subject-based foundation, which may be used in your discussions of what skills are actually important to develop in the primary phase of education:

- managing one's own learning
- problem-solving
- thinking
- research, enquiry and investigation
- invention, enterprise and entrepeneurship
- communication
- social and interpersonal skills
- teamwork
- leadership.

This may offer a possible way forward in the curriculum planning process. Let us take an example from KS2 geography. The road outside the school is getting increasingly blocked with cars dropping off and collecting pupils at the start and end of the day. What can be done about this to create a safer and more environmentally favourable approach? There is no textbook answer here so it can easily involve pupils managing their own learning. There is a problem to be solved. It will require research, enquiry and investigation: why are cars used so much? How far away are they coming from? How can the environmental impact be measured using data from the website on petrol pollution? Communication skill will be used to collect this data and then to present findings to a variety of audiences. This is a sensitive question because they will be challenging activities and beliefs held by the parents using cars, so social and interpersonal skill will be developed. There are many lines of enquiry to follow, so these can be taken up by different teams of pupils who will have to co-ordinate their work. Leadership skill will be developed in teams if real progress is to be made. In addition, of course, a wide range of subject specific geographical knowledge, skills and understanding will be developed. Hopefully, this example will help you develop curriculum discussions with colleagues where greater clarity and understanding of what we really mean by 'skills' can be applied in your educational context.

Discipline

The term 'discipline' is included in this discussion of the curriculum as it is a term not often considered in primary education, at least not in its pedagogical meaning as against maintaining control! The term is used to describe

> a branch of knowledge as systematised into distinct ways of en-
> quiring, knowing, exploring, explaining, creating and making sense,
> each with their own key foci, preoccupations, concepts, procedures
> and products.
>
> (Alexander, 2010: 251)

So, for example, if you read the literature or visit the website of the Royal Geographical Society, you will often see the word 'discipline' referred to when talking about geography because they firmly believe that the subject has a particular way of developing our understanding of the world, as distinct from others such as science or mathematics. This is quite a helpful way of thinking about subjects in that it may clarify the actual learning experiences you provide for pupils within any subject area. This is also related to developing your own knowledge and understanding of what is particular to any subject and therefore being clear about what you hope children may learn.

The final two words are discussed because they are sometimes interchanged and not understood as two quite separate concepts.

Curriculum

Alexander helpfully teases out the curriculum process into three strands: 'what is intended to be taught and learned overall (the planned curriculum); what is taught (the curriculum as enacted); what is learned (the curriculum as experienced)' (2010: 250). If you have not considered the curriculum in these terms before, they may be an additional tool to aid your discussions with colleagues in future development activities you undertake. The author has also found it helpful to engage pupils in this form of discussion as perceptions about the three strands may not always match between learners and teachers. It is also perhaps useful to come back to these three basic strands in your future discussions because so much debate about the curriculum in recent decades has become extremely complicated and confusing. Indeed, many still are; for example, the tension between the statutory national curriculum require-ments for English and mathematics and the non-statutory strategies for literacy and numeracy.

One of the possible reasons for less effective curriculum planning in recent years may well have been the overwhelming of teachers with so many often conflicting messages about what a curriculum is and how it works. Alexander helps to keep it in perspective. The other idea he keeps returning to in his report is the notion that a curriculum should be both local and national. Ideally, he would like to see a national curriculum that actively encouraged educators to take the national frameworks and, where appropriate, build in a local perspective. Some schools do this already, but maybe there is much more scope for this type of curriculum planning to be developed, even if teachers are handed yet another version of a top-down national curriculum. It would also be a very effective way of ensuring local and community perspectives have a much stronger presence in the curriculum. This local/national (and indeed global) way of thinking about a curriculum can be adopted into any national framework without being illegal or increasing the actual content of the curriculum. The key is clever planning and some schools have always been good at this. The key to clever planning is to think creatively about what subjects/areas of learning can be planned together in meaningful and interesting ways and not necessarily stick with the official document's ways of presenting learning. Rowley and Cooper offer some excellent examples and up-to-date case studies of primary schools who are adopting this form of curriculum planning. They argue that in their approach they:

> . . . deliberately avoid the rather sterile and polarized debate about 'topic' and 'themes', and instead search for examples of robust links between subjects; links which take account of the discrete thinking processes at the heart of different subjects and relate them through children's experiences.
>
> (Rowley and Cooper, 2009: 2)

The case studies they provide offer real examples where everyone involved in the education process can make a contribution to the notion of curriculum.

Timetable

This is not the curriculum but the temporal space in which learning can take place. It is mentioned here because the developments of the last 20 years have created a situation where the curriculum has come to govern the structure of the timetable, especially with literacy and numeracy having excessive control, being at its worst when we had the literacy clocks where time was more important than children. It may now be time to ask some basic questions about the way in which the curriculum is timetabled. The following are provided in order to begin debate within your own educational setting:

- Why do we place certain subjects and areas of learning where we do? Are there still good reasons for this or is it now time to rethink?
- How long do various blocks of timetabling actually need to be for specific activities?
- How do whole-school factors constrain how we use time and can they be justified?
- How much flexibility should we have to ditch programmed aspects of our timetable if this will improve learning?
- How predictable should our timetables be? Children need security but does predictability sometimes kill interest?
- How long should blocked aspects of our timetables be? For example, why do most schools plan units of work around half-term blocks when in fact the content may need less or more time?
- To what extent should children be engaged in managing the time they spend on activities?
- What opportunities does our school context provide that we do not as yet capitalize on? An example here would be a small rural school. In large primary schools, some organizational factors can limit the flexibility of timetabling; for example, the need to share an ICT suite between all classes. In small schools, there is potentially more scope for flexibility.
- Finally, who actually controls the timetable and why?

Conclusion

In the world of geography education we spend quite some time discussing the notion of curriculum-making. One reason for this is perhaps the potential of our discipline, which has many opportunities to bring the real world into the curriculum. But equally, any subject has the potential to bring the real world into it. The basic objectives for geographical learning may be well mapped out in terms of knowledge, skills and understanding. But the fascination and opportunity provided by geography is that the enquiries pupils may become engaged in can be topical and regularly changing. These can be identified by both pupils and the adults with whom they work. It leads to a curriculum where all those involved feel they have ownership. The research and learning are up to date and relevant. Curriculum-making enables a wide range of resources to be used to conduct enquiry, analyse findings and present them in a variety of ways. In turn, it means that the curriculum is constantly evolving. This is neatly summed up by Lambert (2009: 4):

> What the primary curriculum requires is a continual act of creation and renewal (what we call 'curriculum making') and teachers

need to do this using the key subject resources they have at their disposal.

All disciplines are constantly changing and it therefore brings the real world of human learning into the experiences of our pupils. If we think of science our understanding of what is sometimes called climate change is constantly evolving and we gain new knowledge and understanding of the global processes at work. Part of the excitement of being engaged in that research is the excitement of understanding the world in new ways. Indeed, one of the strengths of all disciplines is that they are constantly challenging current understanding and searching for new ideas. Perhaps if we were to develop this culture in primary education, we could create a much more dynamic and meaningful curriculum.

References

Alexander, R. (ed.) (2010) *Children, their World, their Education: Final Report and Recommendations of the Cambridge Primary Review*. London: Routledge.

Department for Children, Schools and Families (DCSF) (2009) *Independent Review of the Primary Curriculum: Final Report*. Nottingham: DCSF.

Hargreaves, D. (2004) *Learning for Life: The Foundations for Lifelong Learning*. Bristol: Policy Press.

Her Majesty's Inspectorate (HMI) (1989) *The Teaching and Learning of History and Geography*. London: Her Majesty's Stationery Office (HMSO).

Her Majesty's Stationery Office (HMSO) (1967) *Children and their Primary Schools*. London: HMSO.

Lambert, D. (2009) *The world in the primary school*. Paper presented at the Institute of Education, University of London.

Rowley, C. and Cooper, H. (eds) (2009) *Cross-curricular Approaches to Teaching and Learning*. London: Sage Publications.

15 Creativity

The idea that creativity is an important part of the educational process is of course not at all new. However, it is one of those concepts which can be complex to identify and explain. This is not meant necessarily from the point of assessing creativity as so much of our current 'educational' activity is obsessed with. It is more to do with having a professional understanding of what we mean by the word. We begin with a reading written in the middle of the twentieth century: not that long ago in the greater scheme of things but the language itself is fascinating. It has been chosen as a form of educational writing as its style is so different to the often functional and matter-of-fact styles we use today, whether in textbooks or government documents, but makes some comments very relevant to today's discussions on creativity.

> **1. MARTIN BUBER ON THE CONCEPT OF CREATIVITY**
> On the subject of teaching, the little that I can say is based on external observation and refection rather than on practical experience. Nor is this little that I have to say in any degree original: it has all been said with subtlety and profundity by a great modem philosopher who, at an international conference held at Heidelberg in the year 1925 to consider 'the unfolding of creative powers in the child', spoke on this very subject. As his lecture seems to be quite unknown to educationalists in this country, I shall give some account of its general argument and then emphasize the particular aspect which I find so relevant to the problem we have been discussing.
>
> Buber begins by examining the concept of 'creativity' on which, as he says modern educators rely so much. He shows that it was only fairly late in history that this concept, formerly reserved for the divine action of calling the universe into being, was metaphorically transferred to human activities, more especially to works of genius in the sphere of art. It was then recognized that this tendency to create, which reaches its highest manifestation in men of genius, was present, in however slight a degree,

in all human beings. There exists in all men a distinct impulse to make things, an instinct which cannot be explained by theories of libido or will to power, but is disinterestedly experimental. Buber gives as an example of the manifestation of this instinct, the manner in which an infant will attempt to utter words, not as given things, which he has to imitate, but as original things to be attempted for the first time – 'sound-image after sound-image breaks forth, emerges from vibrating throat, from trembling lips, into the surrounding air, the whole of the little vital body vibrating and trembling, shaking with a paroxysm of outbreaking selfhood.' Obviously such an instinct to originate must be taken into account in the process of education, but Buber points out that it is not the free exercise of the instinct that matters, but the opposition it encounters. Here Buber gives the reader a foretaste of his characteristic mysticism. If, he says, the originating instinct operated in a passive world, it would create things which would then become merely external, objective. Under such circumstances it is a force which goes out from the centre of the person and into the object made, and there it peters out. But nothing comes in – and hence the ironic myth of Pygmalion. Man as creator is a lonely figure. Even if his creations are appreciated by other men, he remains isolated. 'It is only when someone takes him by the hand, not as a "creator", but as a fellow-creature lost in the world, and greets him not as an artist but as comrade, friend or lover, that he experiences an inner reciprocity. A system of education built up solely on the instinct to originate would bring about a new and the most painful isolation of men.' A child learns much from the making of things which he cannot learn in any other way, but there is something he cannot learn in this way, and it is the essential thing in life. He can gain an objective sense of the world from his own creative activity, but what he cannot acquire in this way is a subjective sense. That can only come from a mutual relationship, established by what Buber calls the instinct for communion (Verbundenheit) – an instinct which again owes nothing to the libido or will to power, which is not a desire to enjoy or dominate another person, but which is at one and the same time a giving and a receiving. 'The child, who, lying with half-closed eyes, waits anxiously for his mother to speak to him – his longing springs from something other than the desire for the enjoyment or domination of a human being, and it is also something other than a desire to do something on his own; in face of the lonely night, which spreads beyond the window and threatens to break in, it is the desire to experience communion.'

2. THE PUMP AND THE FUNNEL
Buber fully admits that the liberation of creative powers in the child is a precondition of education, but distinguishes between a specific impulse to originate and a more general spontaneity. All educators recognize the

necessity of not repressing spontaneity, but they leave the child beating his wings in the void. Buber then takes as an example the very subject with which we have been most concerned in this book. In a drawing lesson a teacher using the old method of 'constraint', begins with pre-scripts and approved models which lay down what is unquestionably beautiful, and all he has to do afterwards is to decide how nearly his pupils have approximated to these standards. But the teacher in a 'free' school places, say, a spray of broom in a jug on the table and lets his pupils copy it; or he might first place it on the table, ask them to look at it, and then take it away and ask them to draw it from memory. In either case, the results for each pupil would be quite different. But now comes the delicate, almost unperceived, but all-important stage: criticism and instruction. The child comes up against a definite, if un-academic, scale of values: against a more particularizing, but still clear-cut, knowledge of good and bad. The more un-academic, the more particularizing, this scale or knowledge may be, the more vivid it appears to the child. In the old days, a declaration of legitimacy found the child either resigned or rebellious; now, however, the child himself has already ventured far with the work before he is enlightened by the teacher. By his own experience plus the enlightenment he subsequently receives, he is truly educated and made reverently aware of the nature of the object.

This almost unobserved encounter, this utmost delicacy of approach – perhaps the raising of a finger, a questioning look – is one half of the educational activity. But these modern theories of education which emphasize freedom do not see the importance of the teacher's function, whilst those which are based on the principle of authority neglect the importance of the other half (the child's experimental activity). The symbol of the funnel has merely been exchanged for that of the pump.

The dispositions which, if it were possible to analyse them, one would find in the soul of a new-born infant, are nothing but aptitudes to receive and conceive the outer world. The world engenders the person in the individual. Thus the world – the whole environment, nature and society – 'educates' man: it draws out his powers, allows him to respond to and be convinced by the world. What we call education, conscious and willed, means the selection of a feasible by the individual – means to give the directing force to a selection of the world made under the guidance of the teacher.   **99**

Source: Read, H. (1958) *Education through Art*. London: Faber & Faber, pp. 285–7

We would like to draw out four ideas from this reading. The first is the notion of children, indeed human beings in general, becoming engaged in the process of giving and receiving. This is described in a very human way; for example, the child hoping to hear a mother's voice in the dark. It is an interesting way of beginning to think about creativity in the sense that when we create something it often has most value when it is shared with another human. Of course there may also be times when the sheer act of personal creation is sufficient in itself for the creator. What we are thinking about is the opportunities we provide in educational settings for this sharing process to occur between all participants in the setting. The second idea is the vision of a child 'beating his wings in the void'. The author is rather drawn to this vision because of the hundreds of hours he has spent observing students in the primary classroom. Observing children is of course a central part of this work and the number of wings beating in the void must run into hundreds. By this we mean all those things that we have been privileged to see but which are missed by the student teacher or teacher. Wonderful opportunities for creativity are lost simply because the adults have so many responsibilities in modern learning environments. Children have the ideas but rarely the chance to share and develop them through human interaction. The third is the well-rehearsed discussion on the extent to which teachers tightly control what pupils do against giving them freedom to develop their own ideas. Finally, the reading ends with a consideration of the way in which human beings interact with their world and how they develop their personal understanding of a feasible world in which to live.

Reflection

EYFS:
- How might your analysis of this reading move forward your own ideas about what creativity might be?
- Do you think children become more or less creative as they get older?

KS1:
- What parts of your teaching do you think are especially effective at encouraging pupils to develop their creativity?
- Try to find time to ask your pupils what they think creativity might be and reflect on their thoughts.

KS2:
- Do some areas of learning offer more scope than others to promote creativity? Why?
- By the time pupils leave your school are they more or less willing to take risks in order to be creative?

In this chapter we would like to explore some of the factors deep in the education system that may encourage or hinder children's ability to be creative. There are already many excellent texts on looking at creativity through various subjects (Wilson, 2009); (Fisher and Williams, 2004). However, one writer, Sir Ken Robinson (2001), asks us to examine some of the underlying factors of psychology and human social activity that may encourage creativity. The bulk of this chapter examines some of his ideas and place them within an educational context.

How can we spot creativity?

Impact task

Early career professional:
- What is the most creative thing you have ever done?
- Why do you think it was creative?
- Would other people agree with you?
- What impact may it have had on how you have behaved in the future?

Later year professional:
Thinking back over your career:

- What are the most outstanding examples that you can recall of children being creative?
- What makes you see them as creative?
- To what extent to do think the children were aware of their creativity?

Professional leader:
Think back over your career in education:

- What parts of the learning environment hindered you in encouraging children to develop their creativity?
- How might you ensure that you help to provide a learning environment in which colleagues could encourage more creativity?

Now that you have had a chance to focus more on what creativity may be, consider the extent to which you agree with Fisher and Williams (2004: 13) who offer this list of characteristics that they suggest may be seen in creative people:

- They are flexible;
- They connect ideas;

- They are unorthodox;
- They show aesthetic taste;
- They are curious and inquisitive;
- They see similarities and differences; and
- They question accepted ways of doing things.

If we are honest with ourselves, we do need to reflect on the extent to which we often organize learning that actually encourages even some of these processes to take place. We also need to consider messages from other documents. On the one hand, the word 'creative' can be found in the Rose Review (DCSF, 2009: 16) but in the context of encouraging teachers to think out of subject boxes. It limits the use of the word in the programmes of learning to the arts, when in fact Robinson (2001) argues that creativity exists in all aspects of human activity. On the other hand, Alexander (2010: 226) also notes that:

> The words 'creative' and 'creativity' appeared in the submissions more frequently than almost any others. They were applied both to children's learning and the conditions for teaching, and invariably were regarded positively.

So, if the submissions to the Cambridge Review from many parts of society at large are to be accepted, there seems to be some consensus that creativity needs to be a part of education both in terms of pupil learning and development and the ways in which we organize learning opportunities for them. Therefore, we now turn to the work of Sir Ken Robinson and apply some of his ideas to these educational contexts.

At this point in your reading it may be helpful to pause and actually listen to and watch Sir Ken Robinson giving the summing-up presentation at the final day of an education conference on creativity on 30 June 2006. This can be found at www.ted.com. Hopefully, you will find it thought-provoking and enjoyable and an expression of how many of us feel at a time when education needs a radical overhaul, but not one which is government-led. In his presentation he mentions a book (Robinson, 2009) where he describes how successfully creative people discuss how they achieve this. It is a fascinating insight into how humans develop their creativity and raises many questions about our current systems of education.

> There are many misconceptions about creativity. Creativity is not a separate faculty that some people have and others do not. It is a function of intelligence: it takes many forms, it draws from many different capacities and we all have different creative capabilities.
>
> (Robinson, 2001: 111)

The remaining parts of this chapter discusses some of Robinson's ideas about creativity and place them within an educational context. His writing is designed to appeal to a wide range of organizations and situations so this interpretation is given here to support the school context in particular as other organizations such as international corporations might place a different interpretation on Robinson's ideas on creativity.

In order to promote creativity Robinson (2001: 111) suggests the process needs to include

- The importance of the medium;
- The need to be in control of the medium;
- The need to play and take risks; and
- The need for critical judgement.

In educational contexts, the 'medium' may mean a number of things. First, it may be the actual context in which learning takes place. For example, if the rest of a scheme of work has given pupils clear messages that they have to conform to a particular way of working, then suddenly giving them the opportunity to develop their own ways of thinking creatively is unlikely to be successful. In whole school terms we perhaps need to think of this as an ethos in which new ways of thinking are encouraged. The author (John Halocha) would also argue that this applies to everyone in the organization and not just the pupils, as this can have a mutually positive and re-enforcing effect on the whole environment. Second, the medium can also refer to the actual task in which the children are engaged; for example, if an activity is planned to create specific outcomes, pupils are unlikely to think creatively.

For example, the author recalls a mathematics lesson in which 11-year-old pupils were investigating the properties of triangles. There were open-ended tasks which allowed pupils to gain an understanding of the properties of various types of triangle. One boy questioned the fact that all triangles had 180 degrees as the total of their internal angles. He was adopting a creative approach and was prepared to question an accepted fact. He was given the sharpest 4H pencil and other equipment with which to attempt to draw and measure a triangle in which the internal angles did not add up to 180 degrees. After about 15 minutes of very careful drawing and measuring he returned to me and felt that his research did indeed confirm that it was not possible to create such a triangle! In this case the author knew what the probable outcome would be, but felt it was important that his original thinking should be encouraged as hopefully it would be something he felt was valued and would use in the future. This is an interesting example because it comes from a subject where we might think creativity played less of a part. However, the author thinks most mathematicians would agree that it is in fact a very creative subject when taking it to the bounds of new mathematical understanding. This example also demonstrated that the pupil was in control of the medium in which he was working: he had a clear objective and was given high-quality tools to do the job. During his investigation he was allowed to play with his idea and take risks; one of course being that he might not find such a new triangle. Finally, he exercised critical judgement in the analysis of his findings. The exercising of critical judgement is also a two-way process and this is where the role of the teacher in supporting creativity is crucial. The author hopefully gave him a clear message that he valued his questioning of information and that our dialogue was mutually supportive.

Robinson (2001) goes on to raise five questions which are pertinent to education contexts: Are only special people creative? This basically is a message to be aware that all our pupils have the potential to be creative. It is mainly about giving them as many opportunities as possible to explore their potential to be creative. The author recalls an example of a drama production. To make life easy children can sometimes be given roles where we know they will be successful. In one comedy play we put on in school there was the central character of a dad whose day at the seaside became progressively more and more chaotic. There were some possible candidates but also there was one quiet boy who just seemed to have the characteristics that could be built into this dad's character. He was given the part, found it hard to learn the lines, but the way he creatively found that character in himself was amazing. If only we had video cameras back then! Hopefully, he was able to realize the dramatic creative potential he had in him which no one had previously seen.

Does creativity only happen in special activities?

Robinson (2001) raises this question because we often associate creativity with certain types of activity. A careful reading of the programmes of learning in the final review of the Rose Review (DCSF, 2009) rather reinforces this limited view of where creativity can occur. It is of course included in the section 'Understanding the Arts' but gets no explicit mention in mathematical understanding, apart from the notion that they can begin to solve problems by choosing appropriate methods. Robinson (2001) suggests that creativity is a form of intelligence that may be applied to any activity in which humans find themselves engaged. Perhaps a message for schools is to reflect on the extent to which this is made clear to children in practice, often through more hidden signals. It is also perhaps to do with the way in which teachers approach learning and resources. The author introduces geography students to the 'geograph' website which is a totally free and open-ended website containing thousands of photographs, maps and information about the British Isles. One of the author's aims is to encourage them to think creatively about how they and their pupils might use such a rich and up-to-date resource in order to begin to understand the complexities of life in Britain today. Indeed, some concern might be expressed over the recent Creative Partnerships Initiatives in that they tend to focus on the arts subjects. Perhaps their potential for unlocking creativity might be extended if partcipants were able to realize that creativity can occur in a much wider range of activities.

Is creativity all about letting go?

Robinson (2001) recognizes that there are perceptions that contexts for creativity can only occur if children are given complete freedom. In fact the opposite may well be the case, such as the example of the boy acting in the play. The play environment itself was very structured with all pupils having various responsibilities. Within that the actor was given great freedom to interpret his role. Robinson also suggests that far from letting go, it is often necessary to hang on in for some considerable time for the creative results to come out. Many practical ideas on how creativity can be developed can be found in Cole (2006). This book is included here because it offers many examples of Robinson's views on the creative process at work within the context of art education. However, it would not be hard to transfer the key ideas to other subjects or areas of learning.

Is creativity only about problem-solving?

Robinson (2001) neatly turns this round by suggesting that many creative ideas and activities actually find problems as well as solve them. An example from history might illustrate this well. The author was working with a school on developing links with a school in Italy. The class had agreed on a list of photographs to be taken and sent to Italy as an introduction to their locality. All went well until we arrived at the village war memorial. At this point one pupil remarked 'they (Italians) were not on our side were they? Do you think we should include this photo?' The spontaneous sense of creative social responsibility was amazing because he had been prepared to think of what he knew about history in ways that were relevant to his present context. This example also demonstrated that creative ideas and ways of thinking do not have to be world class to be of value: they have to be relevant and new ways of thinking in whatever context is appropriate.

Can creativity be taught?

The author could never have taught that boy to think in the way he did about history. He believes it was him using some of the features of creativity outlined by Fisher and Williams (2004) and listed at the start of the chapter. However, Robinson is clear in his view that creativity can be taught and that it is not confined to special people. Specific examples of how this might be taught are discussed below.

Robinson (2001) notes the importance of imagination in the creative process but also argues that unless creative imaginings are expressed in some way to the public world, they are not truly creative. In other words, imagination is an important part of the creative process but full creativity also involves actually producing something in the real world: this might be a mathematical formula for others to investigate or a piece of music for them to enjoy. In terms of educational settings how often do we encourage pupils to use their imagination? More so, how often do we encourage them to develop their imagination over time? An example from English may help to illustrate this. So often we introduce an idea we expect children to write about and to do it almost as soon as they have been told it. With a little planning it is quite possible to introduce ideas ahead of time and give pupils a chance to mull over and develop their ideas. At university level, the author gives the example of those students who do remember what I say about starting to think about their final dissertation from year one. Many ideas will be developed and scrapped, but on the evidence of the quality of the final assignments, the author finds strong links between those students who do a lot of thinking and imagining about possible geographical enquiries and their final results.

A further issue which enters the debate about creativity is the extent to which it is original. With the current size of the global population, it almost appears to be an irrelevant question as it would be impossible to ascertain total originality. Robinson (2001: 116) suggests that originality operates on three levels:

- To the person involved – *personal originality*;
- For a particular community – *social originality*; and
- For humanity as a whole – *historic originality*.

An example of the first might be a young child working within a poetic form who is able to find ways that are new for her to describe her garden. Many other people will have described gardens in poetry, but for her, this is a first and she should be proud. An example of social originality could be illustrated from the author's work with the Geographical Association. We have a network of local branches around the country, some of which were founded in the nineteenth century. They all have slightly different ways of organizing their activities but the general pattern is one of public lectures and various types of field visits. However, in about 2005 an entirely new type of branch was founded. It was in an area of extensive social deprivation and one where much social and economic regeneration was planned. Very often these are top-down processes. A group of local geography teachers got together to form a branch in which not just geography teachers and pupils were members, but where people from as many walks of life were encouraged to meet and debate how local issues might be resolved. A huge amount of geographical understanding was developed by everyone but the real strength was in the sense of community and ownership the branch has developed. This soon led to active community participation in a wide range of activities. This example is also described as it may change your ideas about the scale of creative ideas and how the school might be a catalyst for creativity in the community.

Historic originality for humanity as a whole may not be in the realms of primary education (but why not?) but maybe pupils should have specific opportunities to think about how creative ideas can have global implications. One that might be relevant to them would be the invention of the Internet and the implications it is having at a whole range of scales. It could also get them to think about what makes something creative. We had many forms of communication before the web, but the inventor imagined new ways in which technology and ideas could be linked to create something entirely original.

Robinson (2001) places much emphasis on the links between language, imagination and the creative process. Drawing on established psychology he notes the need for people to think symbolically in order to develop new ways of looking at the world. At a practical level in school, what might this mean? From my own experiences both as a teacher and now a regular visitor to schools, I find it fascinating to listen to the language used in all educational contexts, both by pupils and adults. At its worst were the early days of the literacy strategy where one would visit almost any school and hear exactly the same mantra being expressed. Things are improving but I think we have much scope for analysing the type of language that becomes part of classroom everyday life which actively encourages children to develop more creative ways of thinking by empowering them to know that it is good to be different. It would make a fascinating continuing professional development (CPD) research activity as part of a Master's degree programme. It is really a sense of creating a 'can do' environment in terms of encouraging children to develop their creative ability. It is an important concept in the business world and perhaps one that could be adopted more in schools.

Subject task

EYFS:
Choose an activity that you currently arrange for your young children to experience on a regular basis. In what ways might you develop it in order to help children begin to think and act in more creative ways? How would you justify this activity as being a way of improving your practice?

KS1:
Choose a subject you teach where the creative possibilities of it may not yet have been fully explored. Identify a specific activity which you think may have the potential for children to explore in more creative ways than you have expected up until now. Plan a way of introducing this to pupils as a medium, as Robinson (2001) would say, for developing their creative talents.

KS2:
We have discussed the possibility of pupils actually looking at what it means to be creative. Choose a recent example of something that may be considered creative and in which they may already have some interest and understanding. This could be an excellent opportunity to use some of the approaches developed by the Society for the Advancement of Philosophical Enquiry and Reflection in England (SAPERE). It is part of the P4C (Philosophy for Children) initiative in which primary children are encouraged to debate ideas using philosophical methods. The nature of what is creative would be an excellent theme to develop. It could encourage them to reflect on what is creative and start the imaginative processes in their own minds.

To support your initial thinking about these three subject tasks, the discussion in the following paragraph below is provided by Vanessa Richards, an experienced music educationalist and primary music advisor, on how she believes music and creativity may be developed with primary children:

Human beings are inherently musical. You may now be thinking 'I'm tone deaf', 'I can't sing' or 'I can't play a musical instrument'. So where might this innate musical ability have disappeared to and when did you realize you didn't have it? Our current inheritance of how to 'think' about music is coloured by a very strong past tradition in Western art music. Looking back at your own musical education what names would appear? I would think that Beethoven, Mozart and maybe Haydn would be near the top of your list. To consider music lessons within this tradition does a disservice to ourselves as teachers and to our students. Why, for most people, does music still evoke this past – a past where music should be listened to attentively and respectfully? How many times have you heard it said in assemblies (or maybe said it yourself?) 'Please stop fidgeting and listen to the music'? Can we, and should we expect our future musicians to have the same ethic? Do they need to have the same view of music now as they did in the nineteenth century? If a piece of music you enjoy comes on the radio do you stop and listen attentively without moving? Music is an extremely powerful way to unlock the elusive 'creativity' so much admired in the curriculum. The early years of a child's life are the perfect opportunity to show how creativity in music is a good thing and to demonstrate to all children that they have talents.

So what might creativity in music look like? It may well look much the same as you would expect in any other subject. Creativity occurs when we combine things in new and unexpected ways to create new and unexpected results. For example, recording children's voices and performances is not unusual at all in music lessons. What we then do with it can go far beyond the 'use it as evidence for assessment purposes'. Flexibility is the key here and the courage to follow the children and take a risk – the outcome may be not at all what you expected! The author often uses an MP3 recorder such as the Roland Edirol with early years children. This simple, handheld device records at the press of a button and can be immediately connected to either a laptop or portable speakers for children to listen to.

Children are fascinated by the sound of their own voice! I use a computer programme called Audacity, a free downloadable programme which can change inputted sounds. Once inputted from the recorder we can then explore! What happens to Three Blind Mice when we reverse the song? Is it still an effective song? Do we like the sound of it? What would happen if we speed the voices up? The children are curious and inquisitive; they question the accepted way of listening to their voices, the outcome is unorthodox. All these are key characteristics of creativity. You would be surprised at how many questions this simple activity generates and questioning the accepted practice is what creativity is all about. Is the reversed song still music? All music is music. Do not be afraid to experiment, to explore and to take risks. We should aim to celebrate, not stifle, the talents of our future generations.

A final point based on Robinson's (2001) discussions on creativity is how we find a medium in which to become creative. This has a number of important implications for schools. Clearly, not every human being is going to have a large number of ways in which to be creative. Very often we have one talent that is just waiting to be sparked off. If you listened to Robinson on the TED website (www.ted.com) as suggested earlier in this chapter, he is particularly concerned about the way in which current mass systems of education actually set out (not necessarily deliberately) to limit pupils' access to opportunities to be creative, but also how so often we do not recognize the wonderful talents many young people can have. He argues that with all the growing and interrelated complex issues at work on a global scale, we simply cannot afford to let this talent remain untapped if we are to survive and progress as human beings.

Conclusion

Robinson suggests that there are many phases of creativity and that as we move our creative thinking and actions forward we are developing 'successive approximations' on what we hope to achieve. This is an important point on which to conclude. As educationalists we need to remember that creativity is not something we timetable or just plan into a few subjects. Its inclusion within the whole ethos of what we do in schools hopefully gives young people the message that they are very important both to themselves, their community and the wider global society as they each have the potential to make a unique and creative contribution to humanity. Perhaps that is what real education is all about.

References

Alexander, R. (ed.) (2010) *Children, their World, their Education: Final Report of the Recommendation of the Cambridge Primary Review*. London: Routledge.

Cole, R. (2006) *The Creative Imperative: Unravel the Mystery of Creativity*. Lichfield: Primary First.

Department for Children, Schools and Families (DCSF) (2009) *Independent Review of the Primary Curriculum*. Nottingham: DCSF.

Fisher, R. and Williams, M. (2004) *Unlocking Creativity: Teaching Across the Curriculum*. London: Fulton.

Read, H. (1958) *Education through Art*. London: Faber & Faber.

Robinson, K. (2001) *Out of our Minds: Learning to be Creative*. Chichester: Capstone.

Robinson, K. (2009) *The Element: How Finding your Passion Changes Everything*. London: Penguin.

Society for the Advancement of Philosophical Enquiry and Reflection in England (SAPERE). Available online at www.sapere.org.uk/ (accessed 10 January 2010).

Wilson, A. (2009) *Creativity in Primary Education*. Exeter: Learning Matters.

16 The individual child

This chapter focuses on the importance of a child-centred approach for successful development, learning and teaching. It considers the work of many theorists and discusses their influence on new initiatives in early years and primary education.

Every child matters

The publication of *Every Child Matters* (DfES, 2003a) was an important event in the development of understanding young children's development and practice in early years and primary education, linking different services for children and young people up to 19 years of age. It is based on the principle that every child matters and has a right to five outcomes:

- Health, enjoying physical and mental well-being and living healthily.
- Safety, being safe and protected from any form of harm or neglect.
- Enjoyment and achievement, having access and benefiting from opportunities and developing important life skills.
- Contribution, being involved in community and social life, so that they are able to make a positive contribution to society and take some responsibility for their own actions in society.
- Economic well-being, being able to achieve their full potential and not be economically disadvantaged later in life because they have not had opportunities to fulfil their potential.

The publication of *Every Child Matters* (DfES, 2003a) was followed by the Children Act 2004, Childcare Act 2006, Children and Young Persons Act 2008 and further publications (DfES, 2004a, DfES, 2004b; DCSF, 2008a). These all identified the need for a radical reorganization of children's services to improve and integrate services in early years settings, schools and the health services, providing specialized support for families and children (see also Chapter 11, 'Working together'). Most importantly, if every child does matter then care and education for children in both the early years, primary education and beyond must become child-centred (DfES, 2004a). This is a move away from the practices of the last 20 years when the narrow focus of the cognitive curriculum dominated and services to support children were over-stretched and underfunded. It is also a move endorsed by the Cambridge Review of Primary Education (Alexander, 2009), which identifies a further radical change to support the wider social and emotional context of childhood. There is compelling evidence (e.g. Palmer, 2006; Bowlby, 2007; Mayall, 2007; UNICEF, 2007) that children are adversely affected by poor social, emotional and educational contexts and the implications are that if we do not make changes now, then we are creating future problems for both the individual child and society as a whole.

Reflection

Every Child Matters (DfES, 2003a, 2004a) has led to each local authority conducting comprehensive surveys, identifying local needs and producing action plans. However, there does appear to be a danger that each local authority spends considerable time and effort in translating the principles, celebrating existing practice and consulting with service providers, so that individual settings/schools and children may be overlooked and fall between gaps in provision. Financial considerations also must affect the ability of each school/setting and local authority to deliver quality and joined-up services for children and meet the *Every Child Matters* agenda.

Reflective tasks:
- How has your practice changed as a result of the *Every Child Matters* agenda?
- How have you been supported by the local authority and/or government departments?
- What are the challenges you face in achieving the *Every Child Matters* agenda in your setting/school?

EYFS:
- How are the challenges of *Every Child Matters* different in the EYFS?
- How can you work more closely with other stages of learning to support the *Every Child Matters* agenda?

KS1:

- What are the specific challenges facing KS1 in achieving the *Every Child Matters* agenda?
- How can you meet these challenges and support individual children in your care?

KS2:

- How do you overcome the tensions that exist between the cognitive challenges of the national curriculum (DfEE, 1999) and the challenges of meeting the *Every Child Matters* agenda?
- What are the implications of the *Every Child Matters* agenda on your future practice and provision?

Historical perspectives on the individual child

A focus on the individual child is not a new phenomena and identified by many theorists and practitioners throughout the years. Maslow's (1968) hierarchy of needs has already been discussed in Chapter 2 and its importance extends to our discussion of the individual child. Maslow (1968) identifies the importance of individualization in our care and education of children (see also Figure 2.1 in Maslow's (1968) *Theory of Hierarchical Needs*).

> 66 **Basic Needs And Their Hierarchical Arrangement**
> It has by now been sufficiently demonstrated that the human being has, as part of his intrinsic construction, not only physiological needs, but also truly psychological ones. They may be considered as deficiencies which must be optimally fulfilled by the environment in order to avoid sickness and subjective ill-being. They can be called basic, or biological, and likened to the need for salt, or calcium or vitamin D because
>
> a)   The deprived person yearns for their gratification persistently.
> b)   Their deprivation makes the person sicken and wither.
> c)   Gratifying them is therapeutic, curing the deficiency-illness.
> d)   Steady supplies forestall these illnesses.
> e)   Healthy (gratified) people do not demonstrate these deficiencies.
>
> But these needs or values are related to each other in a hierarchical and developmental way, in an order of strength and of priority. Safety is a more preponent, or stronger, more pressing, more vital need than love, for instance, and the need for food is usually stronger than either.

Furthermore, all these basic needs may be considered to be simply steps along the path to general self-actualization, under which all basic needs can be subsumed.   **99**

Source: Maslow, A.H. (1968) *Towards a Psychology of Being*. D. Van Nostrand Company, pp. 168–9

Maslow continues by focusing on self-actualization.

66   Among the objectively describable and measurable characteristics of the healthy human specimen are

1.   Clearer, more efficient perception of reality.
2.   More openness to experience.
3.   Increased integration, wholeness, and unity of the person.
4.   Increased spontaneity, expressiveness; full functioning; aliveness.
5.   A real self; a firm identity; autonomy, uniqueness.
6.   Increased objectivity, detachment, transcendence of self.
7.   Recovery of creativeness.
8.   Ability to fuse concreteness and abstractness.
9.   Democratic character structure.
10.   Ability to love, etc.

These all need research confirmation and exploration but it is clear that such researches are feasible.

In addition, there are subjective confirmations or reinforcements of self-actualization or of good growth toward it. These are the feelings of zest in living, of happiness or euphoria, of serenity, of joy, of calmness, of responsibility, of confidence in one's ability to handle stresses, anxieties, and problems. The subjective signs of self-betrayal, of fixation, of regression, and of living by fear rather than by growth are such feelings as anxiety, despair, boredom, inability to enjoy, intrinsic guilt, intrinsic shame, aimlessness, feelings of emptiness, of lack of identity, etc. These subjective reactions are also susceptible of research exploration. We have clinical techniques available for studying them.   **99**

Source: Maslow, A.H. (1968) *Towards a Psychology of Being*. D. Van Nostrand Company, pp. 172–3

1. One conclusion from all these free-choice experiments, from developments in dynamic motivation theory and from examination of psychotherapy, is a very revolutionary one, namely, that our deepest needs are not, in themselves, dangerous or evil or bad. This opens up the prospect of resolving the splits within the person between Apollonian and Dionysian, classical and romantic, scientific and poetic, between

reason and impulse, work and play, verbal and preverbal, maturity and childlikeness, masculine and feminine, growth and regression.

2. The main social parallel to this change in our philosophy of human nature is the rapidly growing tendency to perceive the culture as an instrument of need-gratification as well as of frustration and control. We can now reject the almost universal mistake that the interests of the individual and of society are of necessity mutually exclusive and antagonistic, or that civilization is primarily a mechanism for controlling and policing human instinctoid impulses. All these age-old axioms are swept away by the new possibility of defining the main function of a healthy culture as the fostering of universal self-actualization.

3. In healthy people only is there a good correlation between subjective delight in the experience, impulse to the experience, or wish for it, and "basic need" for the experience (it's good for him in the long run). Only such people uniformly yearn for what is good for them and for others, and then are able wholeheartedly to enjoy it, and approve of it. For such people virtue is its own reward in the sense of being enjoyed in itself. They spontaneously tend to do right because that is what they want to do, what they need to do, what they enjoy, what they approve of doing, and what they will continue to enjoy.

It is this unity, this network of positive intercorrelation, that falls apart into separateness and conflict as the person gets psychologically sick. Then what he wants to do may be bad for him; even if he does it he may not enjoy it; even if he enjoys it, he may simultaneously disapprove of it, so that the enjoyment is itself poisoned or may disappear quickly. What he enjoys at first he may not enjoy later. His impulses, desires, and enjoyments then become a poor guide to living. He must accordingly mistrust and fear the impulses and the enjoyments which lead him astray, and so he is caught in conflict, dissociation, indecision; in a word, he is caught in civil war.

So far as philosophical theory is concerned, many historical dilemmas and contradictions are resolved by this finding. Hedonistic theory does work for healthy people; it does not work for sick people. The true, the good and the beautiful do correlate some, but only in healthy people do they correlate strongly.

4. Self-actualization is a relatively achieved "state of affairs" in a few people. In most people, however, it is rather a hope, a yearning, a drive, a "something" wished for but not yet achieved, showing itself clinically as drive toward health, integration, growth, etc. The projective tests are also able to detect these trends as potentialities rather than as overt behavior, just as an X-ray can detect incipient pathology before it has appeared on the surface.

This means for us that that which the person is and that which the person could be exist simultaneously for the psychologist, thereby resolving the dichotomy between Being and Becoming. Potentialities not only will be or could be; they also are. Self-actualization values as goals exist and are real even though not yet actualized. The human being is simultaneously that which he is and that which he yearns to be.

(Maslow, 1968: 168–9)

Rousseau (1911) identified the importance of early experiences and care for individual children. He advocates 'tough love' and it is necessary to translate what this means in today's society; it is easy to dismiss his ideas as 'out of date', but they do resonate with the debate in Chapter 1, 'Social development' and the arguments raised by Palmer (2006).

66 The mother may lavish excessive care on her child instead of neglecting him; she may make an idol of him, she may develop and increase his weakness to prevent him feeling it: she wards off every painful experience in the hope of withdrawing him from the power of nature, and fails to realise that for every trifling ill from which she preserves him the future holds in store many accidents and dangers, and that it is a cruel kindness to prolong the child's weakness when the grown man must bear fatigues. Thetis, so the story goes, plunged her son in the waters of Styx to make him invulnerable. The truth of this allegory is apparent. The cruel mothers I speak of do otherwise; they plunge their children into softness, and they are preparing suffering for them, they open the way to every kind of ill, which their children will not fail to experience after they grow up.

Fix your eyes on nature, follow the path traced by her. She keeps children at work, she hardens them by all kinds of difficulties, she soon teaches them the meaning of pain and grief. They cut their teeth and are feverish, sharp colics bring on convulsions, they are choked by fits of coughing and tormented by worms, evil humours corrupt the blood, germs of various kinds ferment in it, causing dangerous eruptions. Sickness and danger play the chief part in infancy – one half of the children who are born die before their eighth year. The child who has overcome hardships has gained strength, and as soon as he can use his life he holds it more securely.

This is nature's law; why contradict it? Do you not see that in your efforts to improve upon her handiwork you are destroying it; her cares are wasted? To do from without what she does within is according to you to increase the danger twofold. On the contrary, it is the way to avert it; experience shows that children delicately nurtured are more likely to die. Provided we do not overdo it, there is less risk in using their strength than in sparing it. Accustom them therefore to the hardships they will

have to face; train them to endure extremes of temperature, climate, and
condition, hunger, thirst, and weariness. Dip them in the waters of Styx.   **99**
Source: Rousseau, J.-J. (1911) *Emile*. London: J.M. Dent & Sons,
pp. 14–15

Reflection

The importance of early experiences is endorsed by many current initiatives
(e.g. DfES, 2003a, DfES, 2003b; DCSF, 2010), research (e.g. Bowlby, 2007;
Mayall, 2007) and writers (too many to list but see, for example, Kerry, 2002;
Johnston and Nahmad-Williams, 2008).

The evidence implies that if we do not provide positive experiences for
children at all stages in the early and primary years, then children's development
and learning is adversely affected (Schwienhart et al., 1993; Sylva et al., 2004).

Reflective tasks

EYFS:
- Are there children in the early years whose experiences are/have/will
  affect their subsequent development? Who are these children and how
  do their experiences affect their development?
- How can you improve experiences for these children?

KS1:
- How are individual children affected by the experiences prior to KS1?
- How can you support individual children at KS1 to overcome the
  problems of their early experiences?

KS2:
- How do individual experiences create differences between children
  in learning and development?
- How can you support children and bridge gaps between them at KS2?

Impact tasks

Plan some development to support individual children in your setting and
overcome their early and current experiences and differences between children.
You may wish to plan using a format as shown in Figure 16.1.

Try out your ideas and collect evidence to evaluate your development,
reflecting on the impact and the implications for future practice in your
setting/school.

Overall aim

Specific objectives

Intended outcomes for pupils, school, yourself

Success criteria

Timescale

Resources/staff

Sources of challenge and support at different stages

Progress review

Ethical considerations

How and when to share learning

How and when to evaluate the project

Figure 16.1   Action plan.

Rudolf Steiner placed individual development high in priority and in particular the child's inner spiritual development. Our next reading is from one of Steiner's lectures and illustrates aspects of his philosophy of life; anthroposophism.

    ❝ The third member of the human body is called the *sentient* or *astral* body. It is the vehicle of pain and pleasure, of impulse, craving, passion, and so on – all of which are absent in a creature that consists of only the physical and etheric bodies. These things may all be included in the term sentient feeling, or sensation. The plant has no sensation. If in our time some learned people see that plants will respond by movement or some other way to external stimulus and conclude that plants have a certain power of sensation, they only show their ignorance of what sensation is. The point is not whether the creature responds to an external stimulus but whether the stimulus is reflected in an inner process such as pain or pleasure, impulse, desire, and so on. Unless we stick to this criterion, we would be justified in saying that blue litmus-paper has a sensation of certain substances, because it turns red through contact with them.

Humankind, therefore, has a sentient body in common with the animal kingdom only, and this sentient body is the vehicle of sensation or of sentient life.

We must not make the same mistake as certain theosophical circles and imagine that the etheric and sentient bodies consist simply of substances that are finer than those present in the physical body. That would be a materialistic concept of these higher members of human nature. The etheric body is *a force-form*; it consists of active forces, and not of matter. The astral or sentient body is a figure of inwardly moving, colored, and luminous pictures. The astral body deviates in both size and shape from the physical body. In human beings it presents an elongated ovoid form in which the physical and etheric bodies are embedded. It projects beyond them – a vivid, luminous figure – on every side.

Human beings also possess a Fourth member of their being, and this fourth member is shared with no other earthly creature. It is the vehicle of the *human 1*, or ego. The little word I – as used, for example, in the English language – is a name essentially different from any other. To anyone who ponders rightly on the nature of this name, an approach to the perception of true human nature is opened up immediately. All other names can be applied equally by everyone to what they designate.

99

Source: Steiner, R. (1996) *The Education of the Child and Early Lectures on Education*. New York: Anthroposophic Press, pp. 8–9

Reflection

Steiner's (1996) writings illustrate the complex nature of individual development, with different factors affecting outcomes. Children (and adults) are a complex mix of emotional, social, cognitive and physical development (see Chapter 1, 'Social development', Chapter 2, 'Emotional development', Chapter 3, 'Physical and spatial development' and Chapter 4, 'Cognitive development') affected by the social, emotional, physical and cognitive contexts and experiences of childhood. Each child, as an individual, will have different needs and challenges and identifying these and supporting children is a demanding, complex, but rewarding task for professionals working with them.

Reflective tasks

- How do you identify the needs of individual children in your care?
- What are the most common specific needs that children in your stage of learning have?
- How do you accommodate these needs in your current practice?
- What support do you need to help you to develop your practice and meet individual needs?
- How can you access this support?

Individualization in the future

The importance of personalized care and learning is now well recognized. Many professionals attempt to implement aspects of Gardner's (1983, 2006) theory of multiple intelligences (see Chapter 4, 'Cognitive development'), but often without full understanding of what it actually means and how it applies to their own practice. Gardner's more recent ideas, embodied in *Five Minds for the Future* (Gardner, 2007) are written much more for educational professionals (see also Chapter 4, 'Cognitive development' for more details and Reflective Tasks associated with Gardner's ideas). The next reading summarizes one of Gardner's Five Minds, respect, which is possibly the most important attribute a child can develop.

❝ **An Order For Mastering The Minds?**
1) Respect. From the beginning, one must begin by creating a respectful atmosphere toward others. In the absence of civility, other educational goals prove infinitely harder to achieve. Instances of disrespect must be labeled as such; each must be actively discouraged and its practitioners ostracized. (An aside on literacy: the first cognitive assignment for all schools is mastery of the basic literacies of reading, writing, and calculation. Because this point is and has long been uncontroversial, I need not elaborate on it here.)
2) Discipline. Once one has become literate, by the end of the elementary years, the time is at hand for the acquisition of the major scholarly ways of thinking – at a minimum, scientific, mathematical, historical, artistic. Each takes years to inculcate, and so delays are costly.

3)   Synthesis. Equipped with major disciplinary ways of thinking, the student is poised to make judicious kinds of syntheses and, as appropriate, to engage in interdisciplinary thinking.

4)   Ethics. During the years of secondary school and college, one becomes capable of abstract, distanced thinking. One can now conceptualize the world of work and the responsibilities of the citizen and acts on those conceptualizations.   **99**

Source: Gardner, H. (2007) *Five Minds for the Future: The Theory of Multiple Intelligence*. Harvard: Harvard Business School, pp. 161–2

A focus on learning styles is also very popular in early years and education. Often, three distinct learning styles are identified: visual, auditory and kinaesthetic (VAK) (Dryden and Vos, 1999). Like multiple intelligences (Gardner, 1983) these are much misunderstood (Gardner, 2006) and there is a tendency for some professionals to interpret these learning styles to mean that children fall almost neatly into one of the three categories and should be taught in different ways to accommodate preferences for learning and they waste valuable professional time trying to adapt their teaching for the myth of VAK (Coffield et al., 2004). In reality, there is little evidence from research, although quite a lot of anecdotal evidence about learning styles, and so they have to be considered careful and tentatively (Revell, 2005). In addition, the idea that individual children need to be taught to accommodate their preferred learning style is one that does not hold out against scrutiny. It is much more reasonable to assume that children should be helped to learn in a variety of ways, so that they are able to develop regardless of the approach used.

Personalized learning stems from Rousseau's view (1911) that education should be child-centred, accommodating children rather than expecting them to accommodate to the educational system. The personalized learning initiative (see DCSF, 2010) involves adapting provision for children to cater for their individual needs, interests, abilities and achievements and aims to support individuals to enable every child to achieve their full potential, meet the aims of the *Every Child Matters* (DfES, 2003a) agenda. All children should have learning personalized so that the effects of personal circumstances, culture and ability can be overcome. Personalized learning (DCSF, 2010) has five components:

1   Assessment for Learning (AfL)
2   effective teaching and learning
3   a Flexible curriculum
4   organizing the school for personalized learning
5   beyond the classroom.

Personalized learning is underpinned by important principles, such as child-centred provision, where the child's voice is important (see Cheminais, 2008), so that children can identify the approaches which work for them. Parent partnership is a key issue, so that parents and child and professional:

- have shared understanding of developmental and educational progress and the support needed to reach the next developmental stage
- are equally involved in planning to support development
- have high, but realistic, expectations of achievement.

Impact tasks

Early career professional:
Identify an individual child in your setting who finds learning difficult. This may be because the child:

- finds sitting still difficult
- prefers to make a model rather than write about something
- would rather draw a picture or annotate a drawing
- likes to be given instructions to follow
- enjoys the unknown and unexpected
- likes a routine.

Adapt your planning for one session/lesson to accommodate the child's individual needs and evaluate the impact.

Reflection

- How did the changes support the child's learning?
- What are the implications of this for your future practice?

Later years professional:
Develop an action plan (see Figure 16.1) to accommodate changes in your practice and provision that will support individual learners over a period of time. This may involve supporting children in developing understanding of how they learn and what affects their learning (metacognition – see Chapter 4, 'Cognitive development'), varying the pedagogical approaches used (more exploratory, play, open-ended, child initiated, etc.), or providing more differentiation by outcome, so that children can start and finish activities at levels appropriate to their individual needs and abilities.
Evaluate the plan, using the identified success criteria.

Reflection

- What impact did the changes make to children?
- What are the implications of the evaluation for your future practice?

Involving children in all aspects of their learning can be a good step towards personalized learning. Many early years setting use the high/scope cognitively oriented curriculum, which is underpinned by the belief that children are active learners who learn best from activities planned, executed and evaluated by themselves (Hohmann and Weikart, 2002). The effects of this have been found to be long-lasting on all aspects of development from childhood and into adulthood, especially where later stages of learning build on the development and move towards short-, medium- and long-term target-setting with children and carers/parents. Target-setting is an important part of the process of learning and teaching. Individual targets, developed collaboratively, provide opportunities for children to be clear about what is expected of them and how they will achieve this. It is important that targets, or success criteria, are, Specific, Measurable, Achievable, Realistic and Time related; that is **SMART** (DfEE, 2001: 15). Additionally, targets need to be flexible so that they can be adjusted if found to be too challenging or too easy.

Subject tasks

EYFS:
Identify targets for children in your setting, related to the EYFS six key areas of learning (DCSF, 2008b):

- personal, social and emotional development
- communication, language and literacy
- problem-solving, reasoning and numeracy
- knowledge and understanding of the world
- physical development
- creative development.

You can use the action plan in Figure 16.1 to help with your planning.

You may wish to adopt the high/scope approach of working with the children to encourage them to take some ownership over their learning and plan what they want/need to achieve, follow out the plan and review their achievements against the targets set. This approach will need to be phased in slowly as children will not be able to work fully in this way at the first attempt.

Evaluate the success of the approach and how well the children met the set targets.

Reflection

- How did the children respond to the target-setting?
- What difficulties did the children face in working towards targets?
- How can you support the children in taking more ownership over their own learning and target-setting?

KS1:

Ask children to identify what the next step of their learning is in one aspect of either English (speaking and listening, reading and writing) or mathematics (number, calculation, space and shape, etc.). This may be best undertaken after children have attempted a task and their achievements and challenges are clear in their minds. Make sure that the target is achievable in a short timescale and is not too challenging for the child. Get them to write their target on a strip of laminated card with a marker pen and keep it with them to remind them of their target. It can be blu-tacked to the table where they work, or put on a small card holder in front of them.

The target can be reassessed by you and the child after a period of time (daily or weekly). Make sure that you use evidence to identify the success. Readjust the target by wiping the card and writing a new/adjusted target.

Reflection

- How well did the children identify and monitor their own targets?
- Why do you think involving children in setting their own targets is important?
- How can you develop the children's skills in target setting in the future?

KS2:

Undertake some concept mapping with children in a conceptual area of science (e.g. plant growth, changing materials, electricity). To do this, identify key words/vocabulary that are important in this conceptual area and ask the children to link these together in a map, which identifies the connections between different areas (see Figure 16.2). Get the children to highlight areas that they struggle to connect and work with them to plan activities to explore those areas over a period of time (a half a term, or one term, or however long the concept is being focused on).

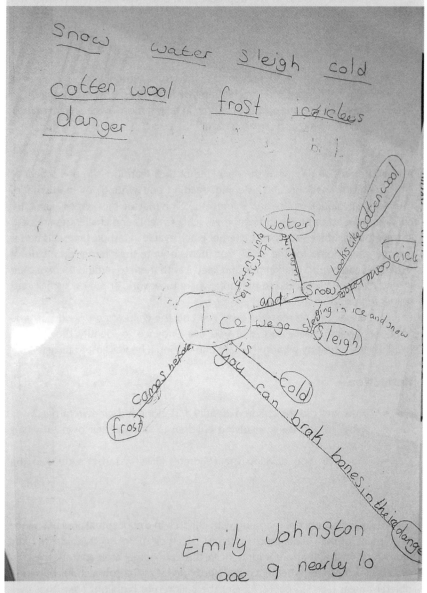

Figure 16.2 An example of a concept map.

After completing the activities ask the children to add to/change their concept map, using a different coloured pen, or to produce a new concept map. Get them to analyse the maps and identify what they have learnt.

Reflection

- How successful were the children in identifying their own achievements and learning needs and understanding their own learning?
- What challenges did the children face?
- How could you overcome these challenges in the future?

References

Alexander, R. (ed.) (2009) *Children, their World, their Education: Final Report and Recommendations of the Cambridge Review*. London: Routledge.

Bowlby, R. (2007) Babies and toddlers in non-parental daycare can avoid stress and anxiety if they develop a lasting secondary attachment bond with one carer who is consistently accessible to them, *Attachment & Human Development*, 9(4): 3017–19.

Cheminais, R. (2008) *Engaging Pupil Voice to Ensure that Every Child Matters: A Practical Guide*: London: David Fulton.

Coffield, F., Moseley, D., Hall, E. and Ecclestone, K. (2004) *Should We be Using Learning Styles? What Research has to Say to Practice*. Learning and Skills Development Agency.

Department for Children, Schools and Families (DCSF) (2008a) *Every Child Matters Outcomes Framework*. London: DCSF.

——— (2008b) *The Early Years Foundation Stage: Setting the Standard for Learning, Development and Care for Children from Birth to Five; Practice Guidance*. London: DCSF.

——— (2010) *Personalised Learning*. Available online at www.standards.dfes.gov.uk/personalisedlearning/ (accessed 13 January 2010).

Department for Education and Employment (DfEE) (1999) *The National Curriculum: Handbook For Teachers In England*. London: DfEE/QCA.

——— (2001) *Supporting the Target Setting Process*. Nottingham: DfEE.

Department for Education and Science (DfES) (2003a) *Every Child Matters*. London: DfES.

——— (2003b) *Excellence and Enjoyment: A Strategy for Primary Schools*. London: DfES.

——— (2004a) *Every Child Matters: Change For Children*. London: DfES.

——— (2004b) *Every Child Matters: The Next Steps*. London: DfES.

Dryden, G. and Vos, J. (1999) *The Learning Revolution: To Change the Way the World Learns*. Los Angeles/Auckland: The Learning Web.

Gardner, H. (1983) *Frames of Mind: The Theory of Multiple Intelligence*, 2nd edn. London: Heinemann.

Gardner, H. (2006) *Multiple Intelligence: New Horizons in Theory and Practice*. New York: Basic Books.

Gardner, H. (2007) *Five Minds for the Future*. Harvard: Harvard Business School.

Hohmann, M. and Weikart, D.P. (2002) *Educating Young Children*, 2nd edn. Ypsilanti, MI: High/Scope Press.

Johnston, J. and Nahmad-Williams, L. (2008) *Early Childhood Studies*. Harlow: Pearson.

Kerry, T. (2002) *Learning Objectives, Task Setting and Differentiation*. Cheltenham: Nelson Thornes.

Maslow, A.H. (1968) *Towards a Psychology of Being*. New York: D. Van Nostrand Company.

Mayall, B. (2007) *Children's Lives Outside School and their Educational Impact: Research Survey 8/1*. Cambridge: University of Cambridge. Available online at www.primaryreview.org.uk/Downloads/Int_Reps13.children lives voices/Primary Review 8–1 briefing Childrens lives outside school 07/123.pdf.

Palmer, S. (2006) *Toxic Childhood: How the Modern World is Damaging our Children and What We Can Do About it*. London: Orion.

Revell, P. (2005) Each to their own, *Education Guardian*, 31 May.

Rousseau, J.-J. (1911) *Emile*. London: J.M. Dent and Sons.

Schwienhart, L.J., Weikart D.P. and Toderan, R. (1993) *High Quality Preschool Programs Found to Improve Adult Status*. Ypsilante, MI: High/Scope Foundation.

Steiner, R. (1996) *The Education of the Child and Early Lectures on Education*. New York: Anthroposophic Press.

Sylva, K., Melhuish, E., Sammons, P., Siraj-Blatchford, I. and Taggart, B. (2004) *The Effective Provision of Pre-School Education (Eppe) Project: Final Report. A Longitudinal Study Funded by The DfES*.

United Nation's Children's Fund (UNICEF) (2007) *The State of the World's Children 2007*. Available at www.unicef.org/sowc07/report/report.php.

17 Learning places

Introduction

We begin this chapter with a reading from Dewey (1899) where he reports on observations in primary classrooms in the USA. As you read it, note down the features Dewey might well recognize in many twenty-first century primary classroom over one hundred years later.

> ❝ Just as the biologist can take a bone or two and reconstruct the whole animal, so, if we put before the mind's eye the ordinary schoolroom, with it rows of ugly desks placed in geometrical order, crowded together so that there shall be as little moving room as possible, desks almost all of the same size, with just space enough to hold books, pencils and paper, and add a table, some chairs, the bare walls, and possibly a few pictures we can reconstruct the only educational activity that can possibly go on in such a place. It is all made "for listening" – for simply studying lessons out of a book is only another kind of listening; it marks the dependency of one mind upon another. The attitude of listening means, comparatively speaking, passivity, absorption; that there are certain ready-made materials which are there, which have been prepared by the school superintendent, the board, the teacher, and of which the child is to take in as much as possible in the least possible time.
>
> There is very little place in the traditional schoolroom for the child to work. The workshop, the laboratory, the materials, the tools with which the child may construct, create, and actively inquire, and even the requisite space, have been for the most part lacking. The things that have to do with these processes have not even a definitely recognized place in education. They are what the educational authorities who write editorials in the daily papers generally term "fads" and "frills." A lady told me yesterday that she had been visiting different schools trying to find one where activity on the part of the children preceded the giving of information on the

part of the teacher, or where the children had some motive for demand-ing the information. She visited, she said, twenty-four different schools before she found her first instance. I may add that that was not in this city.

Another thing that is suggested by these schoolrooms, with their set desks, is that everything is arranged for handling as large numbers of children as possible; for dealing with children en masse, as an aggregate of units; involving, again, that they be treated passively. The moment children act they individualize themselves; they cease to be a mass, and become the intensely distinctive beings that we are acquainted with out of school, in the home, the family, on the playground, and in the neighborhood.

On the same basis is explicable the uniformity of method and curric-ulum. If everything is on a "listening" basis, you can have uniformity of material and method. The ear, and the book which reflects the ear, consti-tute the medium which is alike for all. There is next to no opportunity for adjustment to varying capacities and demands. There is a certain amount – a fixed quantity – of ready-made results and accomplishments to be acquired by all children alike in a given time. It is in response to this demand that the curriculum has been developed from the elementary school up through the college. There is just so much desirable knowledge, and there are just so many needed technical accomplishments in the world. Then comes the mathematical problem of dividing this by the six, twelve, or sixteen years of school life. Now give the children every year just the proportionate fraction of the total, and by the time they have finished they will have mastered the whole. By covering so much ground during this hour or day or week or year, everything comes out with perfect evenness at the end – provided the children have not forgotten what they have previously learned. (1988:48–50)

> *Source*: Dean, J. (2009) *Organising Learning in the Primary Classroom*. London: Routledge

It is fascinating to read that so many of our concerns today were being voiced back in the late nineteenth century. Of particular interest is Dewey's discus-sion of the extent to which pupils remain as individuals once they are placed in a classroom context. He talks of children learning *en masse*, realizing that it was probably not an effective way of designing learning places. Indeed, the issue of personalized learning is discussed in depth by the 'Teaching and Learn-ing in 2020 Review Group' (2006) where they argue for a focus on the learning of individual pupils as a way of ensuring interest, relevance, motiv-ation and a way of ensuring pupils are engaged in the learning process. There-fore, the purpose of this chapter is to help you examine your own classroom organization in the context of curriculum changes and opportunities based on the revised 2011 primary curriculum. If education professionals really are to take control of the curriculum, they also need to reflect on where the learning is to take place and consider what changes need to be made.

Reflection

EYFS:
- What do you think are the most and least effective aspects of the learning environment you create in your workplace?
- What key message are you trying to communicate in the way you design your learning environment?

KS1:
- What changes might you wish to make to your learning environment in the light of recommendations from the Rose Review (DCSF, 2009) of the primary curriculum?
- How can a learning environment help pupils understand the links across the six areas of learning?

KS2:
- To what extent are your pupils encouraged to take ownership of their learning environment?
- Thinking back to the question above, what new opportunities might you encourage in the light of current developments in information and communication technology (ICT)? This links in with your reading of Chapter 10 'The digital world'.

Human beings are very good at getting used to a particular place and getting on with their lives and accepting what is around them. Just think of your journey to visit a friend: you know the way and probably travel there on personal autopilot. In how much detail can you actually recall what you see and pass on the way? It is very much the same with work spaces. Once we arrive in them, we are mainly concerned with getting on with the job that we do there. This chapter offers a range of ways to look afresh at your classroom organization through asking some key questions and challenging what you see, hear and do.

Before looking at your own practice, we need to place classrooms in a broader context. Unless you are in a brand new school, you have probably inherited your classroom from another teacher within a whole school setting. There may be some things that you cannot easily change. For example, staff may have agreed a whole school policy on how classrooms should be set out for literacy lessons. Each classroom may be fitted with fixed storage cupboards round some of the walls which could restrict how you distribute teaching resources. Your school may have been built in the early 1970s when open-plan designs were popular with some local education authorities. This is clearly going to affect how you currently operate and ideas you may have for the future. There is no one definition of effective classroom organization: the tasks are designed to help you create the most effective learning environment through a combination of various features that make up how your classroom is organized. Indeed, the new primary curriculum offers many opportunities to radically rethink how we create learning places relevant to pupils who will spend their lives in the twenty-first century.

Physical features of learning places

The physical features of learning places may be seen as crucially important if we as professionals are to seriously address the need to move towards more personalized learning based on the new primary curriculum. The key issues are discussed in depth in two government documents (DCSF: 2008a, 2008b). They suggest that pupils' involvement and engagement with their learning, opportunities for pupils to talk individually and in groups, and pupils accepting responsibility for their learning and independent working will all be key elements in learning for the future.

Being involved in teacher education, the author (John Halocha) has visited many classrooms around the country. One of the main impressions gained is the extent to which teachers take classroom organization for granted. Sometimes it is suggested to a student that a piece of furniture could be moved to improve ease of movement around the room. They may be anxious about asking their teacher whether they can do this. However, the teacher's reply is often that they had never really thought about why the furniture was there and of course the student can move it! Sometimes the teachers themselves then see how it has improved the learning environment. This section encourages you to ask those questions for yourself and to consider how you can adapt the physical environment to support teaching and learning.

Maslow (1968) argues that basic physical needs must be met before effective learning can take place. A basic starting point therefore is space, heat, light and sound. Look carefully at the space in your classroom. Do pupils have sufficient space in which to carry out a particular activity? How easy is it for you to move around and monitor progress and behaviour? Do you adapt the spaces depending on the activity. For example, a large-scale art construction may be best approached by removing chairs and putting tables together. This may seem obvious but there are many times during the teaching day when small changes to the physical space can improve learning because the children are both comfortable and best positioned to carry out an activity. Managing space can also support behaviour; a simple example being to ensure ease of movement around the room to prevent pupils disturbing each other. Although a carpeted sitting area is very useful in a primary classroom, have a look at the percentage of your classroom that is used for sitting on the floor. Does it take up too much space when you consider the length of time it is actually in use? If the classroom is small, perhaps allow some pupils to sit on chairs near the carpet as a special privilege.

Look carefully at heat, light and sound. Do some pupils spend their day in the glare of constant sunlight and heat, making for an uncomfortable working environment? Do computer screens reflect the glare from windows making them hard to use? Do you allow a high level of noise most of the day, preventing those pupils whose preferred learning environment is quiet from progressing? Equally, these questions can take an environmental focus, raising questions about the hidden messages you are giving children: do you need lights on during a sunny day? Why are the windows open when the heating is on? These are just a few examples which, if you look closely at the learning environment you create, may help you analyse how comfortable your pupils are in order to maximize their learning. It can sometimes be worth asking the question "would I be able to work in that physical environment?"

Health and safety factors also need to be considered. Are chairs and table so close together that children can hurt themselves and each other when they move about? Are children placed so that classroom assistants may hit their heads on storage units when they are working with particular children? Are electrical cables positioned so that people cannot trip over them? Many aspects of health and safety in your school will be considered by management, but it is occasionally well worth taking the time to re-evaluate such physical issues, not least because we often take our working environment for granted.

Room layout is also an important consideration in classroom organization. How much space do children and groups have in order to do a particular activity? In addition, what is the quality of that physical environment? For example, if you are expecting children to produce accurate drawn work on a large piece of paper, is this hampered by the fact that the working surface is not flat enough? Have you placed a distracting activity right alongside a group of children who are expected to work quietly on a task? Often, considering these organizational factors can go a long way to also managing behaviour in the classroom. Room layout is also important when considering access to resources for both adults and children. Layout also gives messages about you. Is there a particular place from which you tend to operate? Do people in your classroom talk about it having a 'front'? Think about how this message is created and the extent to which it is helpful for everyone to have a common understanding of the function of this place. Dean (2009) offers a detailed analysis of these issues in relation to primary learning places based on in-depth research in a range of primary schools.

Although it can take a little time, it may be worth moving furniture around more often in order to establish effective classroom organization. Try to plan ahead to minimize disruption. Hastings and Chantrey-Wood (2002) analysed the layout of primary classrooms and argue that careful and flexible use of space can have positive effects on learning and teaching. Also, have a look at where resources are positioned in relation to each other. Is a stimulus display positioned on a board where maximum use and visibility is obtained? Are resources and materials for a particular activity placed so children have easy access without disturbing others? Can a mobile display board be used to partition the room to help children concentrate on a particular activity? As with many aspects discussed in this chapter, it can be valuable to regularly step back in your classroom and ask, 'Why is that equipment where it is?' and 'How does that influence the effectiveness of my teaching?'

Another factor relating to layout is the nature of personal and group space within your classroom. As you get to know your children you will observe how best they work both individually and in groups. If a child works best alone in mathematics, try to provide a suitable personal space for them. If you have children grouped in a particular way, does this always stay the same? Are there some subjects where the ethos of whole class learning may be most beneficial? For example, displaying images on an interactive white board and using them within geographical enquiry may help to create a shared approach to learning from each other. Also think about the extent to which you give ownership of space to individuals and groups. This can also support the management of the classroom where various people take responsibility for space and resources. Lucas (1990) discusses a way in which teachers can adapt the physical space in classroom to support individuals and groups. Alexander (2010: 306) supports this notion and explains that:

> . . . classroom research also shows that, in England, teacher-pupils and pupil-pupil talk are under-exploited as tools for learning and understanding, and that their potential in teaching for much more than transmission is rarely fulfilled.

The layout of your classroom can also give numerous messages to children about how these forms of interacting may develop. Taking the time over lunch to change the layout from a morning literacy lesson to an afternoon of historical investigation can subconsciously say to the class that there will be a different way of working and thinking in the afternoon. At this point it may also be worth considering how national initiatives affect classroom organization. Literacy and numeracy hours have been present for a number of years. Going into many classrooms one often sees the daily layout of the room dominated by the need for various parts of these, often morning, initiatives. Many schools are now looking afresh at how they are interpreted and it may be worth considering how new classroom layouts can support revised thinking in how English and mathematics are best taught in the primary school.

Resources need to be well organized in the classroom. By this we would include books, subject-specific equipment, ICT facilities, consumables, artefacts, children's property and the teacher's own personal resources. Here are some key questions for you to ask of your classroom:

- Are resources stored in the most suitable location?
- How easy is it for children and adults to access these?
- Does everyone understand the rules in place for managing resources?
- Are resources in good condition?
- Is there sufficient of everything for their purpose?
- Do the resources help to convey the types of learning you are expecting?
- Do you make the most of opportunities for children to learn transferable skills through using classroom resources?
- To what extent do you provide a role model for the use of classroom resources?

The ethos of learning places

James and Pollard (TLRP, 2006) suggest 10 principles for improving teaching based on an eight-year research project entitled Teaching and Learning Research Programme (TLRP, 2006) all of which may be influenced by the ethos of learning places. They argue that effective teaching and learning:

1 equips learners for life in its broadest sense
2 engages with valued forms of knowledge
3 recognizes the importance of prior experience and learning
4 requires the teacher to scaffold learning
5 needs assessment to be congruent with learning
6 promotes the active engagement of the learner
7 fosters both individual and social processes and outcomes
8 recognizes the significance of informal learning
9 depends on teacher learning
10 demands consistent policy frameworks with support for teaching and learning as their primary focus.

Impact task

Early career professionals:
Consider the learning place in which you currently work. What features of the physical environment create an ethos in which some of the above can occur? It may be helpful to map the features next to the 10 statements. How might you further improve the ethos of your learning place to develop these further?

Later years professionals:
How might you engage the learners with whom you currently work to understand and indeed contribute to the ethos of the learning place in which you interact? What impact might you hope this has on learning?

Professional leader:
Reread the 10 TLRP statements. Which of the statements are most apparent in the learning places you lead in? How can you assess their effectiveness? Which statements could be further developed in the ethos of your learning place? How might you achieve this?

Walk into any classroom and you immediately gain an impression of what sort of place it is at that particular moment in time. But what might we mean by the ethos of learning places? It is not just the physical ambience discussed in the previous section. Is it to you perhaps the accumulation of physical, social, emotional, educational and ethical features that can be identified? Does one feature dominate more than others? This can manifest itself in many ways: the author recalls a student who had created a positive, safe and challenging ethos through her unrelenting use of constructive and encouraging language that she used for giving instructions, explaining, asking questions, responding to pupils and generally orchestrating what happened in her classroom. We normally define the ethos of classroom organization from our impressions of what we think may be happening and the language we use to describe it. The first stage is to look beneath the surface of how we ourselves evaluate classrooms. Choose one of the tasks appropriate to your current stage of career and try to reflect on what you really mean by the words you will be using.

A prime concern of many teachers is to create an ethos that encourages effective behaviour as a key foundation for learning. But just how has that particular ethos become established in your classroom? It is likely that it is based on a broader framework of school policy and rules governing behaviour. Another aspect to consider may be the extent to which pupils actually have ownership of the ethos behind the rules for organizing your classroom. There can often be hidden agendas here which help to reinforce the whole organizational structure: a teacher was observed in a school with a strong environmental policy which underpinned many aspects of classroom organization. One was that the waste from the morning break fruit was placed in the recycling tub. Each day two children were allowed to take this and put the contents on the school compost heap. They knew exactly why they were doing this because they were using the contents of composted heaps on their own class garden. This occurred every day and the head firmly believed that many pupils might take this aspect of classroom ethos into organizing their own lives beyond the school. Regular observations showed that very little teacher direction was required and indeed flowed over into paper recycling and the use of electricity in the classroom.

Classroom ethos may also be developed and reinforced through whole school initiatives. The Lincolnshire 'Golden Boot Challenge' encourages classes to compete for a weekly award by recording how pupils travel to and from school each day, with the most points awarded for those who walk all the way from home. Such activities also help to establish continuity of ethos along with a practical introduction to active citizenship which children can begin to understand operates in the real world at a variety of scales.

It may also be worth considering the ways in which you use language in your classroom that helps to create a particular atmosphere in your classroom. This can be looked at both from the point of view of the teacher and the children. What you say as a teacher is not just about how effective your questions are or how you ensure you use the correct vocabulary in a particular subject. It is also about the way in which you speak and use language.

> Schools are unique communities where children learn, among other things, self-respect and respect for others. Despite major advances in the technologies for learning and ICT, primary education is, and will remain, a person-to-person service, with enormous potential for fostering children's personal development.
>
> (DCSF, 2009: 74)

Primary classrooms offer many opportunities for people to interact in a variety of ways. This section is designed to help you reflect on how your classroom organization can be used to manage social organization to enhance teaching and learning. The broader issues of physical layout have already been discussed. We will now consider the social mechanisms that work within them.

Within a given period of time you will probably group your children as individuals, in groups or work as a whole class. Subsets of this can also exist. While half of the class are working as a large group, perhaps the rest are working as individuals. When you are planning, consider the whole variety of ways to organize children. On top of this, also consider the ways in which adult support, including yourself, can best be used within these various social groupings. You may decide that pupils working individually should be given a block of time where adult interaction is minimal and others in the class are getting more support. So often in primary classrooms, one observes the same patterns of child/adult organization at a given time of day. There may often be good reasons for these, but it can be worth asking whether alternative models may provide learning environments where children can experience various levels of autonomy and support. In planning such types of classroom organization, it may be worth mentally tracking the experience that children will have in say a day, a week or a term.

Another layer of organization may now be laid over this way of planning. Look at the range of subjects being taught and decide how to bring a variety of social groupings to them. This is not simply for the sake of variety: it can help children maximize their learning within a given subject. Look carefully at the particular activities you want them to undertake and adapt the social groups accordingly. For example, if you work in a small village school and your class has a wide age range, how might you best group children within a music lesson in which they are exploring an aspect of composition? Should each group include the whole age range or might it be better to group them according to musical ability.

As teachers, we often socially organize classes in order to achieve certain teaching and learning objectives. There may, however, be some opportunities where your prime motivation is in developing children's social interaction. There are a number of factors that you could consider: boy–girl, age differences, personal interests and abilities which may not be directly related to the curriculum, personal backgrounds that perhaps are valuable in schools where children come from a wide and varied catchment area. Citizenship is not statutory in primary schools and teachers' understanding of the concept is often confused or unclear. Taking some of the above factors into account, you could argue a case that your planning and organization is providing children with opportunities to develop skills in citizenship through interacting with a variety of peers who offer alternative views of life and experiences. The key issue here is to encourage diversity not only of experience, but also of how children are encouraged to think about people around the world.

A further important parameter in this social organization is the mix of ethnic and religious groups within your class. We live at a time of globalization where it is crucial for children to develop an understanding of and respect for people with histories, beliefs, traditions and cultures that are different to what they experience in everyday life. The way in which you manage this in your classroom will clearly depend on the cultural mix that is present. Perhaps the most important thing to consider here is the extent to which all the other factors discussed in this chapter may produce types of organization which do not allow children to make the most of opportunities to learn from each other's backgrounds. For example, if you set pupils across classes for literacy, this may group children together for part of the day where they do not benefit from working within a culturally diverse group.

Another factor to consider is how you organize groups within a classroom in your knowledge of children's preferred learning styles within any particular subject. It may be possible not only to place children in environments that encourage learning, but also to expose them to ways in which other children learn and think. An example of this might be when you draw on the vast range of teaching methods advocated through the various thinking skills materials that are now available for primary schools. They allow children opportunities to think about and express their own thinking, normally referred to as meta-cognition. The ideas suggested by the 'thinking on the edge' resources would provide excellent starting points to provide these social experiences.

Subjects such as geography and history naturally provide enquiry opportunities in which children can engage in problem-solving, justifying ideas and analysing information.

Adults play an increasingly important role in primary classrooms. Look carefully at the way in which you plan for adults to interact with children at any given time or session. Do certain classroom assistants always work with the same children? How might some children benefit from working with particular parent volunteers? What do you actually ask adults to do when they work with children? Layered over these considerations is also the extent to which they are able to manage children and allow their personality to shine through. For example, a parent with a strong sense of humour and sensitivity might be just the person to help you draw out a more reserved child, especially if you think they have more developed skills than you in this area.

ICT resources provide numerous ways in which to support your organization of the classroom. The range of resources is beyond the scope of this chapter but is discussed in more depth in Chapter 8. However, there are some underlying principles that may be applied across the curriculum when organizing ICT within the classroom.

ICT should be viewed as a tool for solving problems and providing facilities for children to use, rather than simply an end in itself. Whatever piece of equipment you choose to use, think carefully about why it is fit for purpose and how it can help you provide effective learning environments. For example, if you video a science experiment in which a bridge construction is tested to destruction, children can then replay the video or DVD recording at leisure to study exactly what happened and offer scientific explanations. Photographs of distant places can be projected onto an interactive white board and a whole class can ask questions and offer perspectives on their analysis of the images. A set of wireless laptops can be distributed around a classroom in order for very small groups to investigate selected websites offering materials of use in a historical investigation, leading to posters being produced for display in the classroom. Also see opportunities for other forms of social interaction through ICT. Can children be grouped in order that technical skills can be shared? Put children in groups where they can learn the skills of sharing equipment and taking turns. Provide opportunities for individuals and groups to be responsible for managing the use of ICT equipment; for example, caring for a digital camera on an out-of-classroom activity.

Beyond the classroom

In any chapter on learning places, it is also important to consider organization beyond the classroom. The central argument here is that working with children beyond the bounds of the classroom may provide opportunities to extend the range of organizational styles experienced by your children.

Spencer and Blades (2006) argues that many modern children have more restricted experiences of the wider environment and fewer opportunities to learn how to survive in new and challenging situations. When you are planning out-of-classroom activities, look for opportunities to develop these. For example, on a river walk, instigate a buddy system to add a further layer of safety to those already provided by adults. This will enable children to take more responsibility both for themselves and others. Use field visits to put children into groups that may seem unusual in the classroom: this can enable new social skills to be learnt in situations where the rules are not taken for granted. Use outdoor activities to let children see aspects of yourself as a person they may not be able to see in the classroom. For example, join in the canoeing activities while on a residential adventure week, rather than just leaving it to the instructors.

Use out-of-classroom activities to develop skills that may not be so easy to achieve in the classroom. For example, physical problem-solving challenges such as bridge building over imaginary rivers helps develop team skills while solving large physical challenges that could not be experienced in the classroom. New experiences can also be developed: environmental enquiries can be made much more concrete outdoors: tree hugging not only requires team skills and trust, but also greatly extended use of the senses. Finally, when out of the classroom, organize time for children to sit, look and ponder. You may be providing them with one of the few opportunities they get to look beyond home and school and to begin to understand that the whole wide world is a place for learning.

References

Alexander, R. (ed.) (2010) *Children, their World, their Education: Final Report and Recommendation of the Cambridge Primary Review*. London: Routledge.

Dean, J. (2009) *Organising Learning in the Primary Classroom.* London: Routledge.

Department for Children, Schools and Families (DCSF) (2008a) *Children and Young People's Workforce Strategy: The Evidence Base.* London: DCSF.

———— (2008b) *21st Century Schools: A world Class Education for Every Child.* London: DCSF.

———— (2009) *Independent Review of the Primary Curriculum: Final Report.* Nottingham: DCSF.

Dewey, J. (1899) *The School and Society.* Chicago, IL: University of Chicago Press.

Hastings, N. and Chantrey-Wood, K. (2002) *Reorganising Primary Classroom Learning.* Buckingham: Open University Press.

Lucas, D. (1990) Systems at work in the primary classroom – a retrospective study of classroom layout, in N. Frederickson (ed.) *Soft System Methodology: Practical Applications in Work with Schools.* London: University College.

Maslow, A. (1968) *Towards a Psychology of Being*, 2nd edn. New York: Van Nostrand.

Spencer, C. and Blades, M. (2006) *Children and their Environments: Learning, Using and Designing Spaces.* Cambridge: Cambridge University Press.

Teaching and Learning in 2020 Review Group (2006) *2020 Vision: Report of the Teaching and Learning in 2020 Review Group.* Nottingham: DfES.

Teaching and Learning Research Programme (TLRP) (2006) *Neuroscience and Education: Issues and opportunities.* London: TLRP/ESRC.

Index

Related books from Open University Press

Purchase from www.openup.co.uk or order through your local bookseller

APPROACHES TO LEARNING
A Guide for Teachers

Anne Jordan, Orison Carlile and Annetta Stack

978-0-335-22670-2 (Paperback)
2008

This comprehensive guide for education students and practitioners provides an overview of the major theories of learning. It considers their implications for policy and practice and sets out practical guidelines for best pedagogical practice. This book includes theoretical perspectives drawn from the philosophy, psychology, sociology and pedagogy that guide educational principles and practice. Each chapter contains:

- A summary of key principles
- Examples and illustrations from contemporary research and practice
- Summary boxes that highlight critical and key points made
- Practical implications for education professionals

Approaches to Learning is an invaluable resource for students and practitioners who wish to reflect on their educational constructs and explore and engage in the modern discourse of education.

www.openup.co.uk  OPEN UNIVERSITY PRESS
McGraw - Hill Education

BEGINNING TEACHING: BEGINNING LEARNING 3/E

Janet Moyles (Ed)

978-0-335-22130-1 (Paperback)
2007

The third edition of this highly successful text sets out to explore some of the wider issues to be investigated by beginning teachers - and those who support them - when working with early years and primary age children, while at the same time, exploring some of the delight and enjoyment in the teaching role.

Key features:

- Reflections of the current context of education and care
- New chapters covering teaching assistants and interagency working, as well as children's independence and physical activity
- Cameos and examples of practice in settings and classrooms to help illustrate the many different aspects of teaching

Beginning Teaching Beginning Learning is essential reading for all students and newly qualified primary teachers who need guidance, encouragement and support to challenge and enhance their own learning and practices.

www.openup.co.uk

OPEN UNIVERSITY PRESS
McGraw · Hill Education